FENIAN FEVER

By the same Author

PARNELL

CHARLES GAVAN DUFFY

THE UNFORTUNATE MR. ROBERT EMMET

DUBLIN CASTLE AND THE 1916 RISING

THE CHIEF SECRETARY

FENIAN FEVER
An Anglo-American Dilemma

By

LEON Ó BROIN

*"After the Fenian fever of the last two years,
constitutional conflicts appear flat to the masses"*
Lord Mayo to Disraeli, *12 August, 1868*

1971
NEW YORK UNIVERSITY PRESS
NEW YORK

Published by
New York University Press
Washington Square
New York 10003

SBN 8147–6151–8

Library of Congress Catalogue Card Number: 79-169251

Printed in Great Britain by
R. & R. Clark Ltd, Edinburgh

To Breandán Mac Giolla Choille

ACKNOWLEDGEMENTS

To Breandán Mac Giolla Choille, the Keeper of the Irish State Paper Office, and his assistant Mrs B. Dolan, now the librarian of the Royal Irish Academy, I owe my introduction to the superb Fenian archive in Dublin Castle and, indirectly, the decision to write this book. For that I am most grateful. Mr Mac Giolla Choille is an outstanding authority on Fenian history and I consider myself very fortunate to have had his assistance at all stages. He read my typescript and made suggestions for improving it which I did not hesitate to follow.

For the other material on which I rely I acknowledge with gratitude my indebtedness to Lords Derby and Abercorn, and to the authorities and officials of the National Library of Ireland, the British Museum, the Bodleian Library, the National Trust, the Public Record Offices in London and Belfast, and the University of Cambridge. Robert Blake, Sean O Lúing, Kenneth Timing and Denis Porter were very helpful to me during my search for papers, and my work otherwise has been greatly facilitated by the courteous library staffs of Oireachtas Eireann, Trinity College, Dublin, the Royal Dublin Society and the Dublin Corporation.

Dublin, 1971   Leon Ó Broin

CONTENTS

ILLUSTRATIONS

CHAPTER I

Conspiracy

IN British Government circles in Ireland in the eighteen-sixties the credit of organising what was called the Fenian Conspiracy was given pre-eminently to two men, James Stephens and John O'Mahony, who had taken part in the Young Ireland Insurrection of 1848 and had afterwards gone to the Continent to avoid arrest. Stephens, a clerk in his native town of Kilkenny, had been conspicuous at the barricades of Killenaule, was wounded at Ballingarry and left half-conscious in a ditch. To enable him to escape, a mock funeral was held, and a coffin, supposed to contain his remains, was interred with ceremony. O'Mahony was an unusual mixture, a gentleman farmer from Limerick and a Gaelic scholar who had made an English version of Geoffrey Keating's History of Ireland, *Foras Feasa ar Eirinn*.

In Paris, where for a number of years they exiguously supported themselves by teaching and translation work, Stephens and O'Mahony planned the next stage of the fight to overthrow British rule in Ireland, helped by other Irish refugees and by members of revolutionary societies with whom they were familiar. In 1856 O'Mahony went to America and there founded the Fenian Brotherhood which derived its name from the Fianna, a pre-historic Irish military force. Stephens returned to Ireland and on St Patrick's Day in 1858, following an organising tour that took him through the length and breadth of the country, he held the first meeting in a Dublin timber yard of the Irish counterpart of the American Fenians, the Irish Revolutionary Brotherhood (the I.R.B.).

The structure of Stephens's organisation, later to be called the Irish *Republican* Brotherhood, but still the I.R.B., bore some resemblance to the *Blanquis* who sparked off the French revolts in 1848 and played a part in the Paris Commune; but there were other underground societies also well known to Stephens and

O'Mahony in Paris, all of them influenced by the original *Carbonari* as modified by Mazzini and Young Italy. The Irish Brotherhood was organised in 'circles' with a centre A in charge, who had under him nine sub-centres known as B's or Captains; each of these controlled nine C's or sergeants, who in turn directed nine D's or privates. This, in theory, would have given each circle a membership of over 800 but in practice a circle sometimes consisted of 2,000 men, all of them sworn in individually by their immediate superior officer, the idea being, though it was not always realised, that they should know nobody outside their own section. They solemnly swore allegiance to the Irish Republic and their oath committed them to service whenever called upon. Their opposite numbers in America were not oath-bound. They were merely required to sign a form of pledge and even this was usually not exacted from military officers or persons of any position. The American Fenians were conceived originally as an auxiliary service; to supply the army in the field in Ireland with officers and arms as well as with some reinforcement of volunteers.

The Fenian movement made spectacular progress in the United States, where anti-British feeling was widespread. Britain was believed to have become alarmed at the increasing prosperity of America, to have deliberately sown the apple of discord there and, by intrigue, kept the civil war going. She had recognised the Confederate States as a belligerant power and had permitted privateers for the South—the *Alabama*, which had so effectively driven Union shipping off the high seas, was a classical case—to be built and fitted out in her ports. So bitter were American feelings that the British Foreign Secretary, Lord Clarendon, was hardly listened to when he tried to explain his country's position. At the outset, there was but one feeling of regret, he said, at what was considered an enormous calamity for England quite as much as for America; not one Englishman in 10,000 desired the rupture of the Union. As the war proceeded, opinions and interests divided; there was sympathy for the South making a gallant stand against fearful odds, and in England, as in America, what was strongly felt was unreservedly expressed; but he insisted that if ever a government acted honestly upon a principle which they had laid down for themselves, it was the English Government in the maintenance of neutrality. The *Alabama* might have escaped out of Liverpool by a fraud a few hours before she would have been seized, but for that the Government was blameless. The argument was lost on the Americans. They seemed determined, Clarendon thought, to keep all the old sores open, to ensure that the two countries were not to shake hands and be friends (1), and it was in this atmosphere that the Irish, impregnated with the hatred of England they had brought across the Atlantic, rallied to the Fenian cause in great numbers. From 40 members, all New Yorkers, in 1858, the movement grew to 50,000 at the beginning of the Civil War, with perhaps four or five times that number of open sympathisers. Thereafter progress was on a similar spectacular scale.

In Ireland, the sister organisation developed more slowly because of the remembrance of past revolutionary failures and as the result of the opposition of the Catholic Church. A display of strength was necessary to inspire the people with fresh confidence and this came with the arrival in Ireland in November 1861 of the body of Terence Bellew MacManus, one of the 1848 refugees, who had died in California. People gathered from all parts of Ireland for the funeral procession, and the occasion was used to administer the Fenian oath to many of them. Dr Paul Cullen, the Catholic Archbishop of Dublin, who by tradition and experience was rootedly opposed to secret societies and continental-inspired republicanism, refused the use of the Pro-Cathedral for a lying-in-state and prohibited his clergy from taking any part in the obsequies. The remains, therefore, lay in the theatre of the Mechanics Institute for a whole week; they were visited each day by thousands of people, attracted by the posters displayed all over the city which spoke of giving the world proof that the old cause for which MacManus had suffered was still loved.

The MacManus funeral was a turning point in Irish history; from it the Government recognised that the I.R.B. was a formidable force, and as time went on, they became painfully aware of its rapid expansion not only among ordinary people but inside the British regiments, thus creating an obviously serious challenge to national security. It was reckoned at one period that almost half the soldiers on the Curragh were Fenians, while 200 of the 500 infantry guarding the arsenal at Athlone which contained 30,000 rifles and other military stores belonged to a Fenian group. It was the same story in other parts of the country. The biggest concentration of soldier Fenians, however, was in Dublin, where the Fenians, were expected to strike their heaviest blow: among the garrison of 6,000 the Fenians claimed to have 1,600 adherents, some of them in kilt-wearing regiments who had been recruited in Scotland.

The growing influence of Fenianism in Ireland was notably enlarged when in 1863 Stephens established the *Irish People* newspaper, with an office within a stone's throw of Dublin Castle and with personnel who were effectively those of the Central Secret Committee. Thomas Clarke Luby was the nominal proprietor, John O'Leary the editor, Jeremiah O'Donovan Rossa the publisher and Charles Kickham one of the permanent editorial staff. It was among the subordinate staff of this paper that Daniel Ryan, the Superintendent of the G Division of the Dublin Metropolitan Police, found an informer in Pierce Nagle. While detectives watched the office from the outside, particularly the movements of Stephens under assumed names, Nagle gave Ryan, for the information of his Police Commissioners, a fair idea of what went on inside the building apart from the production of a weekly paper. 'Pagan' O'Leary, for instance, who displayed a fanatical zeal in recruiting soldiers into the Fenian ranks, kept a large chest containing arms and ammunition in a room on the first floor, and Nagle extracted from the office two booklets that were being used to give Fenians a basic education in military matters. One of these was *First Steps to Irish Liberty*, the other was entitled *Military Resources of Ireland*, both of them written by a Charles Beggs, a member of the organisation (2).

Things meanwhile were moving apace in America. At the first National Convention of the Fenian Brotherhood, held in Chicago in November 1863, resolutions were passed proclaiming the Republic of Ireland to be virtually established, acknowledged Stephens as the representative of the Brotherhood in Europe and the supreme organiser of the Irish People, and a constitution was adopted under which the government of the organisation as a whole was entrusted to a Head Centre (O'Mahony) and a Central Council of five members with treasurers and secretaries. Fourteen months later O'Mahony reported to a second Convention in Cincinnati that the organisation was established on so firm a basis that the most malignant enemy could not destroy nor even shake it, and money was pouring in. His optimism seemed to wane in his next words as he urged the importance of depending entirely on Irishmen to accomplish the freedom of Ireland; the efforts of Irish-Americans should be directed towards Ireland and not against the British dominion of Canada as was now being suggested. It was in Ireland that the help of the Fenians was most needed; it was there that English tyranny would receive its death blow. This Convention, as O'Mahony anticipated, was critical of his 'drag chain policy' and increased the size of the Central Council with the intention of curbing his authority, while among the new members of the Council was William R. Roberts, a dry goods merchant from New York, who was soon to lead a breakaway faction. Before that happened, however, a third Convention, held in Philadelphia in October, 1865, abolished the post of Head Centre and the Central Council and set up in their place a President of the Fenian Brotherhood of the United States (and *ipso facto* of the universal Fenian Brotherhood) and a General Congress consisting of a Senate and a House of Delegates: in effect a government modelled upon that of the United States. O'Mahony, by virtue of his new status, proceeded, like any American President, to appoint a cabinet with a secretary of war, an agent of the Irish Republic, an agent for the issue of bonds and so forth, and he sent John Mitchel, the Young Irelander, to Paris to receive money from New York and to see that it was honestly and fairly disbursed in favour of the I.R.B., to the order of Stephens when he was available and to his agents when he was not. It was a marvellous piece of stagecraft, and the emergent Irish in America understandably swelled with pride when they saw the flag of the harp and sunburst flying from the Fenian Capitol in New York City.

In Ireland, everything Fenian seemed to depend on the presence and personality of James Stephens. Extraordinary homage was paid to him; leading men in the movement, even Luby, O'Leary and Kickham, did not presume to hold opinions of their own; his word was law; no one ventured to ask him for explanations of what he was up to. Everywhere he went, and he travelled a great deal in Ireland and America, men were filled with enthusiasm, drilling went on more intensively, and the whole organisation thrilled with expectation that a successful insurrection in 1865 was more than a possibility (3). They had few arms yet in Ireland it was true, only home-made pikes, but the Fenians in the British Army would open the Army depots to them, while they recognised no limits to the possibilities of assistance from their kinsmen in the United States. The Americans were in the ascendant, England was in decline, and the Irish availed of every opportunity to acclaim the fact. Many meetings were held to congratulate the Federal Army on their triumph over the Confederates, though at one of these, in the Mechanics Theatre in Dublin, the congratulationary resolution had to be changed into one of sympathy as the news of Lincoln's assassination reached the organisers. A large American flag across the back of the platform and a smaller one attached to the chair were *crêped*.

The American interest was discernible in the number of army officers, many of them with Civil War experience, who began to arrive. The most distinguished, judged by his subsequent contribution to Fenian history, was Captain (later, by courtesy, Colonel) Thomas J. Kelly of the Army of the Cumberland who was warmly received by the men in the *Irish People* office. He toured through Ireland and satisfied himself that the Irish Fenians were at one with Stephens in their determination that the contemplated revolt must not be deferred. 1865 was the year of action! Other American officers followed Colonel Kelly, and Nagle, the informer, spoke to some of them when they called at the *Irish People* office. They also were certain a rising would take place soon, and sooner than the Government expected; but in his zeal Nagle declared that 'if I can have it in my power the Government won't be taken unawares'. The atmosphere, from the Government point of view, was noticeably worsening. The constitutional parties were being denounced as un-God-fearing, place-hunting, cowardly political agitators, a clique composed of rack-renting landlords, briefless barristers, anti-Irish bishops, parish priests, curates, and hireling, renegade, perjured press-men. The men of Ireland were called upon to spurn such dross; instead to put their trust in God and keep their powder dry. In the country the Fenians were reported to be drilling openly in places; the Dublin men continued to meet regularly in drill halls and in public houses, with soldiers showing up frequently among them; and Superintendent Ryan told his superiors that nearly all the drapers' assistants in the city had assumed an air of careless independence that rendered them almost unmanageable by their employers, who had grown quite timid and almost afraid to rebuke them.

> In many instances they openly express their political sentiments and their minds seem imbued with revolutionary and democratic notions. They seem glad of the death of President Lincoln, and say it augurs well for their cause, as Johnson, Lincoln's successor, is much better disposed to aid them. They are frequently heard to say among themselves that it is time other tyrants too should be dispatched as he was but they do not mention names . . . (4)

Sedition poured out from the *Irish People* and other national journals, while handbills making wild and fierce announcements were surreptitiously distributed in the streets. One of these— aimed at counteracting public interest in a visit from the Prince of Wales—read:

IRISHMEN
693 years of bloody extermination and rapacious plunder by British Butchers (countrymen of the Queen of England's son) demand of you silence and contempt, and not even by your outward appearance to show the slightest participation in the
HOLLOW REJOICINGS THAT WILL BE PARADED BEFORE YOU ON THE 9th by the BASTARD descendants of

FF B

Strongbow and Cromwell, who happen to be born in Ireland, but avow their allegiance to England.

Irishmen, testify your loyalty and devotion to Ireland by meeting in the bonds of Brotherhood to HAVE IRELAND FOR THE IRISH

GOD SAVE THE PEOPLE

By Order of the Vigilance Committee

(2)

The Liberals, on assuming power in 1865, placed Lord Wodehouse, whom the Fenians promptly nicknamed the Woodlouse, in the Viceregal post of Lord Lieutenant. His Chief Secretary was Sir Robert Peel (the 3rd Baronet) and, later, Chichester Fortescue, two gentlemen who, being members of the Commons, were able to speak authoritatively in that house on Irish affairs. Under the Chief Secretary was the Under Secretary, the permanent Civil Service head, through whom the Irish departments, as distinct from those whose headquarters were in London and from the Army and Navy, approached the Chief Secretary and the Viceroy. The Under Secretary was Sir Thomas Aiskew Larcom who was sixty-four years of age and coming up to his retirement. He had been in Ireland since 1826, half of the time in the Ordnance Survey and the other half either as one of the Commissioners of Public Works or in the Chief Secretary's Office. Wodehouse, on the other hand, was not yet forty and at the beginning of a highly successful career in politics. He was a vigorous, independent-minded man who liked to 'run' the Government of Ireland himself. He certainly had no intention of being a figurehead, nor did he want his Chief Secretary to have a seat in the Cabinet, which was sometimes the case. When he heard a rumour that this might happen, he made it known in London that he would prefer to resign first.

'One fact is, I fear, unfortunately too true,' he told his close friend, the Foreign Secretary, Lord Clarendon, 'namely that there

is widespread and increasing disaffection and hatred of the English Government. I am by no means an alarmist, and I have no doubt whenever disaffection shows itself openly, we shall easily crush it, but the seditious spirit which is abroad is doing a vast deal of harm by unsettling the minds of the people. The Fenian organ *The People* which I see every day is ably written, and universally read by the peasantry. It is very superior to the *Nation* which is a poor sneaking rebel, and indeed is better written than most of the Irish papers: of course it preaches open rebellion . . .'
(5) He was writing to a man who knew Ireland, for Clarendon had been Viceroy between 1847 and 1852 and had received the garter for his prompt measures in suppressing the Young Ireland outbreak in 1848, and Wodehouse relied on him to make his views known to the Government as to how the Fenians should be dealt with. Nothing was more difficult than to estimate at its true value information about secret societies. The Fenians were increasing in number, that was certain. It was also certain that their agents were being paid from societies in the United States, and perhaps partly by the Irish in England. They were collecting arms, but not, Wodehouse thought, in large quantities. They were drilling, but in small numbers and very clandestinely. They had been tampering to some extent with the soldiers. Their head-quarters were at Dublin and Cork. Cork was the most disaffected county. The men who enrolled themselves as Fenians were in the towns mostly shopkeepers' assistants and men of that class: in the country railway navvies, quarrymen, in short such men whose employment led them to congregate in masses. The bad feature of this rebellious movement as compared with former plots was that it was sustained by foreign money and connected with wide-spread foreign societies; the encouraging symptoms were that it was hostile to and strongly opposed by the priests, and that as far as he knew no respectable person had joined it or encouraged it. He thought the priests would continue to oppose the Fenians, as long as they dared, but if the movement were to become really serious they would row with the stream.

In Wodehouse's opinion, Fenianism would not become serious unless England went to war with the United States, but in that event he feared there would be an open attempt at rebellion. The danger of such an attempt would depend entirely on aid given by Britain's enemies abroad, though he doubted if that would amount to much. The Americans would attack Canada, where the advantage of nearness to their resources gave them a great advantage over the British, rather than Ireland, where the advantage would be on the British side. Nevertheless there was great reason to be watchful. In the year or so he had been in Ireland he had seen enough to know that the atmosphere was loaded with lies and exaggerations, and that even honest men seemed to lose their power of discernment and looked perpetually through magnifying glasses, but it was impossible not to be painfully struck by the statements which reached him from men of all creeds and parties that it was long since they remembered so general a feeling of discontent with the Government, and by Government they meant not this particular administration but the Queen's Government generally. A feeling seemed to be taking hold of the Irish mind that the Queen's Government was something apart from, and alien to Ireland. This, as distinguished from actual disaffection, he believed had arisen from want of consideration in recent years for the wishes of the landed gentry, and the Irish members of parliament. It would not answer to govern as if Irish opinions and wishes were the mere idle fancies or ignorant prejudices of an inferior race. (6)

In May 1865, after the Prince of Wales' visit, Wodehouse wrote to Clarendon again. He was not a little satisfied that the visit had passed off well and without any disagreeable incident. 'Although I never for a moment felt any serious apprehension', he said, 'it was impossible not to feel anxious, knowing as I do, how many disaffected people there are in Dublin. The newspapers talk a great deal of nonsense about enthusiastic crowds etc., but the true account is this. I had the best means of observing, and I watched narrowly everything which took place. At Kingstown on arriving the Prince was well received though there were a few hisses. From Westland Row Station all through Dublin to the Park gate there were large crowds of people. We passed in an open carriage. Cheers predominated, but many people hissed all the way. The

next day going to the Exhibition much the same but rather less
hissing . . . The conclusion I draw from all this is that the reason
why he was better received on the latter two days than at first
was partly that the disaffected faction was satisfied with having
made open demonstrations of their disapproval on the two days
when he appeared most publicly in Dublin, and partly that the
demeanour of the Prince and the success of the whole affair
created goodwill towards him . . . There can be no doubt that the
rarity of the visits of royalty to this country is a source of much
evil. You know Irishmen well, and I need not tell you that they
are far more moved by sentiment than Englishmen. The Royal
Family have it in their power to render an essential service to the
country by conciliating Ireland. I have heard that the Prince of
Wales has sometimes thought of buying a hunting box in Ireland.
I am sure he could not do a wiser or more popular act. Kildare for
instance is as quiet as an English county . . .' (7)

In a later letter he dealt with the renewal of the Peace Preservation Act. He could not have taken upon himself the responsibility
of advising its discontinuance at a time when the Fenian association was exciting disquiet and alarm. He believed that the movement would come to nothing, but it was undoubtedly increasing
and it would not be wise to give up powers of repression until
they saw more clearly what the course of the movement would
be. (8)

(3)

The Government's information regarding Fenian doings in
America came from the British Minister at Washington, from the
consuls in several of the principal cities, and from Thomas Doyle, a
sub-inspector of the Irish Constabulary who was sent out from
Dublin and who reported direct to the Inspector General of that
force; he had been to America before, in 1859, on a similar
mission. These reports revealed that the United States Government
were unwilling to take active measures to check the Fenian move-

ment, which thrived on a hatred of the English government that was fostered by the Press and by the masses of the American people. Bruce, the British Minister, had approached Seward, the Secretary of State, with no satisfactory result. He was unwilling to take any notice of the conspiracy until a breach of the law was committed, and he complained of the curtness and absence of friendly expressions in the communications received from the British.

Through 1865 the reports became more and more alarming. Squads of Fenians supplied with arms were said to be leaving for Ireland by every steamer. Vessels were being prepared to carry munitions of war to Ireland, and the end of September was named as the time for the insurrection to commence on Irish soil. Rumours were current that privateers were in readiness to sail from American harbours the moment the first blow was struck, and it was reported by the British Consul in Philadelphia, on what appeared to be good authority, that one Fenian regiment had actually embarked for Ireland.

The information acquired as to the state of affairs at home was no less alarming. Early in 1865 Head Constable Talbot, who had insinuated himself into the Fenian movement, reported that the number of drilled Fenians in Ireland exceeded 120,000 and that arms were being stored in several timber yards in Dublin. The Dublin police seized firearms coming from O'Mahony in New York to O'Donovan Rossa of the *Irish People* office; later, money from the same source fell into their possession; towards the autumn a man named Warner, an ex-sergeant in Cork Militia Artillery, who was a B (i.e. a Captain) in the Fenians, came forward in Cork and gave the police particulars of the organisation there. He told them that a rising was to take place before the end of September, that a body of 200 men was to attack every police barrack, slaughter the police and seize their arms, that all Protestants refusing to take the Fenian oath were also to be massacred and that Fenianism was rapidly spreading in the Army. There was obvious exaggeration here, but there were other indications of trouble in store. Farmers in the South had begun to draw their money out of the banks in gold, people generally expected an outbreak, and there was good reason to believe that not merely the army but the militia, the coast guard, the Dublin fire brigade and even the police had many sworn adherents to the conspiracy. Americans in large numbers were coming in. The *Irish People* was becoming more and more inflammatory in every issue. And James Stephens was reminding the Fenians that this year, 1865, must be the year of action.

If there was to be a rising before the end of September, there was little time to be lost. So, while the Admiralty were throwing a cordon of war ships round the coast to meet any possible American descent, the Dublin Metropolitan police and the Irish Constabulary on the night of the 14th September carried out a series of raids on Fenian centres in Dublin, Cork and elsewhere in the provinces, and on private dwelling-places. Their main concern was with the *Irish People* office where they seized anybody they found on the premises, including the informer Nagle— this no doubt for his protection—and a vast mass of documents which they brought over to Dublin Castle and had closely examined by a team directed by Samuel Lee Anderson, the son of the Crown solicitor for the county and city of Dublin, himself a solicitor. They also suppressed the paper. Among their discoveries in Luby's house was a document from Stephens authorising Luby, John O'Leary and Kickham to act as an executive committee whenever he happened to be absent. Luby, apprehending for a long time that the police were likely to pay him a visit, had carefully put this document in one envelope and his love letters in another, and then proceeded to mark the envelopes wrongly, leaving what he thought were the inoffensive letters from the lady he had married in the drawer where the police found it. They also found on Luby's person a letter proposing the destruction of the aristocracy. Another letter, produced at the trial of Luby, suggested that a suitable article for the paper would be one showing how the Swedes, when subject to the Danes, had shown their disgust of the Catholic clergy by passing a law to ensure that any priest entering Sweden would be emasculated. The readers would be left to draw the inference. These letters had emanated from Christopher Manus O'Keeffe, the hard-drinking, half-crazy, illegitimate son of a peer, whose eccentricities were well-known in the Dublin newspaper offices. Luby had kept these letters to show to his friends 'for a laugh', but the authorities took a different view of them and their author was sent to prison with Luby and the other Fenian leaders and stayed there for almost five years.

Lord Wodehouse was more than pleased with the results though Stephens, who had gone to cover, was not among those arrested. By striking at the heads and headquarters of the 'plotters' Wodehouse hoped that the whole conspiracy had been paralysed. He emphasised that it would be a great mistake to treat the Fenian plot as utterly despicable. It might already have done and perhaps might still do much mischief. People fancied that there was nothing in it because they did not see the names of any wealthy people implicated, and no doubt it was more satisfactory that no one of any station, social or professional, was connected with it, but the tradesmen in the towns and the small farmers in the country throughout the South of Ireland were largely tainted with disaffection, and the influence of the landlords and wealthier classes over the masses was not to be compared with what the corresponding classes had in England.

The cause of all the bad feeling, apart from the old deeply rooted antipathy to Englishmen, seemed to be the widespread emigration. The peasantry believed that their poverty and the necessity to emigrate was caused by mis-government, and they had a vague notion that if they could drive the English out, exterminate the landlords and confiscate their land, Ireland would be the Paradise which mouthing agitators had so long taught them she ought to be. They were strongly encouraged in these revolutionary ideas by their friends who had emigrated, and who wrote from America. Thus the feeling of the Irish across the Atlantic and the Irish in Ireland acted and reacted the one on the other till it produced the result seen in Fenianism.

Such a movement struck at the very root of society and was akin to the movement in France which culminated in the French Revolution. What he feared was a peasant uprising suppressed by a military force but causing much misery and bloodshed to individuals. He did not think it would come to this because forewarned was forearmed, but that was what it might end in. The priests were on the side of order, but it was a notable symptom that the exhortations of the priests appeared to be disregarded. People alternated between foolish confidence and childish panic, both equally unwarranted by the real state of things. They fancied that the Government, roused out of apathy, was suddenly determined on doing something, whereas the fact was that the Government had been watching the Fenians for months and had only been waiting for a fit opportunity which had at last presented itself. (9)

At the Special Commission that was set up to try the prisoners taken in the raids of the 14th September, the informer Nagle proved an indispensable witness as to the nature of the Fenian conspiracy. Only a few months earlier the authorities were extremely doubtful as to whether he was worth the modest sums, totalling £41 in all, that had been paid to him since he first offered his services in April 1864. In fact, they discontinued payment in July 1865, an action which produced the following sycophantic letter:

No. 2 Chapel Lane, Sheriff Street. Dublin, 25 July, 1865
May it please your Excellency
With feelings of profound respect I seek an audience with your Excellency. As one of Her Majesty's loyal and faithful subjects I confidentially [sic] trust that your Excellency will assent to my prayer.
Your Excellency must be already aware of the existence of widespread disaffection in Ireland towards the Government of our most gracious Queen known as Fenianism for the purpose of disturbing the peace and well being of society by bloodshed and destruction of property. For the past four years I have voluntary [sic] devoted my entire attention towards the discovery of the hotbed of this secret plot, the fruitful spring of sedition in this country at present and so far have I succeeded that I safely say I have placed in the hands of the proper authorities a vast amount of important information even the chief promoters.
The labour of fidelity to the state and throne exhausted my private means so that I had to be supplied with funds by the Government to continue the good work. My entire ambition is to be a

useful public servant in the employment of Her Majesty's Government and relying on your clemency I approach your Excellency for
to be placed in a civil service situation.

In the next place I have to inform your Excellency of the fact
that those revolutionists in conjunction with their Fenian brothers
in America contemplate on an uprising this year.

For those two fold objects I seek an interview on this or any other
time your Excellency may appoint.

I have the honour to be, Your Excellency's most obedient and
humble servant

Pierce Nagle
English and Mathematical Instructor
Dublin Mechanics Institute (10)

While under police protection Nagle read in the *Irish Times*
that on account of his becoming an approver in the Fenian cases,
a brother of his had been assassinated in New York. He was 'much
affected', Superintendent Ryan reported, and begged that some
protection might be given to his father and another brother who
resided at Fethard, County Tipperary, as he feared that some
outrage might be committed on them also. The story of the
assassination proved to be untrue but the British Consul in New
York found that Nagle's brother and his wife were unwilling to
avow any relationship with the informer for fear of the consequences. Their attitude probably relieved the Consul of the need
to act on Nagle's appeal that they should be given protection and
'suitably employed out of the reach of the Fenians'. To live on in
Fethard was a different matter. The Government could not continue to protect the family indefinitely there, so they were given
their passages to America. The unhappy Nagle himself was naturally anxious to find obscurity outside Ireland too, when his work
was done. The financial arrangements were designed to give
him a couple of pounds a week to enable him to live in London
but, the remittances not reaching him regularly, he told Larcom,
the Under Secretary (24.7.1866) that 'at the present time I am
penniless and need I add friendless . . .' (11) He appears to have
been on the Irish Government's hands until November 1866 when
a lump sum payment of £250 was made to him. (12)

Stephens managed to avoid arrest for nearly two months. On the 9th November, however, a visitor called at the Detective Office in Dublin Castle and told Inspector Hughes that a gentleman, who gave his name as Herbert, and his wife, had been living in Fairfield House, Newbridge Avenue, Sandymount since about the beginning of July. This Mr Herbert used to go into town every day until the *Irish People* was seized, but since that time it had been noticed that neither himself nor his wife were seen out of doors except on rare occasions and then late at night. He described the couple, who seemed to resemble Stephens and his wife and, when some further confirmatory information had been obtained 'a shrewd constable' of the G Division, with the letter E on his collar to give the impression that he was just an ordinary 'bobby', was sent by Inspector Hughes to reconnoitre the area. This led to a decision to effect an early entry into the house. Between six and seven o'clock on the morning of the 11th, therefore, Colonel Lake, one of the Metropolitan Police Commissioners, with the men of the G Division and ten men from B Division, scaled the high wall around the pleasure grounds and surrounded the house. An inspector knocked at the hall door and, in reply to an inquiry from within, announced that they were the police and were seeking entry. Stephens, undressed, came to the door and gave his name as Herbert, but later admitted who he was on being recognised by Inspector Dawson. He said he would not then offer resistance, but had he anticipated their visit he would have put it to the test whether they were men; and if he got out he was damned but they would have it hard to catch him. He told his wife that she might not hope to see him again, and when she said she would apply for permission to see him, he said with harsh emphasis, referring to the Chief Secretary, 'Is it to Peel in the Castle you will go for a favour? Ah no, die first, and so will I.' Three leading Fenian centres were found sleeping in the house— one of them Charles Kickham—and were arrested. Four 6-barrelled revolvers, capped and loaded, were found, and a pocket book belonging to Stephens had some entries of much importance. The prisoners were taken before a magistrate and remanded to Richmond Jail. That night an attempt was made on the lives of two detectives as they entered the Detective Office in Exchange Court. Both were hit, but not seriously. The shots were supposed to have been fired from a house formerly occupied by Stephens' brother-in-law, Hopper. The attack confirmed what Superintendent Ryan had always been told, that in the event of Stephens being arrested some one would lose his life.

Wodehouse hastened to give the good news of the arrest of Stephens, whom he described as the arch-Fenian, to Clarendon at the Foreign Office. 'I regard his capture', he wrote, 'as the heaviest blow we have yet struck against this seditious faction. I am told there is ample evidence against him in the papers seized at the *People* office.' (13)

CHAPTER II

The Escape from the Richmond Bridewell

ON hearing of the arrest, the leaders of the Irish Revolutionary Brotherhood and the members of the Military Council still at large met and decided to elect a military man to fill Stephens's place temporarily. Their choice fell on the President of the Council, F. F. Millen, a native of County Fermanagh who had become a Lieutenant-Colonel in the Liberal Army of the Republic of Mexico. About thirty-three years of age, and five feet ten inches high, Millen was a raw-boned man with long arms and long oval face, a long straight nose, and lightish sandy complexion. He had a quiet, slow manner of speaking and had retained his native accent. The Government speedily heard of the appointment, and Larcom, the Under Secretary, wrote to E. M. Archibald, the British Consul in New York, for any intelligence he might be able to procure respecting this 'General Mellon' and his movements. He wrote on the 24th November but, in circumstances that will appear later, four months elapsed before Archibald communicated some startling information that had been in his possession for more than a year.

Since 1860 Millen had been an honorary member of a 'Friends of Ireland Club', and some of his letters, charged with zeal for the Irish cause, had been published by John O'Mahony in a Fenian paper he edited. In October 1864, by which time he had seen much active military service and had become a General of Brigade, Millen called at the Fenian Headquarters in New York City and introduced himself. He was cordially greeted by O'Mahony whose appearance, however, disappointed him.

> I imagined to myself that O'Mahoney, to be the leader of such an extensive revolutionary movement as the one he directed, should, if found walking in the streets of London or Dublin, be taken for a member of the House of Commons at least; that he should be not only a gentleman by education, but in appearance also, as well as in

address, manners and style; instead of which I found a man who had I met on the street, I might readily have mistaken for an over-worked assistant book-keeper in some second or third rate pook [sic] jobbing house. His tall gaunt frame clothed in the shabbiest description of a threadbare suit of blue, together with his long, not overly well kept iron gray hair, and his unmistakably Celtic, tho' well formed face, rendered him anything but impressive in appearance, as a revolutionary chieftain—at least to me. (1)

In April 1865, having concluded some civilian mission in the United States, Millen told the Mexican authorities that he was taking six months' leave of absence. He did this in order to accept an offer from O'Mahony to go to Ireland or, alternatively, to become the Treasurer of the Fenian Brotherhood. 'The Fenians in Ireland at this period', he wrote in his *Account of Fenianism* (New York, 1866), 'were kept in spirits by the glowing accounts sent to Stephens by O'Mahony of the condition and prospects of the Brotherhood in America, backed by remittances of £100 or £200 at a time' (2) They were also promised the secret assistance of the United States Government. (3)

> On the other hand the Fenians of America were led to believe, through the reports which O'Mahony received from Stephens, that there were in Ireland in 1864 at the very least 50,000 sworn in and organised men ready to take the field 'under able and experienced leaders', and that all they required was some arms and ammunition and a few good military officers to direct them. These items it was supposed the Fenians of America could and would supply. Thus, the one half of the organisation trusting in the other and neither in itself amounting in importance to the value of a row of pins if taken separately, the organisation as a unity went on gathering strength until at length it became really formidable and would have been most dangerous but for the death blows it received through the quarrels of its leaders and the imprisonment of some of the principal spirits of the I.R.B. after the suppression of the *Irish People* newspaper . . . (4)

In order to judge the state of Ireland and to justify to Americans a long contemplated issue of Irish Bonds, O'Mahony sent over a succession of investigators. The first, a man named Cantwell, earned the enmity of Stephens, who denounced him as a traitor and had him expelled from the Brotherhood. The second, whose name was Coyne, produced such a flattering report that nobody believed it. Then Colonel Kelly was sent. He, a stout, square-built fellow about thirty-three years of age, was to become one of the really great figures of Fenianism. A most resolute character he was, according to Millen, the sort of man who, if he failed to rescue Ireland from the Saxon, would not hesitate to *make away with* all the nobility and gentry from the Lord Lieutenant down. Kelly was to forward his report to O'Mahony by special messenger in three months and then take his choice of remaining with Stephens or returning. When the time came he elected to stay with Stephens. He had only been about a month in Ireland when Millen followed him, and soon found himself looked upon as a leader in the movement. The Central Committee had resolved that he would be more useful in Ireland than in New York and agreed to pay him 222 dollars a month, which was the current stipend of a colonel in the American army, though 200 dollars less than Millen said his rank of brigadier general would have entitled him to. His instructions were to present himself, through John O'Leary, the editor of the *Irish People*, to Stephens, who carried the high-sounding title of Central Executive of the Irish Republic (C.E.I.R.) He was to make himself available for military service and to perform such duties as were assigned to him without asking questions. At the end of three months he, like Kelly, was to make a detailed report to O'Mahony on whatever part of the I.R.B. 'the Boss', Stephens, might show him. (5)

Millen, according to himself, left New York 'with a not very friendly feeling towards England' and, when he set his foot on Irish ground, the words of Scott recurred to his memory with a force that nearly brought tears to his eyes:

> *Breathes there a man with soul so dead*
> *Who never to himself hath said*
> *This is my own, my native land?*

His first impression in Dublin when he got there was of the efficiency of British Army units whom he saw in the Phoenix

Park during a display given by the Commander of the Forces in honour of the visiting Prince of Wales. He did not think that the Horse Artillery, in particular, could be surpassed anywhere. 'The velocity and precision of their evolutions was truly surprising.' By comparison, the Fenians he began to meet were a drab lot. All the sense of superiority of the returning Yank asserted itself. One of his letters of introduction was to a man whose place of business was in Dame Street, and Millen had figured to himself that he was one of the leading men in his line in Dublin. He was disappointed, however, to find that he was not so.

> 'but was only George Hopper, the happy-dispositioned, paunchy, merry-souled, joke-cracking, kind-hearted and not overly well-educated tailor . . . now so well-known to the people of Dublin . . .' Similarly, with the exception of O'Leary and Luby, he did not meet anyone among the leaders 'that one could call a gentleman or associated with upon terms of any sort of equality. As far as education and manners are concerned', he said, 'these gentleman might pass in a crowd but they were very far from being what one might expect the leaders of a great revolutionary movement to be'. (6)

Returning from a visit to his people in the North, Millen was told that there had been some 'queer sort of men asking all manner of strange questions' about him, and about the class of people who had been in the habit of visiting him. These were Superintendent Ryan's detectives, he thought, and to avoid falling into their hands, he changed his lodgings no less than eight times in seven months. In doing this he went one better than Stephens, who tried to secure safety by renting four houses simultaneously.

Time hung on Millen's hands. He was given very little to do, beyond preparing estimates of the cost of arming and equipping an army of 50,000 men for the field. These led nowhere. With O'Donovan Rossa he coaxed his way into the Magazine Fort in the Phoenix Park and afterwards from memory made a plan for its seizure by a *coup de main*. He did the same for the Pigeon House Fort after a visit there with Luby, a man who seemed to Millen to be well read in military history and to have no mean knowledge of the principles of strategy. By contrast he had a poor opinion of Stephens as a strategist, and told him that he was sorry he had compromised himself by declaring for action at any particular time. 'A revolutionary movement from the nature of it was a secret one, and such as prevented a leader from saying even to himself, much less to his friends, that he would take action at any given time.' (7)

Millen met the Fenian centres who came to Dublin to interview Stephens, and questioned them about the condition of their circles. On the strength of this, when the time came to write his report, he endorsed Colonel Kelly's optimistic account to O'Mahony of the spirit of the I.R.B. Kelly warned that any further postponement of a rising might result in the collapse of the whole movement. The contingencies in their favour were immense, he declared; the knowledge they possessed of the whereabouts of stores of material and supplies, the work that had been done to infiltrate the garrison; the fact that about half the militia had been won over, the spread of the organisation in England so as to create a diversion—all these capabilities, if properly exploited, under competent leadership, left no doubts in his mind as to the success of the project. (8) Millen was no less enthusiastic. He was personally willing to risk his life upon the issue, he said, and would go into action tomorrow if Stephens should think it necessary. It only remained for the Americans to supply the funds by putting on sale the long promised Bonds, and to apply them as required. A beginning should be made that year, in God's name, or at the latest by early in the spring of 1866.

Of Stephens he said that when they first met they eyed each other pretty sharply for some minutes. The result again was disappointment with the person of 'the Boss'. His intellectual countenance and gentlemanly deportment were pleasing, but he did not come up to Millen's beau idéal of a revolutionary leader, though, on the whole, he preferred him to O'Mahony. He had 'a considerable smartness' and 'some determination of purpose', but he was a man so self-opinionated and dogmatic that even when he knew he was in the wrong he would not confess it. He would prefer to see a project ruined than do that. (9) He was also loth to part with any of his powers and saw to it that the Military Council had little or nothing to do beyond distributing the Irish-American officers, and attending to their needs. Most of these

went to stay with friends and relations, and in that way penetrated to many parts of the island. The Council met every twenty-
four hours, in billiard saloons or in each other's houses or lodgings,
for consultation and to receive a message from Stephens who,
with Kickham and Duffy, was lying low in Sandymount, in a
pleasant little house on the banks of the Dodder. There in this
retreat they 'engaged themsleves passing well until fished to the
surface of the vulgar world's gaze by the impertinent limbs of
British oppression'. (10)

In the emergency created by the arrest of Stephens, Millen also
became the acting C.E.I.R. The Dublin centres wanted Kelly, but
Millen was preferred because of his superior rank and experience,
which had also been the reason for his becoming President of the
Military Council. He protested that he was not the man for the
job, that one of the intelligent centres present would be better,
but this was greeted with shouts of 'No! No!' The General was
the man: he would be leading them soon in the field anyhow and
might as well begin now. So Millen became the provisional head
of the I.R.B. and Colonel Kirwin replaced him as President of the
Military Council. In his new capacity Millen wrote immediately
to O'Mahony to assure him that, despite the arrest of Stephens,
war would begin during Christmas week. Irish pilots were on their
way to New York and he hoped that the expedition would be
ready to sail when they arrived. A few days later Kelly also wrote
to O'Mahony announcing a plan to rescue Stephens.

Within hours of the appointment of his successor, Stephens
from custody took steps effectively to countermand it. He was the
Boss and intended to remain so. Through his sister-in-law, Doty
Hopper, he sent out a pencilled message, ordering Millen to return
to the United States immediately and there to take command
of the expedition to Ireland. He was to travel back with the first
of the ships, whose landing was to be the signal for a universal
rising, *but not sooner*. This looked like a device to get Millen out of
the way and was recognised by Millen as such. He was convinced
that Stephens was jealous of him. As late as the end of October he
had asked for leave to return to America and had been refused,
Stephens then saying that he could as soon do without his right

arm as let him go. Now, a few weeks later, he was being sent home with a prohibition against his returning. He protested, but his colleagues accepted Stephens's decision and a story was put into circulation by Kelly that Millen had intended to abscond with all the available funds, which he had insisted should be handed over to his control. (11) He had also become unpopular because he had been seen playing with the affections of a lady who was engaged to an imprisoned Fenian officer.

Millen attended no more meetings of the heads of the I.R.B. in an official capacity but he delivered to Colonel Kirwin a grand plan of Dublin Castle and of the Magazine and Pigeon House forts which he had got from Stephens. These were, he said, the only preparations, if preparations they could be called, that Stephens had made for a rising. And while waiting for a boat he also gave Kirwin, who visited him almost daily, the benefit of his views as to the course of action he should observe as President of the Military Council.

When he got to Yankeedom, as he called it, Millen was 'not a little grieved and chagrined, and disgusted too', at finding that the Fenians there were at sword's point with each other. O'Mahony's leadership had been questioned by an important section led by William R. Roberts and General Thomas W. Sweeney. Of his personal position Millen had at first no reason to complain. He was accepted by O'Mahony as Stephens's representative and came to be considered as the chief of O'Mahony's War Department, but Archibald, the British Consul in New York, stressed that this was an acting appointment. Millen, formerly a keeper of a liquor or small grocery shop, did not appear, he said, to be held in much esteem by the Fenian leaders. (12) He was, however, invited on to the platform at a Convention O'Mahony called in January 1866, at which cheers were given for him, for the Irish Republic and for Stephens. This Convention rejected Roberts, Sweeney and company and pledged prompt and efficient aid to 'the men in the gap' in Ireland. But frustration followed frustration and the expedition to Ireland that Millen was to lead was deferred until O'Mahony abolished the Expeditionary Bureau, a step which, according to Millen, disgusted the Fenians completely with O'Mahony's administration. The men who had assembled from various quarters of the United States and had waited in New York to take part in the adventure, returned home wiser and sadder, while the pilots who had come out from Ireland continued to walk about the city doing nothing, and without the means of returning to their native shore.

(2)

Stephens was less than a fortnight in the Richmond Bridewell when he vanished. The first person outside the prison to hear of the escape was a constable of the E Division. At 5.20 in the morning of the 24th November he hurried into the Detective Office in Exchange Court alongside Dublin Castle and said that he had been sent by Mr Marques, the Governor, to say that James Stephens, confined in the Bridewell on a serious charge, had disappeared. The men of the G Division were immediately sent to watch the railway stations and Fairfield House, where Stephens had lately been living, and one went to the Bridewell for particulars. Mr Marques told him that about half past four the night watchman reported that he had discovered two tables, one upon the other, close against the inside of the outer wall of the prison on the West side, and that, upon examination, he discovered Stephens's cell open. There were seven doors, including the door of his cell, to the place where the tables were found. The door of the cell was secured by a strong stock lock, and also a very large padlock on the outside of the door: all of these were found open, and two keys were found in them. The wall at the place where the tables were discovered was about seventeen feet high, the tables one on top of the other were about five feet high, and from that to the top of the wall was therefore about twelve feet. The tables had been taken to the place from the lunatic department of the prison. A prisoner in the cell next to Stephens's told the G man that about ten minutes after the clock struck one he heard the footsteps of one person in the corridor the door of Stephens's cell unlocked and then the footsteps of two persons moving away. It was evident to the detective that Stephens could not have removed the padlock on the outside of his cell door, or placed the tables in position on his own: therefore he must have been aided by someone inside connected with the prison.

That was the substance of Superintendent Ryan's preliminary report on the escape. He added to it that at Fairfield House Mrs Stephens and her father were removing the furniture as if they were going to reside elsewhere. Mr Hopper could scarcely credit that Stephens had got away. If the story were true, Stephens would go to France, and not by the ordinary route either, so that the police would never lay hands on him again. (13)

It had of course been 'an inside job'. The prime movers in it were John J. Breslin, a prison hospital steward, and Daniel Byrne, the very night watchman who had apprised the governor of the escape. This man was a Fenian and through him contact was established with the Fenian body outside. Copies of keys were made to enable entrance to Stephens's corridor and cell to be effected, a night for the operation was fixed and a group of armed Fenians under John Devoy helped the escaping prisoner over the wall and away to comparative safety.

Lord Wodehouse was bitterly mortified at the escape.

All the work of months is undone in a moment, and I expect more trouble than ever with much less hope of success. I am only surprised that the Fenian warders who let Stephens out into the street did not let out all the others. They were not I suppose worth the trouble. I was in a fool's paradise about the safety of the prisoners. The Governor long ago applied for a military guard. I desired one to be furnished. I *now* find out that the Governor subsequently told the military authorities he did not want a guard, and it was never posted!

The Inspector of Prisons who I *knew* constantly visited the prison since Stephens and company have been there, reported that they had made arrangements for eight policemen to be stationed in the prison. They were reduced to *three* without my knowledge. They were posted so that they would not communicate with the part of the prison where Stephens was! The Governor now says that besides two warders now under arrest he suspects *three* others. I never heard of these suspicions till now. . . . At present the case wears a most ugly aspect of neglect and treachery combined.

I need not describe to you the outburst of exultation of the disloyal all over Ireland, and the general mistrust amongst all who have anything to lose which Stephens's escape has caused.

I feel like a general who has let his camp be surprised in the night and lost half his army, but the lesson to be learnt is: more vigilance and caution, and I shall do my utmost to repair the disaster. (14)

When the first annoyance of the escape was over, Wodehouse began to philosophise. He now thought that the trial and punishment of Stephens would not have had as much permanent effect as he had hoped. It would have been a great but momentary triumph of the law, but the effect would have worn off very quickly. The problem they faced was one of widespread disaffection. 'The whole mass of the peasantry are sullenly or actively disloyal,' he told Clarendon; 'so are the small tradesmen, the artisans, and the railway and telegraph clerks, porters, engineers etc. . . . In England people altogether underrate the potency of the old hatred of the Saxon . . . The heart of this people is against us, and I see no prospect of improvement within any time that can be calculated.

'You will say, what is the use of this Jeremiad? I think it is of this use: the next best thing to curing a disease is squarely to look the evil in the face, and not deceive oneself into crying "peace" where there is "no peace".' (15)

When Clarendon tried to encourage him with kind words, Wodehouse thanked him. 'I am not given to despond,' he said, 'but I need them in the discharge of this most hateful and discouraging office.' His impression, which Clarendon confirmed, was that the sedition they now faced was worse than in 1848. They both agreed that the Suspension of Habeas Corpus Act, whatever else it might do, would not stamp out the rebellion as in 1848. The American element was too strong for that. There was also the spread of Fenianism in the forces to contend with. Soldiers convicted of Fenianism would have to be punished most severely.

One of the few satisfactions was the unshaken fidelity of the Constabulary. Wodehouse hoped that Gladstone, the Chancellor of the Exchequer, would grant the additional pay that was about to be recommended. 'What sum of money would it cost to hold Ireland if the Constabulary were disloyal, or ineffective? Timely liberality now will confirm them in their fidelity, but if they are treated in a niggardly manner we shall commit an *irretrievable* mistake, for it would be impossible in the present temper of this people to hope to reconstitute a force with the *esprit de corps* which pervades the force now, officers and men.' (16) He did not feel the same way at all about the Dublin Metropolitan Police. Despite what he was told locally he suspected that treachery alone could account for their failure to get Stephens. (17)

The arrest of Stephens had been a sensation comparable to that of O'Connell in 1844. People had got into the habit of thinking that, like O'Connell, Stephens had entrenched himself in an unassailable position, that he was too clever, too knowledgeable of the ways of the enemy to fall into his hands. The report of his arrest was therefore received first with incredulity which gave way to a deep depression. Then, just as suddenly and completely, the nation was electrified by the news that he had escaped. This was, in John Devoy's words, the Fenians' 'one proud day'. (18) Depression was replaced by joy. Exaggerated opinions of the genius of 'the little fellow'—Stephens was only five feet seven—were again commonplace. Perhaps he had permitted himself to be arrested so that he might show the Government that the prison had not yet been built that could contain him. And as a counterblast some loyalists put out the story, equally groundless, that the Government had let him go and that he was now their tool.

(3)

Stephens lay low in Dublin from the 24th November until the 13th May 1866, most of the time in the house of Mrs Butler, a fashionable dressmaker, overlooking the Kildare Street Club, the very centre of Unionism, while the police searched high and low for him, following every clue, no matter how ridiculous. He was 'seen' everywhere, in Paris, Caernarvon, in the Dublin streets, and in a monastery in Harold's Cross. Jokes about him were made at the expense of the police. Rumours about what he intended to do next multiplied. He would lead an attempt at rescuing the Fenian prisoners in Mountjoy, possibly on Stephen's Day, his special day. That day passed without incident. Then St Patrick's Day, the 17th March, became a likely day for some sensational move, perhaps a rising. The police observed that, for greater safety, Fenians were meeting in the Phoenix Park instead of in public houses. Seditious placards and pamphlets were circulating, and threatening letters issued to loyal people. Songs 'of a decidedly Fenian nature' were being sung, a printed prayer for the safety of Stephens was receiving avid distribution, isolated attacks were made on the police, and informers went in dread of their lives. However, nothing untoward happened on St Patrick's Day, but by that time Parliament had suspended Habeas Corpus, and the police had begun to make wholesale arrests and to seize arms. By the second week of April the number of persons in custody reached the maximum of 669.

The effects were magical, according to the Commissioners of the Metropolitan Police. 'Fenian meetings were abandoned; drilling ceased; the menacing tone of Fenianism, so much heard in the streets and public houses, was silent; the public alarm subsided; people resumed their ordinary pursuits, and before the end of May Fenianism was forgotten and apparently extinct, or at least was no longer active.' (19) In America, however, the enactment of the Habeas Corpus Suspension measure and the arrest of many Americans had the opposite effect. It incited the American Fenians to action.

The Lord Lieutenant had thought that Stephens's escape might have led to a rising; but the Commander of the Forces in Ireland, Sir Hugh Henry Rose, was of a different mind. He had come to Ireland in July 1865, with a most distinguished reputation earned in the Crimea and Indian Mutiny. He was a strict but fairminded disciplinarian and had been sent over to help in arresting the spread of Fenianism, and particularly its infiltration of the Army. He did not rate too highly the chances of Stephens and the Fenian body. 'I feel persuaded', he told his chief, the Duke of Cambridge, 'that Stephens acts and thinks as a fugitive; only anxious at present for his escape; and that his fear of imprisonment and impending punishment are too lively and recent to admit of his thinking of heading an outbreak in Ireland.' He was sure there would be no rising for another reason. 'The Fenians as a body', he said, 'are preparing and waiting for what will never arrive—ironclads with an army and leaders from America.' They would not compromise themselves in the absence of this aid. He felt, too, that the Fenians had made a great mistake which would turn to the Government's advantage. Having imbibed free-thinking notions about religion in America, they had thrown over their clergy who would have nothing to do with a Red Republic. Fear of being denounced by their clergy and countrymen probably explained the remarkable fact that Fenianism had so far committed no outrage except some shots that were fired at two detectives.

Among the Fenians there was some support for a rising at the end of 1865 or in the opening days of 1866, before what was left of the American officers were arrested, and while the Fenian elements in the British Army could be used to seize the Dublin barracks and hand over their military contents. This was considered preferable to a delay that would leave the initiative with the Government, and would make success dependable upon a problematical American descent. However, the majority of the Dublin officers, whom Stephens saw in twos and threes, decided the other way, and the country centres, when they were consulted subsequently, came to the same conclusion. 1865 was not to be the year of action after all; it would now have to be 1866. Stephens attributed this decision to the centres but he had apparently made up his own mind that circumstances did not favour a rising at that time, particularly with the American Fenians divided as to whether their major field of activity should be across the border in Canada rather than across the ocean in Ireland. Devoy was critical of Stephens's judgement, which was affected he said, by his overweening confidence in himself and his constant self-assertion. Nobody questioned his decisions, however, and the organisation he directed was the most completely despotic system in the world. (20)

The decision to postpone the rising was a particular disappointment for Devoy who believed that the Fenians held a trump card in the disaffection they had spread among the forces of the Crown. With the grandiloquent title of 'Chief Organiser of the British Troops' that Stephens had given him, Devoy directed this work, in succession to 'Pagan' O'Leary and Roantree, from October 1865 until the middle of February 1866, by which time, according to himself, Fenianism was widespread in the army and in good shape. Thereafter it declined and disappeared, principally, he believed, as a result of the postponement of the fight. (21) An insurrection in 1865, or during the first weeks of 1866, might conceivably have failed, but a fight at that time would have found Ireland in better condition from a military point of view than she had been in for several hundred years previously, and England at a great disadvantage. (22)

CHAPTER III

Fenianism in the Army

AFTER the escape of Stephens, Rose, the Commander of the Forces in Ireland, told the Commander in Chief of the Army, the Duke of Cambridge (who was a first cousin of the Queen) what had gone wrong. The military situation was favourable and the troops behaving well, but on the civil side there was room for criticism, and the Governor of the Richmond Bridewell was particularly blameworthy for allowing the Fenian leader to get away. The prison administration generally was defective; it was not in the hands of the Government of Ireland, but chiefly in those of the Corporation of Dublin and of Superintending Authorities. The result was the appointment of inefficient staff, and the improper control and management of prisoners. Two warders had been arrested for complicity in the escape, and Lord Wodehouse, of whom Rose thought highly, had told him that three more were suspected. A full inquiry was being made into the whole discreditable business and Wodehouse was already resolved on superseding the Governor, Dominick Marques. There would be no real remedy, however, until the prison system was fundamentally altered. One of Rose's officers had seen in the Governor's room a portrait of William Smith O'Brien, who was convicted of rebellion in 1848, with an inscription that it was from the 'captive' to Mr Marques. That was bad enough, but the Deputy Governor of the Jail told the officer that he did not know whose portrait it was!

What Rose forecast happened. The governor was dismissed, the local inspector of prisons severely reprimanded, and Byrne the night watchman committed for trial. No suspicion fell on Breslin, who had played the major part in affecting the escape. And the Lord Lieutenant resumed his statutory right to appoint the intern officers of the Dublin prisons. This pleased Rose exceedingly. The Corporation, which could not administer the sewerage, were

certainly not equal to so important a charge! (1) He was thinking
of the state of the Liffey, a beautiful river, he said, as it flowed
through mountain passes and between the hills of Kildare but
which was offensive to sight and smell in the centre of Dublin.

While doing everything that was asked of him, Rose, as we saw,
did not share the Lord Lieutenant's view that the escape of
Stephens might precipitate an outbreak. Nor did he think that it
called for reinforcement of the army, though Wodehouse thought
it did. A reinforcement, he felt, was undesirable; it would cause
nervous people to believe that the situation was more serious than
it actually was. Nevertheless, as he found himself obliged to
strengthen the garrisons in Dublin and in a few places in the
South, he asked the Duke of Cambridge for two extra regiments.
Simultaneously he stopped all furlough.

A most elaborate plan for the establishment of a republic
involving widespread military action had been found lately on a
clerk in the Crown Solicitor's office, and Rose feared that this
was indicative of the spread of Fenianism into almost every civil
department, rail, roads, stations, telegraph offices and the post
office. The situation was not judged to be at all as bad as it had
been in 1848, but there were 33,000 men available in the army
then as against about only half that number now. (2) It was impossible, of course, to foretell the future, especially a future that
depended on Irish passions, but these passions would never lead to
cool or deliberate operations, to open content in the field,
though they might be productive of a sort of *jacquerie* which was
congenial to the habits and antecedents of the Irish.

When it came to gauging the extent to which Fenianism had
actually penetrated the Army, Superintendent Ryan, in January
1866, said that almost all the men in three regiments he named
were Fenians. This Rose declared to be a gross exaggeration,
although it might have been a more accurate picture of the situation six months or so earlier. He had assumed the command in
1865 on the death of Sir George Brown, whom he described as 'a
very fair gallant old soldier' who was under a fairly common
delusion that the British uniform could not possibly cover a
traitor. He would not listen to numerous proofs brought to him

by commanding officers of Fenians in their regiments, and this had produced a considerable slackness which Rose had worked hard to remove. 'I soon became aware', he said, 'of the extent and danger of Stephens's intrigues in the army, and of the necessity of counteracting as vigorously as he plotted them.' (3) So, by the end of January 1866 he was in a position to repeat to the Commander in Chief that the body of the army in Ireland was sound. 'There is more Fenianism than there ought to be', he added,

and I think that exemplary punishment of Fenian soldiers who have violated their oaths of allegiance and have committed a double crime of treason, that is as civil subjects and as soldiers, is necessary. This is the more necessary because there cannot be the slightest doubt that the Fenian conspirators have not lost sight of the so obvious policy of causing their agents to enlist into regiments where, provided with plenty of money, they have a more favourable opportunity of tampering with soldiers and gaining information useful to their employers, than if they were out of the Army. (4)

As things stood, soldiers found guilty by courts martial of treasonable conduct could receive no more than two years' imprisonment while individuals charged before the civil courts were more sternly dealt with. The Military Act cried out for amendment.

In the process of combating Military Fenianism, as it tended to be called, the Government were able in serious cases to keep the 'Fenian' regiments out of Ireland, sending in others which were not placed, as Irish soldiers were, in 'antagonism to the designs and hopes of the masses of their countrymen', and of the individuals who were anxious, by every means in their power, to seduce 'the impulsive and credulous co-religionists' serving in the ranks. (5) The quoted words are Rose's. In 1848, when no less than 100 soldiers in Irish regiments were reported for disaffection, Sir Edward Blakeney said that 'it would be better to take no notice of it'. Rose took an entirely contrary view. Temporising and condoning such grave crimes in soldiers, the violation of their first duty, was most dangerous. Whenever an instance of disaffection occurred it should be dealt with promptly: otherwise the trouble was bound to spread. (6) He had put the whole officer corps on its guard, and police detectives, as well as the army agents, were going among the troops in search of Fenian activity. Two soldiers of the 4th Dragoon Guards had had themselves sworn in as Fenians and divulged what they thereby learned of the secrets of the Brotherhood. One thing they discovered was the untrustworthiness of the warders in the Richmond Bridewell—this was before Stephens escaped—but the information, though it had been passed to the civil authorities, was not acted upon.

By similar means some of the principal trouble-makers were detected. These included Colour-Sergeant Charles MacCarthy, Sergeant Thomas Darragh and Corporal Chambers. Mac-Carthy's was regarded as the most serious case. 'It was a case of deliberate, deeply planned treason, than which nothing could be worse' (7) for MacCarthy was 'the source, a very dangerous one, in the Army of Fenianism', one of the paid Irish Republican agents. (8) He had obtained a false key of the magazine at Clonmel with the intention of taking out battery guns deposited there and of using them against British soldiers. Rose would have liked to have had him shot for this but, with Darragh and Chambers, though formally sentenced to death, he was given a life sentence.

For much less serious offences, such as shouting 'Hurrah for the Irish Republic', soldiers were taken out and flogged before their comrades and took their punishment with extraordinary fortitude. John Devoy knew a man named Curry who never winced or moved a muscle as the lash fell on him. How did he do it? 'Be jabers, John,' he said, 'I had a sixpence between me teeth.' (9) Rose was opposed to the abolition of flogging in the army. It was always to be avoided, he believed, but it was indispensable as a summary example in dealing with hard, irreclaimable men. After all, the only alternative he could think of was capital punishment, and 'that, of course, was impossible' in these less serious cases. (10)

The agents among the troops had to watch their steps. The first of these was Private Patrick Foley of the 5th Dragoon Guards who acted as a spotter without any extra pay for nearly twelve months and whose information led to the numerous arrests, including that of Devoy, that were made in Pilsworth's public house in James's Street in February 1866. He, and Private James Mears of the 8th Foot, also identified Fenians in Mountjoy Prison. From the moment, however, that he came forward as a witness in the public courts his life was at risk, and, as he had no comfort in his regiment, he had to remove to England where things were safer for a time.

(2)

Fenianism in the army was only one feature, albeit a distinctive one, of the political condition of the country that Rose had had to concern himself with since coming to Ireland. He had not served in Ireland since 1833 so he considered it safest to rely on the opinion of the Government of the country at whose head stood 'an authority with such great and impartial judgment as Lord Wodehouse'. (11) Because of his position Rose was able to go direct to Wodehouse, though by doing so he offended Larcom, the Under Secretary, who would have preferred a more orderly channel of communication. But direct contact with the Commander of the Forces doubtless suited Wodehouse, too, because of his desire to exercise personally the control he supremely held. It was from Wodehouse that Rose, early in December 1865, learned directly of a letter from America that had been intercepted, which spoke of an invasion force and likely landings in Galway and Kerry before St Patrick's Day (17th March 1866). The invading force would consist principally of devil-may-care Irishmen who had served in the Confederate Army, many of them from Cork. They had arms and training and could be relied upon to put up a tough fight. 'You ask me,' the letter said, 'are the priests mixed up in the business; the Fenians on this side of the water are too go-ahead fellows to care much which part they [the priests] take. I dare say they will watch the fighting and be guided by the result.'

To meet the invasion was a matter in the first instance for the Navy, of course: their job would be to prevent any American invaders from reaching the Irish coast. So the Admiralty, who had actually wanted to reduce the number of warships already in Irish waters, were prevailed upon to act with discretion. There was an ample sufficiency of suitable anchorages on the coast, though these were not perhaps the most agreeable stations for the officers. Rose knew from experience that the latter would represent that the idea of a descent or landing was out of the question, absurd, and so forth, and would try to pass the buck to him. He repeated therefore,

> that not to employ steam ships of war and to employ land troops, *troupes de terre*, in watching and defending the Irish coasts, their numerous anchorages and landing places, would be to use one finger instead of five. All the initiative and the most important by far part of the defence of sea coast is the specialty of vessels and especially steam vessels of war. I cannot draw up a memorandum on the subject of the defence of the coasts of this country without knowing how many vessels of war, steam or otherwise, are stationed on the Irish coasts. If an idea exists among Irish American Fenians of a filibustering descent on the Irish coasts, nothing is as likely to prevent it as the knowledge that there are ships of war in strategical stations . . . (12)

The rumours of a rising at or about Christmas 1865 increased so much that Wodehouse thought it necessary seriously to consider what steps should be taken if an outbreak should take place in Dublin, which was constantly mentioned with Cork as the place where it would begin. 'In 1848', he told Rose,

> a regular programme was prepared so that in the event of any sudden attempt, especially at night, the military and police authorities should know what to do at once. I would suggest that such a programme should be prepared without delay and that the Heads of the Police and the Constabulary should be made acquainted with it. I can hardly believe in the probability of so mad an attempt but prudence requires that we should not neglect any precaution. The garrison of Dublin ought on no account to be diminished . . .

He added that there were confident statements current among the Fenians that a filibustering expedition was on the way from

America, and would arrive shortly. In those circumstances he did not think that Rose, who wanted to get in some shooting, should be long absent from Dublin. (13) Rose accepted this and his decision pleased Wodehouse; although, as Rose said, 'it is a shrieking bore to give up the woodcocks, with whom I believe the Fenians to be in league'. (14) He might go away for one day. Would that be all right? But Wodehouse could not take it upon himself to say whether it would or not, for, as he said,

> we have been for months constantly beset with rumours of outbreaks which have never taken place, and if we wait till we are free from them, we may remain in Dublin for months. I don't venture to go away myself at present, but as I conclude that General Cunyngham [the officer commanding the Division at Dublin and the Curragh] is here and that you have confidence in him, I shall leave it to you to suit your own convenience. There are all manner of rumours of an attempt at rescue or 'something' tomorrow night or next night. I can't believe in such folly, but I should be glad if you would tell General Cunyngham and ask him to be specially on the alert in your absence.

Wodehouse had spoken of a 'programme' and he explained to Rose that what he had in mind was the desirability of considering what points the troops should occupy if an outbreak did occur. Probably this had already been done but the chiefs of the police and constabulary might with advantage be told what points they should specially watch and what course they should take if any sudden movement occurred. He did not feel himself a good judge on such essentially military matters. 'I quite agree with you', he added, 'that a general rising is only likely if an expedition landed, but a *handful* of men might kindle the flame. It is, I am sure you concur with me, wise to be prepared even for not very probable contingencies when there is so bad a feeling abroad amongst the mass of the Roman Catholic population . . .' (15)

Rose agreed, and Wodehouse was able to tell Sir George Grey, the Home Secretary, that the disposition of the military force, made after most careful deliberation, was well calculated to suppress quickly any attempt at a rising, though no doubt 18,000 men was not a large force. There was, he said, a general sense of

FF D

insecurity which perhaps the presence of troops in districts to which they could not send them at that time might diminish. He was particularly worried about Ballina, which he thought was a security risk, but Rose had told him that he had not 100 men to send there. It was in following up this that Rose was encouraged to apply, as we said already, for two extra infantry regiments. When these, the 59th and 64th, arrived within a couple of weeks, they were housed, one at the Curragh, the other at Birr and Templemore. Meanwhile Rose was paying attention to the defence of the Pigeon House and Magazine forts.

(3)

A Constabulary watcher in the United States, Sub-Inspector Doyle, who had warned his Inspector General that 'a storm from this country threatens yours and that it is only prudent and wise on your part to put your house in order for the event' (16), said on the 7th October 1865 that he did not believe it possible for the Fenians, earnest though they were, to send any large body of men to Ireland that winter. One of their chiefs had recently advised against precipitate action, saying that Irish Freedom was a boon worth waiting for; if they took the necessary time to strengthen and mature their power, they could as certainly expel English dominion from the soil of Ireland as the stars were gleaming in the heavens as he spoke. (17)

They had an army organised, though in scattered divisions, and had collected large sums of money, and the crushing blow the organisation had received by the recent proceedings of the Irish Government might compel them to make the choice of fighting very soon or give up the business altogether. Yet Doyle could see no indication that they were about to embark for Ireland except as individuals. (18) The news from Ireland of arrests, of informers, of naval ships on the southern coast and of troop movements had disheartened them (19) and reinforced his belief that there would be no invasion in 1865. (20) There was talk of there being privateers ere long to create havoc among English shipping, but he did not know what importance to attach to these stories. Steamships of the privateer class could readily be purchased; the American Government were selling many of the ships that had lately been used in the War and which were no longer needed. But the Fenians had other uses for their money, too. They had just acquired splendid premises in Union Square at a monthly rent of a thousand dollars. (21)

Since the previous December Head Constable Martin Meagher from Ireland had been helping Doyle to watch the Fenian headquarters and to keep an eye out for Stephens who, it was thought, would come to America. Things were 'far from happy' with the Fenians. The leaders, split into two factions over where the battle for Irish freedom should be fought and over O'Mahony's issue of Republican Bonds which the Senate, led by Roberts and Sweeney deemed to be irregular, illegal and unconstitutional, had started to heap abuse on each other, and O'Mahony had gone so far as to describe the Senate as 'a faction instigated by corrupt motives and British gold'. He had put up a poster on the headquarters in Union Square denying admission to the Senators, and they had retaliated by deposing him and setting up house for themselves on Broadway. (22) President Roberts, as he was now styled, had signalled his appointment by openly declaring war on England. This, Doyle thought, might mean action in February 1866. A letter written by an avowed Fenian announcing an early attack on the cross-border town of St Stephen had come his way and he had sent particulars of its contents to the authorities in New Brunswick. To his chief in Dublin, Colonel Wood, he said it was clear that the Senate wing planned an operation across the Canadian frontier while O'Mahony remained committed to fighting on Irish soil. The Government at home would, therefore, have to watch two fronts simultaneously.

Doyle, and Consul Archibald whom Doyle saw from time to time, kept Dublin posted about the Congress that O'Mahony convened in January 1866, but which was not recognised by the members of the Senate. The important meetings of this Congress were supposedly held in secret, and the entrance to Clifton Hall where it was held was guarded by a company of O'Mahony's regiment, the 99th State Militia, but the newspapers were 'pregnant with information'. The outcome was an endorsement of O'Mahony and his plans. Ireland, not Canada, was to be their venue for the battle; and to his message giving this news Doyle added 'Need I say more—one word—Prepare!' (23) O'Mahony was going to Europe to meet Stephens and Mitchel; he would be followed there by Head Constable Meagher. (24) O'Mahony had also engaged passages for ten Fenian officers on the *City of New York* calling at Queenstown, and Doyle asked Wood to 'meet them' there. (25)

Stephens was expected to try to heal the rift in America, but if the letters appearing over his name in the newspapers were genuine, that likelihood was now remote, for in them he scouted the idea of an invasion of Canada as un-Irish, and foreign to the proper object of the Fenian organisation. Archibald, drawing attention to this development, told Clarendon, the Foreign Secretary, that, despite the wranglings among the Fenians, their ardour in the common cause showed little sign of diminishing. 'The Prophecies of St Columbkille', which had been secretly and extensively circulated, were continuing to exercise a pernicious influence on the minds of Irishmen everywhere. 'Although a manifest imposture and throughout a rhapsody of nonsense' they were artfully designed to operate on the superstitious feelings of the Irish and to propagate a belief in what was foretold of the consummation of events. (26)

(4)

The Irish Government, considering in the middle of January 1866 that the immediate danger of an invasion had passed, proceeded to thank everybody for their special services during the previous four months, the Admiralty whose ships of war had kept cruising off the southern coast in weather that was often vile, the military who had supported the police at every point, and the resident magistrates who had demonstrated their courage and efficiency. It only remained for the Special Commission that had been appointed to try the Fenian prisoners, among them some obviously dangerous men who gloried in their treason, and to sentence them to long terms of penal servitude. Lord Wodehouse had seen to it that these men would not get away as Stephens had done. They were most carefully watched in prison; even at night-time they were seen every quarter of an hour.

For the success of the Commission the Government relied heavily on the politically disreputable Judge Keogh and on Judge Fitzgerald. These men had to be watched as closely as the prisoners. Keogh was receiving threatening letters and this worried Wodehouse for 'there are scoundrels amongst these Fenians quite capable of shooting him from behind a wall. I mention this for your own private information', he told Clarendon, 'as it would only encourage the concoctors of threatening missives if they thought we took notice enough of them to be afraid'. (27) When the judges went to Cork they had to be guarded with particular care and escorted from and to the railway station by the resident magistrates, the mounted constabulary and an escort of dragoons. Since Stephens's escape Cork city had been excited, an effort to hold a torchlight procession in his honour had had to be suppressed, and trouble was expected to break out with the arrival of the judges. Placards were posted up calling Keogh a second Norbury and a perjurer, and urging the people to give him and Fitzgerald the reception they deserved. However, apart from a little booing, everything passed off quietly.

From the Speech from the Throne on the 6th February 1866, it appeared that the constitutional power of the ordinary tribunals would be found to be sufficient to repress the Fenian conspiracy. But inside a fortnight the Government—apparently influenced by Sub-Inspector Doyle's reports from America that a crisis was at hand—changed its attitude dramatically, rushing a Bill through Parliament to suspend Habeas Corpus in Ireland. (28) Probably no statute was ever previously passed with such celerity. The case for doing so was made to rest on a letter of the 14th February from the Lord Lieutenant in which he declared that he could not be responsible for the safety of the country if power was not given forthwith to the Government of Ireland to seize men of a most dangerous and reckless class who, undeterred by the punishment of so many of their leaders, were actively organising an outbreak with a view to destroying the Queen's authority.

This new crop of trouble-makers he described as Irishmen, imbued with American notions and possessed of considerable military experience, acquired in the American civil war, that was admirably adapted to train them for conducting an insurrection. There were 340 such men known to the police in the provinces, and those known in Dublin came to about 160—in round numbers, 500 in all. That figure was being augmented by fresh men constantly arriving from America. In Dublin there were also several hundred men who had come over from England and Scotland who were receiving one shilling and sixpence a day while they waited for the time of action. They could be observed at the street corners. Three regular arms factories had been discovered in Dublin, and the police believed that several more existed. The disaffection of the population in certain counties such as Cork, Tipperary, Waterford and Dublin was alarming; and a most dangerous feature of the movement was the attempt to seduce the troops. 'Are we to allow those agents to go on instilling their poison into the armed force upon which our security mainly depends?' he asked. The suspension of the Habeas Corpus Act would have a most salutary effect, he said. It was remarkable that the Fenian leaders were saying that there was no time to lose, as if they did, the Act would be suspended and they could be held in custody for an indeterminate period.

The suspension, limited till the first of September 1886, was carried in the Commons by 346 votes to 6, the only serious opponents to it being John Stuart Mill and John Bright. But even before the Bill passed in the Lords and was signed, the powers it conferred were put into operation. On the 16th February a large number of arrests was made in Dublin and its vicinity, while many of the American men hurriedly left the country to avoid being taken up. By these events, the arrests and the departures, the alarms of 'the peaceable and well-affected part of the community' subsided, and the insurrectionary spirit began to show signs of decline. That was still roughly the situation when a renewal of the suspension for a further term was later considered.

(5)

In April 1866 the Government sought, through their representative at the Vatican, Odo Russell, to put pressure on the Pope through the Secretary of State, Cardinal Antonelli, to deal with what Lord Clarendon called 'that truculent body, the Irish Priesthood'. He believed that it would make all the hair the Cardinal had on his head stand if he knew the truth about the subversive doctrines they held and the rebellious spirit they encouraged, for it was impossible to expect that the people who were taught to be as tigers to their governors should at the same time be as lambs to their pastors. Hatred and defiance of authority had been instilled into them, and the Church, though it might be the last to suffer, was quite sure to be treated in the same way. The priests as much as the people had been looking to America for relief from the yoke of England and the establishment of a republic in Ireland, but the first thing the Irish did on arriving in America was to emancipate themselves from their priests and their religious obligations, and it was these men who as Fenians had returned to Ireland meditating a bloody social revolution and denouncing the clergy as actual enemies to their schemes. The clergy, of course, denounced them in turn, but it was too late, for the Fenians knew well that the ground had been prepared for them and how easily they could reunite their forces among men who had been taught to conspire. Clarendon wished that Cardinal Antonelli had the will or the means to ascertain the truth and he would find that this was no exaggerated statement of priestly doings and their results in Ireland. He had heard privately from Lord Wodehouse that the priests had in many places joined the Fenian movement and were known to be receiving the confessions of Fenians. If Cardinal Antonelli wished to help the

Government he should send peremptory orders to his friend
Archbishop Cullen to put some check upon his socialist clergy. (29)

(6)

Towards the middle of March, Stephens and Colonel Kelly
got away from Ireland on a two-masted coasting collier. They
did so despite the exceptional vigilance of the authorities and a
proclamation offering two thousand pounds for Stephens's
capture or a thousand for information leading to his arrest. The
journey, long and hazardous, took them first to Kilmarnock, then
to London by train, where they rested at a hotel near Buckingham
Palace before embarking on the final leg that brought them safely
on the 18th March to the French capital. The Government
speedily heard of their arrival and Wodehouse, at the request of
the Home Secretary, sent a Dublin detective who knew the
Fenian chief to accompany a London policeman to Paris to enable
him to make an identification. More London men were to follow
at intervals to make acquaintance with Stephens so as to be able
to follow him wherever he went: *one* could not do much
good. (30)

Stephens relaxed in Paris for a few days in the company of
well-to-do anglophobes like the Marquis de Boissy and Jules
Sandeau, and renewed earlier contacts with the French Republican
Left. He may never have been a convinced Communist but he had
joined the Red resistance to Louis Napoleon's *coup d'état*. He
may now have met Cesare Orsini (the half-brother of Felice
Orsini who had attempted the life of Napoleon III eight years
earlier), who enrolled him later in New York as a member of the
International Workingmen's Association; Orsini passed on this
news item to Karl Marx, who told Engels about 'this most
doubtful of our acquisitions'. (31)

From Paris Kelly sent a defiant message back to Ireland which
was printed in the *Irishman* for all to read. 'The next time James
Stephens touches the Irish soil,' it ran, 'he will show the British

that their barbarous treatment of Irish patriots but added fuel to the national flame already kindled all over the island . . . Sir Hugh Rose, the British Commander in Chief in Ireland will find, when he attempts to commit such devilish barbarities as those of which he was guilty in India, that he has not sepoys to deal with . . .' (32)

On the 19th March 1866 Sub-Inspector Doyle called to see Archibald, the British Consul in New York, at his request, and found him in very confidential communication with one of General Sweeney's colonels. 'In the coming war', said Doyle, 'he proposes to stand well with both sides.' (33) This was apparently F. F. Millen, who, as we saw, had been ordered back to America by Stephens 'to prepare the expedition to Ireland', and who for a twelve-month had been playing a double game. A letter Archibald had written to Sir Thomas Larcom tells the whole unsavoury story:

British Consulate
New York, March 13, 1866.

Secret and Confidential
Sir,

In your official letter to me of the 24th November you called my attention to the appointment by the Fenians in Ireland of a person called General Mellon as Chief, in succession to Stephens after the arrest of the latter, and requested me to furnish you, for the information of the Lord Lieutenant, with any intelligence I might be able to procure respecting him and his movements.

In my reply to you of the [?] of January I mentioned that Mellon, or rather Millen, was still here, holding an acting appointment as Military Secretary under Sweeney, and that should he be sent over to Ireland again, I should give you timely notice of his departure.

I have lately discovered that I was mistaken in reference to the person described to me as General Millen. Three or four days ago General *Millen* himself called upon me, when I recognised him as personally known to me, having brought me, about a year since, a letter of introduction from a highly respectable merchant of this city, a personal friend of my own, to whom Millen brought letters of introduction from New Orleans, on his way home from Mexico where he had served in the Juarist Army. Such numbers of people come to me constantly with letters of introduction that I had quite forgotten the name of Millen and his short interview with me.

The object of his late interview with me was to furnish me, for the service of Her Majesty's Government, with valuable information in reference to the military arrangements of the Fenians in the United Kingdom, their numbers and distribution, and secret places of deposit of arms.

I have had two interviews with him. He began by himself stating (as you mentioned in your letter to me of the 24th of November) that he had been elected by the Fenians in Dublin to succeed Stephens after his arrest and that, while in Ireland during the past year, he had the control of the military organisation of Fenians, and is acquainted with all the details thereof and that he came out as a special envoy to report the state of military affairs in Ireland and attended O'Mahony's convention in January in that character. I was misinformed in stating that he had been holding an acting appointment under Sweeney—his connection being solely with the O'Mahony and Stephens faction.

It appears that jealousies have grown up between himself and Stephens who fears that Millen was desirous of usurping his, Stephens', authority—and O'Mahony has been trying to adjust the dispute. Millen shewed me letters from O'Mahony to him of recent date on this subject. The result has been that, without deciding against Millen, O'Mahony has relieved him, since the 6th inst. from his rank of *General*—or rather from the *full* pay of it—confiding in his fidelity to the cause and relying on his continued services—or to this effect. In this position of affairs Millen, without breaking with O'Mahony, or exciting the distrust of his colleagues, proposes to furnish H.M. Government with the fullest details of all the information he possesses in reference to the military organisation, enrolments, arms, &c. &c., in England and Scotland as well as Ireland. Of course he looks for compensation, and intimates that he would like to have a small Colonial appointment. I have said that I could make no such stipulation with him, but I suggested that I should send him home so that he could be in immediate communication with H.M. Government, and, if required, go to Ireland; telling him that the Government would, no doubt, grant him such compensation as they might consider adequate to the value of his information after proof of its usefulness.

To this proposition he assents. He is a man of about thirty years of age I judge—a North of Ireland man by birth—intelligent, and frank in his manner and, I think, considering his antecedents, may be able to give very valuable information. He is married but has no family, and wishes to take his wife with him.

Before coming to a conclusion on the subject, I have thought it well to consult Sir Frederick Bruce, and am now awaiting his reply to my letter. If he concurs in my views Millen will go from here on the Inman Steamer of Saturday next the 17th instant. He will go in the confidence of O'Mahony and with the ostensible object of promoting the plans of the Fenians in Ireland.

As regards the operations of the Fenians here, I have to report that the leaders of both factions are making the most of the Canadian excitement to levy contributions of money. I hear reports of steamers being purchased, and torpedoes being constructed &c.: but I believe very little is being done by O'Mahony beyond raising money, and sending off, as best he can, some cases or packages of small arms to be smuggled into Ireland. Some of the newspapers here, for political purposes, are magnifying the Fenian preparations.

I have the honor to be your most obedient, humble servant

E. M. Archibald

P.S. I write you hurriedly as I send this by our special messenger to Boston who is obliged to leave immediately. My object in writing is to forewarn you of Millen's departure. He will probably report first at the Foreign Office, unless on his arrival at Liverpool any agent of the Government may be directed to communicate with him. He will pass under the assumed name of Francis Martin. (34)

Extraordinary precautions were taken to maintain secrecy regarding Millen's betrayal. When his first statement reached Wodehouse from Clarendon, he told Larcom that the greatest care should be taken to keep the name of the informant secret. 'You had better divulge it to *no one* here. Copy out the information as to the individuals yourself and give them to the Police without saying how you got it. We cannot be too secret.' And he enclosed a cheque for £500 from Fortescue, the Chief Secretary, which may have been intended as an initial payment for Millen (2.4.1866). Larcom did as he was told. Archibald had also written directly to him (35) to ensure that there would be no delay in taking action. For greater security he had met Millen at a distance from the Consulate, both to receive promised information and to make arrangements for future contacts. He had accepted Millen's stipulation for secrecy as regards himself and his communications, and had given an undertaking that, in the event of Millen going to Ireland at the instance of the Government, which he was prepared to do, he would under no circumstance be brought forward as a witness.

Millen gave Archibald four addresses in Dublin where Stephens was likely to be found but by this time Stephens had left the city. He also supplied the names of the men who had helped Stephens to escape from the Richmond Bridewell: these included Byrne, the warder, who was already in prison, awaiting a second trial, if evidence could be produced against him. Millen mentioned a Captain O'Reilly who had just arrived from Ireland with a message from Stephens withdrawing the charges he had made against Millen and begging that Millen be sent over with the expedition O'Mahony was fitting out and which would not sail for another four or five weeks. Very little had in fact been done as yet, he said, beyond negotiations for the purchase of a steamer. He mentioned a David Bell as the only member of the I.R.B.'s Civil Executive Council still at large; and of the Military Council, apart from himself (the President), those still free were Colonel Halpin, Colonel Daly and Captain (or Colonel) Kelly. A civilian named Nolan and 'the delicate young man' Edward Duffy (then out on bail) were two of Stephens's best organisers. Miss O'Leary and Mrs O'Donovan Rossa were functioning as pay-mistresses: they made frequent visits to Paris and brought back funds to Ireland for the payment of men and the purchase of arms.

Millen supplied a table, three and a half pages long, showing the location of Fenian centres in Ireland, the number of men in each, whether they were fully or partly drilled, the arms they possessed, and in some instances the names of the centres. He also provided the names and addresses of circles in America with the numbers of men who had signed for active service when called on. He said that a plan was in contemplation to arm five or six hundred desperate men in Liverpool with revolvers and to pay their passages on an English steamer which they hoped to take possession of on the passage and turn into a privateer. An outbreak could be confidently looked for that year (1866), but he would give a warning in good time, so as to enable the Government to suppress it with as little bloodshed as possible. There was no danger of anything until the crops were well in the ground.

The Dublin police were given an opportunity, as usual, of commenting on Millen's information. In a lengthy minute Superintendent Ryan said the apprehension of Halpin, O'Reilly and Kelly would place every Irish-American officer of note in Ireland in the hands of the Government. That done, the conspirators would have no leaders and would be entirely incapable of doing anything worthwhile, until O'Mahony and his expedition went to their help and this they should not be permitted to do. (38) He thought that Miss O'Leary and Mrs O'Donovan Rossa should be arrested and detained; but Wodehouse shrank from such a doubtful measure. His idea was that they should be arrested, searched by 'polite policemen' who would pay every respect to their sex, and released. 'It is a ticklish work to meddle with women,' he said. (37)

CHAPTER IV

American Fenians on the Move

THE proposal to raid Canada first came into the open at the special Fenian Congress held in Philadelphia in October 1865. It is not evident where the idea originated, but B. Doran Killian, an able Fenian lawyer, sounded out President Andrew Johnson, the successor to the assassinated Lincoln, and Seward, the Secretary of State, as to how they would react if the Fenians were to seize some portion of the territory lying north of the frontier of Maine simultaneously with a rising in Ireland. In an amiable discussion the President and the Secretary of State replied somewhat ambiguously, but significantly, to the effect that in such a contingency the Government would acknowledge the *fait accompli*. Killian, in a letter to Seward on the 18th November, tried to tie the Government down to something more specific, by indicating the area in Canada that the Fenians contemplated seizing, but Seward saw through this ruse and gave no written reply. The priest who brought the letter to him received, however, a verbal reply which confirmed that given earlier to Killian, with the result that the Fenians went ahead with their plans, confident that they had the American Government behind them. (1)

When the British Foreign Office heard what the Fenians had in mind, they instructed Sir Frederick Bruce, their Minister in Washington, to make an early *démarche* with the object of putting the United States Government in a position to deal with attacks from American soil. Knowing the extreme delicacy of the question, and the reluctance of the American Government to make any official declaration about it on account of the importance of the Irish vote in the impending elections, Bruce wrote nothing but gave the substance of the London despatch to Seward in conversation. In doing so, he emphasised that he was not looking for any information that he could not obtain otherwise but was letting him know, as if he did not already well know, the intentions that had been imputed to the Fenians, and that Chicago had been mentioned as likely to be their rendez-vous.

Seward told Bruce that he thought the Fenian affair much exaggerated, and that nothing would seem so much to give it importance as that it should become the subject of official correspondence. Bruce thought that if Seward were pressed to make any formal declaration on the question it was very likely that he would accompany it with some expressions of sympathy with the national aspirations which underlay the movement, rather than lose for his party the support of the Irish at that critical moment. A declaration of that nature would be represented by the Fenian agitators as favourable to them and, by the attention it would excite, the American Government would be more embarrassed in taking measures to preserve quiet on the frontiers, should any measures for that purpose become necessary.

Bruce felt that there were larger considerations which made him inclined to work with, rather than in opposition to, Seward, who justly had the reputation of being more pacific in his views than any person likely to be put in his place. Therefore, unless otherwise instructed, he proposed to continue to communicate in a private and friendly manner such specific information as he obtained that might seem to call for vigilance on the part of the American Government. Seward would more readily undertake, and more easily defend, measures of precaution, when he could state that they had been taken as *proprio motu* for the vindication of international obligations, and not at the request of Her Majesty's Government. (2)

Lord Clarendon, the British Foreign Minister, approved of this approach. (3) So long as the security of the British Provinces from persons seeking to produce confusion and to imperil relations could be obtained by friendly and unofficial communication H.M. Government had no desire to remonstrate officially. But he noted from the accounts in the public press that the Fenian agitators in the United States had recently set up a so-called Executive Government with all the paraphernalia of ministers appointed to several departments and had established or were about to establish in one of the centres of the American Union the seat of such government. This, he said, must surely be looked upon by the American Government as a proceeding not only unheard of in the history of the world but as one incompatible with the dignity of the United States and with their international obligations towards Great Britain. Practically these proceedings might be of little real importance as regards the tranquillity of Ireland against which they were avowedly directed, but the tendency which they manifestly had to keep agitation alive and to embitter the feelings of the people of the United States against Great Britain was not only lamentable in itself, but might eventually impair good understanding between the two governments.

The Government of the United States during the Civil War had very justly felt itself entitled to call upon the British Government to prevent any hostile incursions being made from the borders of the British North American Provinces upon the territory of the United States by persons who had repaired to those Provinces for that purpose from the Confederate States; and the British Authorities had done their utmost to prevent or punish outrages of that description, notwithstanding the difficulties interposed by the extent of frontier which it was necessary to watch and the secrecy with which the conspirators devised and carried into execution their plans; and their exertions in this respect were highly appreciated by the Government of the United States.

But in the case of the so-called Fenian Government the locality in which it was established was well known, and their acts and intentions were not sought to be disguised and, therefore, the Government of the United States were not hindered, as were the British Government, in taking, against disturbers of the public peace and against conspirators designing injury to a friendly nation, such measure of precaution and repression as circumstances might appear to call for.

He counselled Bruce to watch the proceedings of the Fenians with the utmost vigilance. (4) Bruce was doing so; he told Earl Russell, the Prime Minister, about the time he received Clarendon's despatch, that no movement could be made on a scale sufficiently extensive to cause serious alarm without timely notice of it being obtained. He was sure that a raid could easily be resisted and defeated from the Canadian side; he was keeping the Canadian Government informed of such intention as he received on that subject. (5) 'I am fairly run down with informers,' he said. 'I think I may say I am bearing the brunt of the Fenian invasion.' (6) Letters from O'Mahony were being brought to him for inspection. 'As long as funds are abundant, numerous military and other hangers-on will be found and ready to aid in their expenditure.' The State elections were now over, the Irish having everywhere cast their votes with those of the minority Democratic Party and, their military services being now no longer needed, public opinion would daily grow stronger in opposition to the Fenians. (7)

Bruce resisted any suggestion that the United States Government should be pressed into taking action under Section 6 of the Neutrality Act. The arrest and trial of Fenians in America would give importance to the movement, and would be the most effectual means of healing the dissensions of the Fenians, while the members of the Government who, from personal motives did not wish to lose the Irish vote, would be tempted so to deal with the question as not to throw the Irish element on the side of the opposition. 'It is to be recollected moreover,' Bruce said 'that there is a considerable sympathy for the Irish as an oppressed nationality and that there is much irritation against Great Britain not only on account of the *Alabama* and *Shenandoah* but on account of the organised system of blockade—running which furnished those supplies for the Confederates by aid of which it is generally believed the civil war ... was materially prolonged.'* It would be wiser to leave it to the United States Government to deal with this difficult question in its own way. He had good grounds for believing that the Government was more on the alert and better prepared to stop any Fenian enterprise than was

---

* The Confederate States employed the *Alabama*, the *Shenandoah* and eleven other vessels effectively to drive Union shipping from the high seas. The *Alabama*, emerging from the port of Liverpool, despite an appeal to have her detained, alone captured upwards of seventy ships, most of which she destroyed. The *Shenandoah* had a somewhat similar record. The British were accused of connivance, claims for damages were made and ultimately settled by arbitration.

FF E

generally supposed. The Fenian cause had been much injured by
the dissensions among its leaders and by the charges of treachery
and corruption they made against each other. 'These evidences of
incapacity and bad faith produce in the practical Anglo-Saxon a
feeling of contempt and distrust which is very damaging and
appeal efficaciously to the spirit of antagonism to the Celtic and
Roman Catholic idea which is a far deeper and more enduring
sentiment than the superficial sympathy which has been evoked
by irritation against England.' (8)

The position at the end of 1865 was that Seward was believed
to want peace and would use his influence in that direction but
was afraid of appearing friendly to the British. (9) He had assured
Bruce privately that it would be seen in due course that his
government had taken more measures of precaution than was
supposed, but he would not say what these were, nor would he
say what steps he had taken with respect to General Sweeney, the
Fenian titular Secretary of War in the Roberts camp who was a
regular official of the United States army, and who was knwon
to have his plans for 'a warlike demonstration on Ireland by way
of Canada.' (10) in an advanced state.

Clarendon repeated that he did not object to Seward being told
that the friendly intentions of the American government were
recognised but Seward should not be surprised at the people of
Britain having some doubt about those intentions when they read
of proceedings so entirely without precedent as those of the
Fenians in America with their Senate, their House of Representatives, their tax collectors, their paper money et cetera, et cetera—
in short, their open and notorious organisation in the heatt of a
friendly country for the invasion of Ireland and wresting it from
the British Crown. (11) Clarendon recognised the impolicy of
pressing the Americans unduly but, some day, he told Bruce,
the Fenians, when they were drunk, might determine upon a raid,
so Seward might be told confidentially that he was not being
written to, because it would be embarrassing to him either to send
a bunkum answer that would please the Irish, or a curt answer
that would annoy the British, but he was being relied upon to
take real and bona fide measures to prevent Fenian follies from

assuming the form of active outrage. (12) He hoped that the Fenians were cutting their own throats in the way most agreeable to all honest men on either side of the ocean. (13)

Early in January 1866, Bruce referred to Seward's timidity at a time when Fenianism appeared to be declining (14) and, a month later, he sent to London the substance of a conversation he had had with President Johnson. (15) Clarendon had told Bruce (16) to tell the President that they did not wish Fenian meetings or their rantings to be interfered with, for the more they wrangled with each other the better their true character and objects would be understood, but the British Government did wish that the Fenians should not be permitted to arm vessels or make raids on Canada as such attempts would give trouble and be the cause of great annoyance to loyal subjects of the Crown. 'It won't do,' he had said, 'to despise these fellows or to consider that they would be incapable of making the attempts I allude to, as the evidence taken at the trials in Ireland shews that they are hardly reasoning beings and may commit any amount of rash folly from sheer incapacity to understand the consequences of their own acts.' In reply to these remarks the President told Bruce that the Fenian movement met with no sympathy on the part of the American Government, which on the contrary was anxious to discourage it. Johnson was much dissatisfied with the *imperium in imperio* the Irish wished to create in the United States; the attempt to combine particular nationalities on the American continent was contrary to American interests, and was inconsistent with their duties as American citizens. He did not think the Fenian affair was as formidable as was supposed; it would die out for want of fuel. He dwelt on the inconsistency of the Irish who, while invoking aid on their own behalf as an oppressed race, were themselves the most bitter opponents of all attempts to improve and elevate the condition of the Negro in the United States. (17)

Bruce thought that the Government of the United States was on the alert; that President Johnson was friendly to England, indeed 'our best friend in the administration'; and possible evidence of this was the dismissal of Sweeney about this time from the U.S. service. The reason publicly given for his dismissal was his

absence without leave from his regiment but the British Foreign
Office thought otherwise, though it would not do to attribute
to the American Government a motive different from that which
they themselves gave. (8) Roberts and Sweeney believed that if
they could get a foothold on Canadian soil on which to raise
the Irish flag they would be recognised by the American government as belligerents. A similar belief inspired the rival Fenian
wing as they sought to bring off a serious rising in Ireland. In
either eventuality Seward could not be relied upon. Bruce's
diplomatic colleagues were telling him that Seward was more
disposed to go to war with Britain than with France—that is, if a
foreign war was to be fought with anyone. He thirsted for
popularity and hoped for some shuffle of the cards which would
give him a chance for the Presidency. (19)

Clarendon, sharing the opinion that Seward's influence in the
Cabinet was unfavourable to Britain, was happy to learn that
Bruce, supported by some useful and reliable American friends,
had made an impression on the President which would prevent
him from being misguided. Of Seward, Clarendon said that he
never knew whether to class him among their lukewarm friends
or their covert enemies. 'I suppose he varies with public opinion
which in America can never be reckoned upon for 24 hours and
that we must not reckon upon him for doing us a good turn
...' (20) He, Clarendon, could not help hoping that the tone
towards England was slightly on the mend. The British were
perfectly able to take care of themselves, of course, and did not
fear a Fenian invasion, but so long as an Irish Republican Administration in the heart of the United States remained unmolested,
nothing would persuade the Irish people that the organisation
was not viewed with favour by the Government, and that the
time was not far distant when that favour would be openly
manifested. Hence the excitement in Ireland did not naturally
abate, notwithstanding the suspension of Habeas Corpus.
President Johnson, in Clarendon's eyes, was 'a man of purpose ... the most powerful and least responsible despot on
earth' and Clarendon hoped that Bruce could see him more often
without exciting jealousy in Seward. If, as seemed likely, he took

a proper view of the dignity of the United States he could not like the *imperium in imperio* which the Fenians, the lowest and most worthless of American citizens, had set up. (21) Bruce duly sent 'a proper message' to the President through a friendly channel.

Clarendon's next few letters to Bruce expressed concern over the rumoured fitting out of Fenian vessels and the maintenance of a large Irish army which was being kept together, and the rabies against England fostered, in order that the American Government would be able to speak louder and more insultingly to Britain whenever the time came to re-present the Alabama Bill. Seward would be contemplating with satisfaction this fine Irish *corps de réserve* in readiness for the quarrel he meant to pick whenever it suited his electioneering or other purposes. Things would have been quiet in Ireland were it not for the vast sums of money transmitted from America. 'Stephens, I believe,' he said on the 24th March, 'has at last got to Paris and will probably be in America as soon as this letter. He will give fresh impetus to the subscriptions and I fear there is a good deal of trouble in store for us.' (22)

He worried about the effect of American behaviour upon domestic and foreign public opinion. Britons were surprised and indignant while European diplomacy regarded what was being done by the Americans as all but a declaration of war against England. He hoped that the feeling manifested in Canada would put some check upon Sweeney, the 'doughty commander of the army of invasion and the rest of the swashbucklers', but Stephens, talking freely in Paris, had declared that the troubles in Ireland were only beginning. 'Surely,' said Clarendon, 'the American Government must see that this *imperium in imperio* may be productive of future inconvenience to them, that they are shortsighted in allowing it to develop itself?' And for Bruce personally he gave this warning: '*Pray* don't disregard the threat of assassination, and don't walk home at night unarmed or alone. If a motion in the Irish House of Representatives is carried that murdering you will be useful to the cause, you may be sure that some Patriot will be told off to do the deed.' (23)

Clarendon's concern increased in the following days as a Consul reported that the Fenians had bought thirteen steamers. If this were true an official remonstrance would have to be made to the American Government. 'I have no doubt that our policy of abstaining from that course has been judicious,' he told Bruce, 'but it must not be carried too far, for if Canada is invaded or any other great disaster leading perhaps to war between us and the United States should occur, we shall be blamed in Parliament for having so long remained spectators of what was preparing, and Seward might turn round on us to say that he was not bound to take care of our interests when we ourselves were indifferent about them . . .' He did not ask for a remonstrance to be sent all the same, and Bruce's friendly go-between unfortunately being ill, that mode of approach was closed; instead Clarendon suggested that Bruce might be justified in writing directly to the President now that the Fenian conspiracy had assumed 'most gigantic dimensions'. (24) At the same time, for self-protection, forseeing that he would have to have something producible handy, he asked Bruce to write him a despatch stating fully what he had and had not done respecting the Fenians and 'the reason why'.

(2)

Sweeney had a plan to seize a Canadian port and use it as a base for operations against England on the oceans and in Ireland: this was divulged to the American newspapers which also published the intention of the Canadian authorities vigorously to repel any attack. Doyle, the Irish Constabulary man in New York, sent the cuttings to his Inspector General and said that the port Sweeney had in mind, he thought, was St John's, New Brunswick. New Brunswick and Nova Scotia seemed vulnerable on their own but war ships had now gone to both places. (25) From what he saw in the newspapers it was apparent that the Fenians of Canada (who ought to know) did not relish Sweeney's plan of invading their country. They were loud, however, in favour of O'Mahony's

plan of carrying the war from their doors to the heart of Ireland.
(26) Doyle urged that adequate preparations should be immediately
completed in Ireland. He repeated the need for the suspension of
Habeas Corpus so as to make it possible to arrest Fenians wholesale, particularly the American officers who were going over on
every boat, and to keep them locked up till all danger was over.
It was vital that the Fenians should not be allowed to have any
early success in Ireland; this would be exaggerated and would
inflame the American Fenians to mischief. (27)

Doyle wrote on these lines in the early days of February. By
the 2nd March the news had reached New York that Habeas
Corpus had in fact been suspended, and Doyle reported the
American reaction. The Fenians were excited. They knew now
that 100 of their officers had been taken up in Dublin, and
O'Mahony had rushed out circulars from his Headquarters
calling for immediate retaliation. 'Brothers,' he wrote,

> the Time for Action has arrived! The Habeas Corpus is suspended in
> Ireland. Our brothers are being arrested by hundreds and thrown
> into prison. Call your circles together immediately. Send us all
> the aid in your power at once, and in God's name let us start to our
> destination. Aid! Brothers, help! for God and Ireland!!! (28)

A month later Doyle ventured the opinion that the spirit of the
Fenian movement had been crushed. 'The rigorous measures of
your Government', he told Wood, 'in suspending the Habeas
Corpus Act and securing O'Mahony's officers, has done much to
calm down wild enthusiasm, and we hear no talk now of directly
and immediately invading Ireland.' (29) The Fenians who had
come back from Ireland were saying that the time for sending
the promised expedition was past, and some of them were
bitterly assailing O'Mahony for his failure to send the expected
succour the previous September. (30) Fenianism was not dead,
however, he said, but there was much reason to hope that it
would not recover from the effect of the blow it had received.
Wood, on reading this, briefly expressed disagreement. Fenianism
would never die. America would not allow it to happen. England's calamity should be the Fenian opportunity, a remark which

drew from Wodehouse, the Lord Lieutenant, the comment that the opportunity would be far to seek. (31)

On the 12th April Doyle had really exciting news to impart. (32) Some hundreds of the O'Mahony Fenians had that day concentrated at Eastport on the frontier of the State of Maine with the intention of seizing the island of Campobello in the Bay of Fundy. The island was considered to be debatable territory, and an attack on it might provoke an international dispute and perhaps a war from which Ireland might benefit. A second, and important, reason for the move was to steal the initiative from the Roberts faction who were known to be preparing for an invasion of Canada but had so far made no move. The O'Mahonyites were determined to show that *they* were the men of action.

The attempt was frustrated, however, by the appearance of six British warships to defend the island. An American naval vessel also arrived along with a company of American artillery under Major General George Meade. These took possession of the arms which had been brought independently to Eastport on a steamer O'Mahony had chartered, and compelled the Fenians to disperse. No arrests were made; no blood was spilt. And a fiasco, which used up forty thousand dollars of Fenian money, ended as mildly as it began. The only achievement was the capture of a Union Jack that had been flying from a customs post!

On both sides of the border the movement had been anticipated. The British were aware through their local Vice Consuls of Fenian activity in the frontier towns. They also knew of the chartering of the arms ship and the date it was due to arrive at Eastport. Their information came from many sources; but notably from within the O'Mahony camp where they had a special informant, a man who in later times was to earn exceptional notoriety as an *agent provocateur*. This was Red Jim McDermott who was in confidential relations with O'Mahony and was consulted by him. (33) The Americans had their own sources of information. Seward was as chary as ever about disturbing the Fenians because of their political importance; when ultimately something had to be done, he simply directed restraining action which, as we saw, took the form of depriving the Fenian raiders of their arms. When things quietened down the arms were given back to their owners.

By the end of April, the Campobello affair was considered to be at an end, and the tide setting strongly against O'Mahony and for the Roberts-Sweeney faction. (34) The British were delighted at the turn events had taken. The appointment of General Meade to the Maine frontier was a good symptom of the determination of the American Government to stop the Fenian enterprises. The officers of the regular army were far more to be relied upon in such matters than politicians, who were always guided by the strength of the Irish vote in their districts. (35) Clarendon had already pictured President Johnson as 'a man of great energy and purpose, who rose every day in public estimation' (36) and now Seward, too, was raised somewhat in their good books as the result of a reassuring letter from Bruce. They had all read with interest Bruce's excellent and most accurate portrait of the American Secretary of State, Clarendon said, and with such a man it must be a long time before intimacy and confidence could be established, but when they were required and his *modus operandi* understood, he might not be more difficult than another to get on with.

There had been a wrangle with the Americans about the citizenship rights of Irish-American prisoners. Many of these were naturalised in the United States, but were born in Ireland and fell to be treated therefore as British subjects. 'Once a Briton, always a Briton.' Lord Wodehouse was very sticky on this doctrine of indefeasible allegiance and declined all communication with the American Consul in Dublin about it. 'The consequences would be obviously disastrous,' he told Clarendon, 'if Irishmen could return from America to plot against the Queen and shelter themselves under letters of naturalisation.' (37) The Irish-Americans were 'real bad fellows, regular filibusters', and Ireland was calmer as a result of their being under lock and key. (38) Clarendon did not disagree, but he was most anxious to avoid the rupture with the United States that the Fenians were striving to provoke. Accordingly, with Wodehouse's concurrence, he proceeded to make an agreement with the American Government for the release of the prisoners on their undertaking to board the first available ship bound for the United States. A despatch from Seward on the subject was considered reasonable and not otherwise than friendly, (39) and Clarendon complimented Bruce for his handling of the American Secretary of State. 'You have dealt very skilfully with him about the Fenian question,' he wrote, 'and I am sure that no written application and still less remonstrance would have led to the same result.' (40)

(3)

On the 10th May Stephens arrived in New York 'with the air of a Napoleon after his first campaign' (41) and was enthusiastically welcomed. Doyle could not foresee what effect his presence would have. Stephens had said that his mission was to heal the wounds inflicted by the divisions on the organisation of the Brotherhood and to secure united action against the common enemy. (42) He had also come to ensure a flow of money to John Mitchel in Paris—the channel of supply to Ireland—who had received no American remittances whatever for a couple of months. Over the whole of his time in Paris he had in fact received for transmission to Ireland a mere fraction of what had been promised.* Doyle did not doubt that Stephens was sincere in his

* John Mitchel (1815–1875), one of the leaders of Young Ireland, was sentenced to fourteen years' transportation in 1848 for treason felony. In 1853 he escaped from Van Diemen's Land to the United States where, in the Civil War, he took the Confederate side. Towards the end of 1865 he was appointed to Paris at an annual salary of 2,500 dollars to take charge of the financial deposits of the Fenian Brotherhood and to see that they were honestly and fairly disbursed for the purposes of the Republican organisation in Ireland and for the defence of men imprisoned for revolutionary conspiracy. He was to maintain 'diplomatic duties' towards the French and other governments, to pay great attention to the practicability of an invasion of Ireland from America, to send full information on the land and sea forces available for the defence of British domination in Ireland and to investigate the possibility of procuring arms and ammunition in France. It impressed upon him, though this was hardly necessary, that a revolutionary organisation in Ireland was absolutely essential to her liberation. 'Without it,' O'Mahony told him (10.11.1865), 'even an American or French war [with

intentions. The degree of success he would achieve was another matter. 'A large proportion of the Fenians were tired of giving money with no results but prisoners, convicts and ridicule.' (43)

Stephens had little chance of securing or imposing unity on the opposing Fenian elements. Before leaving Ireland he had issued a formal document to Fenians everywhere denouncing the so-called Senate for 'madly and treacherously' raising the cry of 'to Canada' instead of 'to Ireland' in defiance of 'the wise and loyal' O'Mahony, and in a letter, that was also published about the same time, he assailed the Senate wing, calling them dogs, fools or rogues, and carrion. They were guilty of cowardice and treason, and right-minded Fenians should cut and hack away the rotten branches. Clearly that particular party were not likely to be won back by Stephens who, by the time of his arrival in New York, had also something to say to O'Mahony, who had been anything but wise in his most recent adventure. He reprimanded him, forced his resignation, and dismissed Killian for being jointly identified with what the press called the Campobello fizzle. There was to be no diversion whatever from the design to which Stephens was committed of liberating Ireland by direct action on Irish soil. The fight would begin there on the very day he set foot in Ireland again. There were 200,000 in the gap, he told the Americans, a quarter of them drilled; all they needed was money for arms and war material, and this America could help to supply. The balance in the O'Mahony treasury had dwindled enormously, the result, Archibald said, of squandering and embezzlement, (44) and Stephens was not improving the position by living in state in one of New York's largest hotels.

With Roberts and Sweeney cutting the painter, Stephens found himself occupying the position O'Mahony had vacated. He was simply the leader of a faction. (45) To try and change this position he went on a propaganda tour of the cities of the interior and was

---

England] might fail to free her ... The Canadian raid I look upon as a mere diversion ... Unless it bring the United States into war with England it can only end in defeat to those that engage in it. But it is worth trying in the hope that it may lead to such a war.' (See 'Fenian Papers in the Catholic University of America' *Journal of Cork Historical and Archaeological Society*, Vol. LXXV, 1970.)

thus engaged when on the night of the 31st May Sweeney launched
the attack on Canada for which he had long prepared and which
now took the British somewhat by surprise. Archibald had
received 'communications principally anonymous from different
quarters', the substance of which he promptly reported to Lord
Monck, the Tipperary-born Governor General of Canada, and
to Sir Frederick Bruce, as well as to the Consuls at Buffalo and
Chicago; but from the known fact of the poverty of the Sweeney
Exchequer and the falsification of earlier reports of an intended
invasion he did not place much reliance on what he had just heard.
He had reported to Washington information he had received
about the forwarding of arms and ammunition to different
points on the frontier, and some seizures were made by the U.S.
officials, but otherwise there seemed to be no active movement
on the part of the Fenians and, as Stephens had loudly denounced
any attack on Canada, it seemed improbable that anything of the
kind would now be attempted. (46)

'But,' said Archibald,

early in the present week there were telegraphic announcements in
the newspapers of Fenians having gone northwards from Nashville
and Stephensville [?], of their having subsequently reached Cincinatti
and with accessions to their numbers had proceeded towards
the shore of Lake Erie. On Wednesday there were reports of their
concentrating at Buffalo but the authorities there could not bring
themselves to believe that these men would attempt to cross over
to Canada. But in the course of Sunday night and early yesterday
morning about 1500 men crossed the Niagara river a short distance
below Buffalo, damaged the rail-road leading from Fort Erie to
Chippewa and moved down the left bank of the river towards the
latter place, having telegraphed to their brethren in the different
U.S. centres to reinforce them . . .

On Thursday morning I received confidentially from Sir Frederick
Bruce information which had been communicated to him from a
reliable source that some of the best drilled of the Fenians were to
assemble at St. Albans near the Vermont frontier where arms had
been secreted and from thence could make an attack on Canada.
This, by Sir Frederick's instruction, I telegraphed in cypher to Lord
Monck. In verification of the report 300 Fenians arrived at St.

Albans from Boston early yesterday morning and others have followed from Boston and proceeded from New Haven. At the same time two companies of U.S. regular troops were sent from Boston to St. Albans to keep the intruding raiders in check.

During the whole of yesterday, telegrams were being constantly received from Buffalo and other points which have been published in the newspapers of this morning. Of these I enclose several copies. The statements are as usual conflicting and exaggerated. The latest telegram from Buffalo which is dated at 3 a.m. of this day reports the dispersion of the Fenian force into guerilla bands and the abandonment of the invasion as an organised movement.

On the whole it is perhaps fortunate that this movement has taken place. The Canadians will speedily dispose of the invaders if they can but come into contact with them and the certain failure of the project will reflect on the Roberts-Sweeney faction a discredit and ridicule similar to that which followed the fiasco of the O'Mahony invasion of New Brunswick. (47)

For a few days the excitement caused by the newspaper reports of this collision and bloodshed inside the Canadian frontier excited the American Irish and was productive of men and money to support the expedition. But the full dimensions of what had happened were gradually apprehended. It had been assumed by the Fenians that the U.S. Government would connive at the attempt. That delusion was ended when President Johnson issued a proclamation against the Fenians, following a protest from Bruce to Seward in which he urged most strongly the propriety of arresting Sweeney and the other leaders as a means of preventing any further attempt. In pursuance of this Roberts and Sweeney were arrested, the movements of persons, arms and ammunition destined to violate the laws of the United States in certain areas forbidden, and many arrests made on the frontier areas. Most of the men thus taken were glad to accept a discharge and free transportation to their homes in exchange for an undertaking not to participate again in an armed invasion of Canada. (48)

The prosecutions of Roberts and Sweeney were not proceeded with, and Roberts went to Washington to agitate for a change in the neutrality laws. He argued that the American administration, particularly the wily Seward, was a dirty tool of the English

Government, and that but for their treacherous interference the
Fenian assault on Canada would have been successful. This view
was to some extent also held in Dublin Castle. Observing that the
raid had always been celebrated as a triumph by the Roberts
party, Samuel Lee Anderson, a Crown Solicitor, believed that
Colonel John O'Neill, who led the Fenians across the Niagara,
did in fact gain a substantial advantage in a fight with numerically
superior forces. These included a volunteer element with some
students from the University of Toronto. At one stage in the
action O'Neill withdrew his men a few hundred yards to reform them, and the volunteers, thinking they had them on the
run, charged after them. The Fenians, mostly Civil War veterans,
met them with a volley and then countercharged, forcing the
volunteers to turn and flee. They had covered about three miles
before the pursuit was called off. (49) It was with this incident
particularly in mind that Roberts protested in Washington against
the interference of the United States which had turned the scales
against him, and led to the arrest of O'Neill. Stephens was already
in the capital and secured an interview with Seward. He was not
at all displeased at the embarrassment of the Roberts-Sweeney
faction and openly denounced their invasion attempt. They were
traitors to the Irish cause; men who had tried to sell the Irish vote
to political demagogues. (50) He then resumed his extensive tour,
promising that before the year was out there would be an Irish
army fighting on Irish soil. He would be there with them and
ready to fight to the death.

Meanwhile Bruce warned Lord Monck not to assume that the
danger to Canada had passed. It had been checked, but at Buffalo
and other places there were considerable bodies of men ready to
act, and the Fenian organisation subsisted. 'This country,' he said,
'is full of desperate men, the scum of Federal and Confederate
armies, who are ready to join en masse any cause for the sake of
plunder and excitement. Any incidents that awoke popular
sympathy might lead to fresh attempts in greater force, and the
very small force at the command of the Government in the North
would be powerless to check them if led by a man of determination. If the militia of the state of New York is called out, the

affair will get mixed up with the politics of that state where the Irish are powerful, and I for one, will not answer for their conduct. Indeed Hemans writes me word from Buffalo that the Irish in the regular army were in a state little short of mutiny at the time of the expedition to Fort Erie.' Such being the state of the case the Government would have little to depend upon but the moral support of the more respectable section of American opinion. Those in that section most opposed in principle to filibusterism were unanimous in advocating delay and lenity in the treatment of the prisoners in the hands of the Government of Canada where public opinion had been outraged by the death of twenty-five of their soldiers and the expense to which the country had been put unnecessarily.

Bruce strongly supported the attitude of American conservatives. The important thing was to avoid creating a false sympathy for the Fenians. The proceedings of the Canadian Government should be marked by great calmness. 'Let the prisoners be tried by the ordinary forms of law, and let these trials be postponed as long as possible in order to allow the present excitement to abate.' If possible no blood should be shed. The existence of the Fenians in Canadian hands was not without some value, as hostages. (51) In this matter, also, it was not safe to disregard the wishes of the American Government. They had acted as fairly as could be expected, and nothing but the President and his advisers stood at that moment between them and a most serious movement. They must strengthen the President's hands by acting in concert with him, or be prepared to see him carried away by the current. (52)

There had been sympathetic murmurs in Congress to which Roberts had alluded when declaring that his projects were only being postponed. Bruce did not think much of the sympathy thus shown which might be justly ascribed to the approaching elections, and to the desire to catch the Irish vote. Nor did he think that the American Government thought differently. Their prime anxiety was to avoid complications arising out of the Fenian proceedings. They had no real feeling for the Irish element in the community, nor did they really care about the fate of the prisoners. But they knew the risk of exciting the sympathy of the masses, and the use that would be made of it by unscrupulous politicians, and in advising delay and lenity they advised what was best for their interest, as for the British interest. (53)

Bruce had to ensure that the Foreign Minister in London correctly understood the position and approved of the line he was taking. To Clarendon, on the 18th June, he wrote 'I beg Her Majesty's Government not to disregard this sympathy (in the House of Representatives) and above all not to be misled by the notion that this Fenian movement is a temporary madness which may be considered as extinguished by the late failures. On the contrary I dread its influence far more at the polls than I do in the field, and I only trust that the incapacity its leaders have shown and the desire for action and excitement so strong in the Celtic race, will continue to blind them as to the true course they ought to pursue here, with a view to embroiling the two countries . . .' As he had done to Monck he recommended that the prisoners taken by the Canadians should be treated leniently on the ground of their being misguided dupes. 'If we do this,' he argued,

we shall strengthen the hands of the United States Government in acting against the leaders and the reaction against these organisations which their open interference with the law is so well calculated to produce. The Government here would be no doubt glad to drop the proceedings against the leaders if they could say that our severity had been sufficient punishment for the mischief done, but our severity will increase rather than diminish Irish animosity against Canada, and tend to produce on this continent that antagonism between the Irish race and British rule from which we suffer in Great Britain. Whereas the punishment of the leaders, even if slight, by the authority of the United States, will be a great check to these filibustering schemes, and will place the Government in direct opposition to the more violent section of the Irish people. In dealing with this delicate question it is necessary for the future and the effect on opinion here which are the main points to be considered, and the question of the punishment to be inflicted on the misguided dupes that have fallen into our hands should be decided in view of these considerations and not of the very natural resentment these proceedings call forth. I am very glad to see that Lord Monck fully appreciates this matter in its political bearings. (54)

1b James Stephens

1a Colonel John O'Mahony

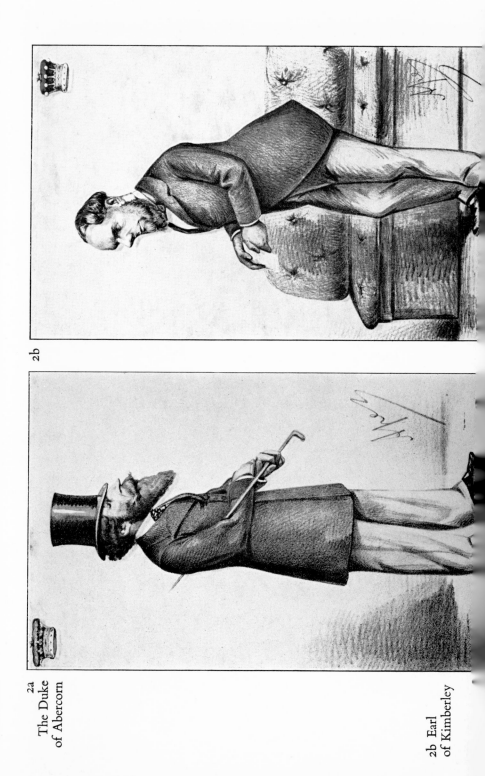

2b

2a
The Duke
of Abercorn

2b Earl
of Kimberley

Lord Clarendon was well pleased with the way things had gone. The United States Government had acted in a most friendly and efficient manner with respect to the Fenians, and he directed Bruce to convey to Seward, and to the President if he saw him, the best thanks of Her Majesty's Government. Bruce would know best in what form or to what extent this should be done; to express themselves too warmly might damage the American Government in the eyes of English-hating citizens.

'We are not out of the wood yet,' he told Bruce on the 30th June, 'as political capital can be made against the President by supporting Fenianism, and I see by the telegrams of to-day that President Roberts, fresh from the police court at New York, has been introduced on the floor of the Senate by Senator Wilson. 'I hope,' he went on, 'the Canadian Government will act humanely with the prisoners—such seems to be the disposition of Lord Monck, and your excellent advice to him will probably improve that disposition. 'I lost no time in writing to Wodehouse about releasing any American citizens and I send a copy of his answer. Of course he must look a little at home interests, but I can answer for his earnest desire to help you to the utmost of his power . . .' (55)

Wodehouse fully appreciated 'the great importance of conciliating President Johnson and Seward', and already, except where imperative duty required the detection of prisoners, he had directed their release. But, he told Clarendon, 'if we were to release at once the whole batch of the United States "citizens" the measure would be attributed by the Irish to everything but the true cause'. (56)

As these words were written the Liberal Government had already been defeated in a Liberal House of Commons on Russell's Reform Bill (26th June 1866) and had given place to a new administration headed by the 14th Earl of Derby. As Derby's party was in a minority he had difficulty in forming a government and Clarendon told Bruce that the new administration would consist of the Old Party *pur et simple*, and the general opinion consequently was that it could not last. (57) It did in fact last until the end of 1868, under Derby and subsequently under Disraeli.

FF F

Clarendon was succeeded in the Foreign Office by Lord Stanley, Derby's son, and on bidding goodbye to Bruce he thanked him for the admirable manner in which he had performed his duty under circumstances often most trying and difficult. He did not know anyone who could have established such good relations as he had done with Seward and the President, and he was sure that no one could have made those relations better. All this he had explained to Stanley, and he thought that, together with the seals of the Foreign Office, the new Minister would take all Clarendon's confidence in Bruce. He prayed Bruce to give his best compliments to Mr Seward. 'Tell him too that I hope my successor will feel as I have always done viz., that European affairs concern us little in comparison with our relations with the United States, not alone on account of our material interests but because I am convinced that if a thorough good understanding could be established between America and England the cause of good government and progress would be promoted throughout the world, and there is no single interest rightly understood between the two countries that *ought* to be antagonistic.' (58)

In his letter of thanks and farewell to Clarendon, Bruce said that he had been finding Seward more courteous of late. The tone of his despatches about Fenian prisoners had changed, since Bruce had told him of the difficulties this was making for Lord Monck who had his own Fenian prisoners to deal with. Bruce urged that more attention should be paid to the influence of priests in Ireland. He was convinced that in America and in Ireland alike they were the great fomenters of discord, if not the instigators of revolution; and the animosity of the Irish was the greatest danger to British relations with the United States. (59)

CHAPTER V

A Change of Government

THE re-emergence of Lord Derby as Prime Minister involved changes in the Irish Executive. Wodehouse, who had become the Earl of Kimberley on the 1st June, and Chichester Fortescue were succeeded by two ascendancy Irishmen, the Duke of Abercorn and Lord Naas, as Lord Lieutenant and Chief Secretary. Naas had been Chief Secretary on two previous occasions, but Abercorn was a newcomer and Kimberley wished him joy with all his heart of the detestable office he had assumed. 'I hardly know how decently to conceal my delight at quitting it', he told Clarendon,

and I have had more cause to like it than most of my predecessors, for the administration of affairs here has been unusually interesting, and I have had the opportunity of acquiring some credit. Moreover the Irish country gentleman (who is to be the prop of the new Government!) has treated us very fairly, treatment which I am ungrateful enough to ascribe chiefly to his terror of the Fenians.

I am more than ever convinced that the sooner the vice-royalty is abolished the better. Lord Derby's programme is meagre enough, but a Tory policy is a difficult thing in these days to devise. (1)

In the shake-up Larcom remained Under Secretary, and Rose, who was raised to the peerage as Baron Strathnairn of Strathnairn and Jansi, continued to command the army. He had received this favour after an initial refusal. Derby had told him that the time was inopportune: his claim in point of Indian service was too remote, and that of Irish too recent. 'Should the Government last,' Derby told him, 'your claim shall be fully considered whenever you shall have closed with credit, as I am sure you will do, the duties of the appointment which you now hold.' (2) But within three weeks Rose was given what he had asked for. Naas and Larcom were old acquaintances: they had worked together before in the same relationship. Naas, otherwise Richard South-well Bourke, was the son of the 5th Earl of Mayo. He was forty-four years of age, twenty-one years younger than Larcom who had reached the age of retirement but stayed on under pressure both from Naas and Kimberley. 'After you left us,' he told Kimberley, 'I acted on your suggestion to remain a few months, hoping constantly they would be my last. Lord Naas, however, entreated me to remain . . . and declared he would not remain if I did not . . .' (3)

To Abercorn as he assumed office Derby said that he understood that all was looking well in the South of Ireland; therefore, the best thing Parliament could do for it was to leave it alone (4) but, in his first letter to Naas, (5) Larcom presented a different point of view. The Fenian business would require early parliamentary consideration. The Habeas Corpus Suspension Act would expire on the 30th September and there were still 400 men in prison, compared with a maximum in April of 660. Naas's first consideration would be whether it was necessary to renew the Act and Larcom thought he would come to the conclusion that it was. The Cattle Plague was an anxious subject too; and the Orange period—focussed on the 12th July, the anniversary of the Battle of the Boyne—was just beginning. Already there had been an unpleasant affair in County Armagh.

Naas had told his constituents at Cockermouth that all that Ireland wanted was the knowledge that the law would be fairly and impartially administered, that evil-doers would be punished, and the right-thinking and loyal encouraged: but he was not too sure that the continuation of the Habeas Corpus Suspension was justified. In fact, as he took office, it seemed that all popular apprehensions with regard to Fenianism in Ireland had disappeared; nevertheless he took the advice tendered to him by Larcom and the police and pushed the continuing Bill through Parliament without any difficulty. The original Act was the child of the Liberals, now in opposition, and Naas in the House of Commons soft-soaped them by saying that they had used the powers conferred by the Act with great boldness but also with great moderation. He gave particulars of the number of persons arrested and discharged on condition that they left the country; towards those that still remained in prison it was not the intention of the Government to exercise any harshness; on the contrary, they would be dealt with in a spirit of forgiveness.

Naas pitched his case for continuing the Act rather on the fact that the conspiracy still existed on the other side of the Atlantic. It was there the movement had its origin; its organisation was at once numerous and wealthy, and it made no secret of the fact that its object was to endeavour by every means in its power to separate Ireland from British dominion. Since the passing of the Act the attempted invasion of Canada would have shown the House how desperate were the designs of the conspirators, and to what extent they were prepared to go. He had read with some astonishment a speech made at Boston by the man Stephens. He had said that he would not give up the cause of Ireland; soon or never was their motto; and he solemnly declared that some time that year he would be on Irish soil, and the struggle would take place. It was evidently necessary that the Government should be prepared. Stephens had not said that it was his intention to land in Ireland with a number of men from the other side of the Atlantic; that would be too absurd, but he had stated that it was by Irishmen on their own soil that he expected to be assisted in his rebellious designs. He had also stated, though Naas believed this to be utterly unfounded, that there was a sufficient number of men in Ireland, enrolled and drilled, to carry on a successful war with the great power of the United Kingdom. In Ireland, Naas was happy to say, the movement appeared to a great extent to be dying away; but there were unmistakeable signs of its existence, and he regretted that there was in Dublin a press which weekly disseminated the most treasonable writings and the boldest sedition.

John Francis Maguire, a leading Catholic member from Cork, opposed the Bill. The state of things on which the former government justified the suspension of the constitution in Ireland no longer existed; the supremacy of the law had been sufficiently vindicated in the ordinary tribunals of the country, and there was likewise an utter absence of political excitement of any kind whatever. The American Fenians talked about a fleet of ironclads, but no one in Ireland expected to see it. As to the alarming statement of Stephens, it had to be remembered that Stephens, O'Mahony and Roberts were all quarrelling one with the other, and that Stephens himself was, he believed, erroneously regarded by many people in America as a spy of the English Government. Therefore, but little importance ought to be attached to any statements he might utter. The name of the organ of the Fenian movement was almost obliterated from the memory of the people; the leaders were undergoing the severest punishment next to that of death; the organisation had broken down, the conspiracy was shattered and no idea of armed resistance any longer existed in the country.

Gladstone, for the Liberal Opposition, supported the Bill, though most reluctantly, he said. It was satisfactory to see that perfect tranquillity prevailed in Ireland, but with threats still used on the other side of the Atlantic, with a possibility that if they repealed the Suspension Act many of those who had left for America in consequence of it would return, or others in their place, he thought that as a prudent man he ought to accede to the application of the Government.

The Bill, having passed in the Commons, was introduced in the House of Lords by the Prime Minister. He, too, regretted that the condition of Ireland was not such as to justify the Government in allowing the Suspension Act to expire, and also eulogised the manner in which it had been put into force and administered by the Earl of Kimberley. Kimberley replied for the Liberals. If he had remained in office he would have recommended the adoption of the Bill by Parliament. No one except those intimately acquainted with the facts could be aware how formidable the Fenian conspiracy had been. Since 1798 there had not existed so dangerous a condition of the public mind as in the past year. The persons who had been the promoters of the scheme had not been the poorer and more ignorant classes, but the class which was best described as artisans and small tradesmen; whilst in the south-west of Ireland, if a rebellion had broken out, there was no doubt the farmers also would have been ready to take part in it.

(2)

For the first month after the cross-border invasion the Canadian Government thought that the end of the Fenian Brotherhood was in sight, but by early August they had come to the conclusion that another invasion was being prepared. This time a deciding factor was believed to be the approach of the annual congressional elections and inducements held out by the contending parties sufficient to prevent the American Government from interfering as energetically as they had done on the former occasion. The Governor General therefore appealed to London for more regular troops as a matter of urgency. While this request was being dealt with at Horse Guards the Prime Minister wrote to Naas: 'I am afraid trouble is brewing in America; Lord Monck seems alarmed, and *telegraphs* for *immediate* reinforcements to a considerable extent, which I know not how we are to send him . . .' (6) Naas, in his reply, warned that in selecting regiments for Canada they could not be too careful in avoiding those which had lately been quartered in Ireland, for he was sorry to say that any regiment in which there were many Irishmen was inevitably tainted with Fenianism. This prevailed to a greater extent than he had any conception of until he came to Ireland and he believed that Lord Strathnairn and his military men were in error in under-rating it. He would send more detailed information on 'this very unpleasant subject' in a few days, but meanwhile he stressed that there were some regiments whose presence in Canada would be looked on with delight by the Fenian leaders.

It was precisely two regiments in this category (the 53rd and 61st) that, in the absence of the Duke of Cambridge and without the knowledge of the Cabinet, Army Headquarters directed to proceed to Canada. When they heard the announced decision, Derby and Naas were flabbergasted. Such blindness! said Naas. It was incredible, said Derby, that the Horse Guards should be such slaves to red-tape as to send those two regiments merely because they stood first on the service roster; and Naas wondered how they would act if called on to fight the American Fenians. However, Naas seems to have been inclined to let the 53rd go. The

Irish soldiers in that regiment had been very much tainted by
Colour Sergeant McCarthy—the man Lord Strathnairn would
have so liked to have shot, and who had been sentenced to penal
servitude for life—but as it was a Shropshire regiment there was
not a very great proportion of Irish in it. The case of the 61st
was different. It was equally tainted, and as its depot had been
for some time in Ireland there were a great number of Irishmen in
it. Should it be prevented from going to Canada? There was a
dilemma here. The moral effect of stopping the regiment could
be worse than letting them go, as it would proclaim to the world
the very doubtful faithfulness of these soldiers in the hour of need.
Perhaps if the news from Canada improved within a few days the
embarkation might be countermanded on the ground that a
second regiment was no longer essential. (7)

The Prime Minister decided the issue. It was too late to make a
change in either case, independently of the bad effect it would
produce; and certainly they had no accounts from Canada which
would warrant them in withholding any part of the reinforcements they had ordered earlier to be sent. They could only hope,
therefore, that the services of those regiments would not be
required, and that, if they were, military discipline would prove
too strong for their Fenian propensities. The Duke of Cambridge
had warned the authorities in Canada of the possible state of the
two corps, and would take an early opportunity of passing them
on to the West Indies. (8)

On the question of the effect of Fenianism in the army as a
whole, and this was a matter that arose incidentally out of the
Canadian request, Naas thought that this ought not to be disregarded. The disease could be eradicated by wise measures in a
few months if the Horse Guards could be persuaded to take them.
This meant making further use of Army Intelligence which in
Ireland was directed by Lieutenant Colonel Feilding, a brother of
the Tory Lord Denbigh and an Assistant Adjutant General
attached to the Dublin and Curragh Division. He, with Captain
Whelan of the 61st Regiment, had already been ferreting out the
Fenian elements among the troops. At the end of August Naas
gave the Prime Minister an account of a conversation he had had

with Whelan. 'He is fully impressed with the idea that the late convictions have not stopped Fenianism in the army. He says that the evil had been too long at work, too deeply rooted in the minds of the Irish soldiery to be got rid of in a few months. It has been done with great skill and extraordinary prudence. A Fenian agent has been for some time at Malta, another at Gibraltar. Pagan O'Leary, now a convict, was for 18 months at the Cape, and he [Whelan] assures me that their emissaries await the arrival of every regiment coming from abroad and immediately commence operations with more or less success.' (19)

Naas recommended that Whelan, who was now with his depot at Chatham, should be employed full-time with a small staff of fifteen or twenty men to watch and defeat the efforts of the Fenian agents among the soldiers. Whelan was a quiet sensible man, he said. (10) The Fenians saw him in a very different light. According to John Devoy, Whelan, though an Irish Catholic, was

> an expert suborner of perjury. It was he who deceived all the informers except the two willing ones, by the infamous methods which prevail in Irish conspiracy cases. He went from cell to cell in Arbour Hill Military Prison, where the soldiers charged with Fenianism were on starvation diet, telling each man that the others had all turned informers and that I had supplied to the Castle a list of all the men I had sworn in. Several of them broke down and he schooled and drilled them in the evidence they were to give, turning mere taproom conversations, with outsiders present, into 'meetings', and making them put the word 'Fenian' in when necessary —a word that was never once used in the talks between the soldiers and the civilian organisers. (11)

One of Feilding's agents established a connection among the East London Fenians through an American agent whose acquaintance he had made. He had taken a lodging in Whitechapel where the Irish abounded, and reported that 'business' was being actively carried on by American agents. At the end of October or early in November it was intended to send Irishmen, in small bodies from all parts of England, into Ireland, in a more secret manner than was done the previous Christmas, and Stephens was to arrive at the end of November. Everybody seemed most sanguine and fully expected 'a good stir'. Minute descriptions of Foley and Abrahams, two of Feilding's men, had been sent over from Ireland and the knife was to be used against them. When Feilding heard this he directed Foley to go to Liverpool at once, to ingratiate himself with the Fenians there under a feigned name, and to report to him in Dublin at an accommodation address. He did this because he had learned through the grapevine that it was in Liverpool and its neighbourhood that the organisation of the Fenians was being completed. Telling this to Naas, with whom he was on the easiest of terms, Feilding said: 'I have written privately to the A.A. General at Headquarters to ask him to keep back the discharge of these men so that I may still have a hold on them . . . I should feel obliged by your writing to the War Office urging upon them the necessity of dealing most literally with all my informers, and suggesting that before *definitely* deciding on the sums to be given to each individual, some of us should be consulted . . . as it must be obvious that no one could better judge the best reward for each individual, than those who know their habits and tastes as intimately as I do.' (12)

A few days later he told Naas that he was afraid that Foley had fallen into the hands of the Fenians. He had asked Captain Whelan to inform the London Police of his suspicions of foul play and to request an inquiry to be made. (13) Foley was in no immediate danger, however; and in December Feilding recommended an annuity for him, a capital sum to set him up in a trade, and a free passage to one of the colonies if that was where he desired finally to go. He had expressed a preference at one time for permanent civil employment in England, in some Government office, such as messenger or porter; he could read well and write fairly, but was not qualified enough to be a clerk. (14) Foley drops out of the official picture at that point, but according to Devoy he died in misery in Boston, befriended by John Boyle O'Reilly, one of the soldier Fenians he had informed against. (15)

The new government had taken office in August. By the 24th November, continuing its conciliatory policy at an accumulated pace, it had reduced the number of prisoners held in custody in

Ireland to 73. Fenian prosecutions had virtually ended, the Crown Solicitor, Samuel Lee Anderson, was specially thanked and rewarded for his exceptional services, and the informer Pierce Nagle was allowed to take his departure, with a lump sum of £250 in his pocket. (16)

But almost simultaeously

affairs assumed once more an alarming character. Fenianism began to revive throughout the country, especially in the South and West. Money was being collected; penny a week subscriptions were being taken up ostensibly 'for a distressed family' while raffles were frequently held and lectures given under the same pretence. Revolvers were being sold at 15/- and rifles at 13/- each. It was reported that arms were being imported on an extensive scale, packed as merchandise. Fenian emissaries from England and America were again pouring into the country. The 'Public House' by night and the streets by day were filled with strangers of this class. Local agents were again active. Serious fears of an insurrection were very frequently entertained, and applications by the loyalists for military protection were again received from many towns and districts. The Police reported that in Dublin the Fenians counted upon 30,000 men ready to rise at a moment's notice, and that 'a burst would be made'. Money was again being drawn from the Banks in some places: on one day as much as £1400 from the Savings Bank in Drogheda. (17)

And the American papers reported that Stephens was about to leave for Ireland, if he was not already on the way.

Because the Habeas Corpus Suspension Act only operated in Ireland, the cities and towns of Britain, particularly those in the north-west, became more important as Fenian organising areas, and were, on that account, closely watched. From Liverpool on the 19th November there came to Dublin Castle this statement made by John Wilson an informer:

... for several months I was in the habit of giving information relative to Fenians to Superintendent Ryan of the G. Division of the D.M.P. but, being a conspicuous member of the Brotherhood and being at large whilst a number of my associates were arrested and lodged in gaol, I became suspected and at my own suggestion

I was arrested and lodged in Mountjoy Prison where I was kept for
about a fortnight, released and sent over to England. I arrived in
Liverpool on the 8th of July last . . . On Friday night last I attended
a meeting at Pitt at the house of a man named Power . . . There
were upwards of 50 centres present . . . and soldiers. There was a
receipt produced . . . for 500 stands of arms with belts and accoutre-
ments—these had been received in Dublin. (Bottles of the 'liquid'
were also produced and its destructive character demonstrated). . . .
The Fenians are determined to be in arms in Ireland in December . . .
Stephens is expected every day in Ireland. Money is coming in from
America. One of the soldiers said if there was a disturbance his Irish
Brigade (the 64th) would seize the arms and ammunition chest in
Liverpool, and that every man of the Brigade would be true . . .
I have heard from several members of the Organisation that they
intend to fire the warehouses along the docks. . . .

Naas, on reading this report, noted that it was very important
that the names and description of the centres mentioned should if
possible be ascertained. They should be watched by McHale, an
Irish Constabulary Head Constable operating from Liverpool,
and if they came to Ireland and were recognised, they should be
arrested at once. McHale was to get orders that in case of any
information coming to him suddenly as to the departure of a
Fenian agent of importance for an Irish port he should send a
policeman in the vessel with the suspected person and telegraph
to have police ready to meet the vessel. To enable this direction
to be implemented four sub-constables were sent to Liverpool by
the Inspector General (18). The situation in America was likewise
kept under surveillance, and some extra police sent out to ensure
that the Government had early intelligence of any of the Fenian
leaders making for Europe. (19)

CHAPTER VI

The Watch on Stephens

BY the end of October two of the Fenian prisoners,—both of them citizens of the United States—James Lynch and Father John McMahon, had been convicted by a Canadian Colonial court and sentenced to death upon a charge of being 'actors' in the June assault on Fort Erie. The American Elections were only a few days off, and were therefore very much in Seward's mind when he raised this matter formally with Bruce. The Government of the United States, he said, was required by the highest considerations of national dignity, duty and honour to inquire into the legality, justice and regularity of the judicial proceedings, and asked for a copy of the record. At the same time he expressed the hope that the British Government would examine the proceedings with a careful regard to the rights of the United States and to the maintenance of good relations between the two countries. Such relations were always difficult and delicate in States that are adjacent to each other without being separated by impossible borders. For that reason it would be very gratifying if the execution of the sentences on the Fenians could be suspended meantime. The offences committed were in their nature eminently political, and sound policy coincided with the best impulses of a benevolent nature in recommending tenderness, amnesty and forgiveness in such cases. This suggestion was made, Seward added, because the same opinions were proposed to the U.S. Government in the recent Civil War by all the governments and publicists of Europe and by none of them with greater frankness and kindness than by the statesmen of Great Britain. (1)

Bruce referred Seward's dispatch to London and drew attention to the inconsistencies in it. (2) Party interests required that the Americans should make a show of taking the prisoners under their protection and so be able to claim credit for any clemency that might be shown to them. He had told Seward that his own opinion was in favour of clemency as a matter of policy, but that the feelings of the Canadian people, who after all were the sufferers by the Fenian raid, would have to be consulted. He confirmed later in writing—the elections were over by this time and the President's message to the new Congress being drawn up—that the fate of convicted Fenian prisoners would be referred by the Canadian Government to London for decision, and would be dealt with so 'as to secure peace and harmony between peoples living in such immediate proximity and separated by a long frontier so easily traversed'. (3) 'As far as I can ascertain,' he told the Foreign Secretary, Lord Stanley,

> none of the leaders are amongst the prisoners and I have little doubt that they were duped by the assertions of the leaders and the reticence of this government into the belief that the expedition was secretly countenanced by the Government of the United States. I do not think anything is to be gained by the infliction of severe punishment on this class of offenders. It would make them martyrs and obtain for them a sympathy which at present is not felt by the Americans. Unless an insurrection breaks out in Ireland there does not appear to be much risk of any further attack on Canada and should such an event contrary to expectation take place this [the American] Government will interfere with greater effect if we do not weaken the influence of the President among the Irish by pursuing a course opposed to the wishes he has expressed. For in that case he might be induced to seek to recover his popularity among them by conniving at their designs and by taking no effective steps to prevent their crossing the frontier.
>
> His position is one of much difficulty. It is to be recalled that at the close of last session of Congress very violent resolutions were passed by the House of Representatives calling on the President to interfere on behalf of the Fenian prisoners in Canada. Had he done nothing when the sentence of death was pronounced on Lynch and McMahon, he would have been attacked by the dominant party in Congress for his neglect and while losing his hold on the Irish vote he would have been ultimately compelled to interfere with pretensions even more untenable and in terms more offensive than those contained in Mr Seward's note. For such is the resentment in this country on all questions affecting England that it may be assumed as certain

that they will be invariably dealt with in a worse spirit by Congress than by the executive. . . . (4)

Stanley, in no doubt what should be done, wrote to the Prime Minister.

My dear father,
. . . the President [of the United States] is in a bad way, and inclined to flatter the Fenians. It is essential that the two men under sentence in Canada should be spared, so far as their lives are concerned. I have written to Carnarvon in this sense. The only passage in Bruce's despatch with which I disagree is that where he lays stress on the necessity of considering the feelings of the Canadians in this matter. That is just what I would not do. The Canadians are naturally angry, and therefore bad judges: they know we must defend them, and are therefore practically irresponsible. . . (5)

The death sentences were commuted to terms of imprisonment.

(2)

All this time Doyle, the Irish Constabulary man, continued to report on what he saw in New York and read in the American newspapers. He also summarised some of the flamboyant speeches in which Stephens pledged himself formally and solemnly to lead a rising in Ireland before the end of the year. (6). Now or never was the time to aid the Fenian cause, he declared, for if not now aided the Irish race would vanish from the face of the earth. Doyle's reports continued to impress upon the Irish Government the necessity of being on their guard. Vigilance in Ireland was a plain duty. It was not to be overlooked that the steamer bought by O'Mahony for the Campobello expedition remained at the disposal of Stephens with the arms he had been able to procure. She lay idle just then—at the beginning of July—but it would be possible to run this vessel and others suddenly towards the Irish coast with Stephens and his followers and the restored arms on board. If such an attempt were contemplated it might be expected towards the early part of October, not sooner. (7) As August came along, Colonels Gleeson, Kirwin and Burke, Captain Condon, Major Comerford and other Fenian officers arrived from Ireland, and reported that the organisation in Ireland was in a healthy condition and the men determined to fight that year or never. (8) Doyle believed that Stephens's influence in America was on the wane. He was supported by only a section of the former O'Mahony wing, and was distrusted chiefly because he made no attempt to account for the large sums of money that had come into his hands for war purposes. (9) He could no longer collect money on mere promises to fight, and this might impel him to risk a rising, though that depended upon whether the Irish peasantry were still under his influence. The means at his disposal were ridiculously and notoriously inadequate despite the return to him of the Fenian arms seized at Campobello but Stephens insisted that his strength was in Ireland where he wanted it to be; all he asked from America was officers and funds. (10)

Towards the end of August Doyle reported that Sweeney and Roberts were not pulling well together and a new split seemed imminent. Sweeney had failed to account for the funds of the Canadian campaign, and had removed the War Office from Roberts's Headquarters to his hotel. (11) On the 4th September he was deposed as Secretary of War by a Congress of the Senate wing at Troy which confirmed Roberts in the office of President with the old policy of conquering Canada and of employing privateers as the best means of ultimately overthrowing British rule in Ireland, of confiscating estates there and of establishing the Irish Republic. Stephens was still pursuing his mission in the Western States while Colonel Kelly looked after his New York Office. (12) Two more Constabulary men joined Doyle at this time to help him to watch Stephens. He might conceivably act on his pledges, and on that account it was vital to ensure that he did not leave for Europe unnoticed. Doyle supplied particulars of the sailings of French ships and mentioned the importance of having French-speaking 'friends' aboard these vessels. Stephens was no mean strategist and it would be worth while paying reliable under-stewards to keep him under cover. (13)

3a Sir Thomas Larcom

3b The Earl of Mayo

4a President Andrew Johnson
Paived from life by William Cooper

4b William H. Seward
From a Daguerrotype by M. B. Brady

When Stephens returned to New York in the middle of September it was noticed that he had allowed his hair to grow long so that it curled over the collar of his coat. His beard also had grown longer. (14) He had his own detectives at his headquarters so that Doyle and his assistants had to act with the utmost caution. (15) A 'friend' of Doyle's named Tully had been seized and an attempt made to hang him as an English spy, before he could be rescued. (16) Doyle nevertheless continued to be a close observer of Stephens's considerable 'nervous activity'. 'I saw him yesterday at his headquarters,' he told Wood, . . .

> The windows were open of necessity to admit air, and they look out on the City Hall Park which is public. During two hours he came frequently under my view—now speaking with him who had just come in and who soon left, now speaking with one who did not leave; now in a writing attitude and soon on his legs again—now walking into the front office where there were several men, some reading papers; here he would not sit but converse a few minutes with one or more, then return to the former room, exchange a few words with some one there and again resume a writing or sitting attitude, soon repeating the routine over again. Thus was he engaged during two hours when circumstances advised that I should stay no longer . . . (7)

The next French steamer would sail on the 22nd September but Doyle did not expect that Stephens would depart so soon, Nevertheless Doyle's assistants were seeing all these steamers off. and arrangements had been made so that at the shortest notice they could travel on them. The Fenian steamer was still lying quietly in dock. (18) On the 28th October the last great Fenian meeting was held in New York. There were 50,000 persons at it, and Stephens announced that it was the last time he would speak to them before returning to Ireland. 'My last words are that we shall be fighting on Irish soil before the 1st January and that I shall be there in the midst of my countrymen.'

When Stephens was not seen for a day or two at his office in the first week of November one of Doyle's 'friends' went to his lodgings to negotiate, as it were, for a room there. The landlady had no room immediately available but she told him that Mr

Stephens was preparing to go to Ireland, and that she expected
his room would be vacant in three or four weeks. Consequently,
Doyle told Wood, his Inspector General, that Stephens would
soon be in Ireland unless his heart failed him. To thwart his tactics,
the valley of the Suir, Waterford, Carrick, Clonmel and Cahir, the
West of Cork, and Dublin should be occupied *strongly*. These
were Stephens's strongest points. The peasantry would be
deterred more by one regiment they could see than by five that
might be ready elsewhere and of which they only heard. Before
any rising could take place the arms etc., in America would have
to be smuggled into Ireland and distributed among the Fenians,
hence the importance of watching the coast also. (19)

Both sections of the Fenian Brotherhood continued to be
active, the Roberts party organising with the professed intention
of making another raid on Canada, the Stephens circles collecting
money for the insurrection in Ireland. This insurrection was to
follow a plan which Doyle outlined to his superiors, and which
was independently confirmed by an informer who was in communication with the Consul at New York. (Whether this was
General Millen or not is not clear.) 30,000 Fenians were to take
possession of Dublin; the Castle was to be attacked by a body of
picked men supplied with bottles of liquid fire; the Lord Lieutenant and the chief officers of State were to be seized as hostages;
and all inferior officers hanged. The barracks and outlying
posts were to be simultaneously attacked, and the arms there
obtained to be at once distributed among the Fenians. The
same course was to be adopted in other towns. After the capture
of Dublin, 30,000 men were to march upon Athlone. The railways and telegraphs were to be torn up, the Atlantic cable alone
being spared. Fenian emissaries were already being sent to Ireland
to seek employment in the respective localities assigned to them.
The informer stated that privateers had been promised to Stephens,
and that he had received offers of assistance from French revolutionaries and from Kossuth, the leader of the Hungarian revolt.
The Consul at New York also reported on the authority of
General Millen that a revolutionary movement in England was
proposed simultaneously with that in Ireland. A design was enter-

tained of destroying the English docks and arsenals by means of liquid fire.

Stephens was introduced by Colonel Kelly to a Monsieur Pelletier, a former member of the French legislature, living in New York, and in his house Stephens and Kelly frequently met General Gustave Cluseret, 'a specialist in wars and revolutions' (20) who in June 1848 had helped to suppress the workers' revolt in Paris. For carrying proletarian barricades and ruthless exploits against the insurgents under their red flags he was awarded the Legion of Honour. Later he was struck off the Army list for being involved in the mysterious disappearance of military stores. Returning to civilian life he managed an estate for a while, but lost the job when an entire flock of sheep under his charge likewise disappeared mysteriously. So he went back to the wars with a somewhat shady reputation, serving in Italy under Garibaldi and in the American war on the Federal side where he achieved the rank of Brigadier General. (21)

He had already been in negotiation with the Senate wing but, with the collapse of the Canadian invasion, his services were available when Stephens approached him. Cluseret, in later years, described the meeting. The Fenian leader was 'a man of superior merit but vain, despotic, and over-bearing beyond any man I ever saw. As regards action, he was worth nothing. I left the house, much disturbed in my mind.' (22) The first part of that judgement confirms an Irish view of Stephens. J. F. X. O'Brien, in his unpublished memoirs, describes conversations with Thomas Clarke Luby and John O'Leary in Portland Prison.

I learned that Stephens had taught them to accept him as a genius without compare, that if he chose to set himself to the work, he could surpass the greatest men such as Raphael, Michelangelo, Shakespeare etc. One of his great ideas was to build a city at or near Killarney in a style of architecture which would harmonise with the scenery of the place. Luby said that, while ashamed of the influence Stephens had exercised over them, he was afraid that, if they were released and circumstances again brought them together, Stephens would soon regain such ascendancy . . . Stephens was in truth complete master of Ireland. It was a case of One-Man Power. In the intense yearning for nationality, the Irish people have, in my time, in the pursuit of it, conferred such like power upon two other remarkable men, O'Connell and Parnell. . . . So far I have met Stephens thrice . . . and I am bound to say I could not understand how he succeeded in imposing himself on many, in my opinion, his intellectual superiors. He never impressed me particularly. I perceived how he ruled and subjugated the mind of others and thought there must be more in the man than I was able to discern, and I was open to be convinced by experience. My belief now is, he never was the man he was taken for. . . .

However that may be, and it was easy for O'Brien and others to be discerning after the event, Stephens put it to Cluseret to lead the Fenian insurgents in Ireland—he was to be known as the Commander in Chief of the Army of the Irish Republic—and Cluseret accepted the offer on conditions, one of which was that his Adjutant General should be Octave Louis Fariola, a young Belgio-Italian who had served with distinction as a Colonel of Engineers in the Federal Army. Cluseret had little faith either in Stephens or his movement but he availed himself of Stephens's proposals in order to obtain a passage to France where he had some business to transact. Fariola was a professional Republican and a member of one of the most secret of the Continental revolutionary clubs. He met Stephens early in November, at Pelletier's table. Unlike Cluseret, he was a man of almost childish simplicity; he readily accepted Stephens's story of the 50,000 men who were ready to rise in Ireland, and agreed to start at once for Europe in order to interest, if possible, the Continental revolutionaries in the movement, and also to select a staff of foreign officers for the army of the Irish Republic. So warmly did he take up the cause that before he left New York he induced a friend and former Belgian military association of his named Vifquain to join him with the rank of Brigadier General, to which they had both been brevetted in the Federal Service. It was expressly stipulated that as Cluseret, Fariola and Vifquain were neither Irishmen nor Fenians, they should keep aloof from the conspiracy proper, and that they should not be required to appear in Ireland until a *de facto* government with headquarters at

Limerick had kept an army in the field for a reasonable time. This they would accept as proof that the cause had the support of the people. And they would then lend their aid as regular soldiers. On this understanding Fariola sailed for Europe on the 14th November, just eight days after his arrival in New York. (23)

Despite the utmost vigilance, Stephens was not seen by Doyle or his men after the 20th November. He left his lodgings on the 18th, and it was rumoured that he had probably withdrawn to the house of a friend there to remain until the moment arrived for his departure, as he had done after the escape from the Richmond Bridewell. Another possibility was that he had already gone to Ireland in a freight ship and might be landed on the coast of Cork from a small boat. The British Admiralty were informed. The American newspapers began to speculate along similar lines, and Doyle allowed his assistants to return to Ireland. He stayed on himself until the middle of December by which time all trace had been lost of Stephens, although a little earlier Pierrepont Edwards, the British Acting Consul in New York, had heard that Stephens had not yet left. 'My informant,' he told Larcom,

is *General* Millen, the successor of Stephens in Ireland who is at present here ostensibly with the object of aiding the latter in his promised expedition, and with whom I am negotiating for the supply of certain information in reference to the Fenian organisation which might be of great value to Her Majesty's Government in preventing any attempt at an uprising. (24)

Edwards paid Millen a sum on account and from him he learned that Kelly, Halpin, Gleeson and others were making preparations to leave for Ireland. They would cut their hair short, shave off their moustaches, and change their style of dress before going. Colonel Kelly was optimistic about the outcome; he was a much more dangerous man than Stephens. He was much less scrupulous too, and had expressed his determination to assassinate the leading men who had been their principal opponents, in the event of the rising being a failure. (25)

There was no love lost between Millen and Stephens at this time, obviously. Millen told Edwards that Stephens was arbitrary, egotistical and tyrannical towards everybody he might have anything to fear from, and his friends were getting quite disgusted with him on that account. Millen himself was convinced that Stephens had no intention of going to Ireland at that time. On the 7th December he attacked Stephens in the columns of the *New York Times*, describing him as 'a political humbug if not a cheat, and a rascal besides. He would not fight.' The reason for this outburst was explained by Pierrepont Edwards to Lord Stanley, the Foreign Secretary. He had received a letter from Millen in which he stated that in consequence of having been detected in his communications with the Consul, he had quarrelled with Stephens and feared that this fact would interfere with his future opportunities for obtaining information in New York of a nature likely to be of use to Her Majesty's Government. Millen, at the same time, said that, should their quarrel result in an open rupture with his party, he was determined to expose through the press what he believed to be the dishonesty of Stephens. There could be little doubt, Edwards believed, that, coming from a person known to have been intimately connected with Stephens, this would have a damaging effect on Stephens's cause. Much excitement had already been manifested by the Irish Americans on the defection of Millen, and threats of vengeance against him and the British Consul were being freely indulged in.

Edwards enclosed a copy of a report that had been made to him by Millen. This described a recent meeting held in Colonel Kelly's room at Fenian Headquarters 'on account of some one having informed them that the British Consul in New York had a spy at Headquarters. I have noticed on several occasions lately,' Millen wrote, 'that many things of that kind have been said, and I know that many men reported to be English and Canadian detectives have been spotted and followed from day to day.' (26)

In an earlier despatch Edwards described how, about the 25th November, Millen called on him with the manuscript of his history of Fenianism, which he proposed to place at Edwards's disposal for transmission to Lord Stanley, provided he was at once paid the sum of £500.

Mr Consul Archibald had omitted to inform me what in his estimation would be a reasonable remuneration for this document; but as I considered the sum proposed to be excessive it was at length agreed between Millen and myself that £250 should be the amount at which the manuscript should be parted with, leaving it to be afterwards decided by Her Majesty's Government whether the nature of the information contained in it was of sufficient value to justify the increase of the amount to the sum first demanded.

Bruce, the Minister in Washington, had agreed to this course.

In addition to the document in question Millen is to continue for the space of three months to furnish to me reports on Fenian matters, unless in the meantime Your Lordship should be of opinion that his services can be turned to better account in Great Britain, where he is to proceed to any place which may be designated to be made use of as Her Majesty's Government may deem proper, subject however to the conditions which formed part of his original agreement with Mr Consul Archibald.

The Ms. in question is not quite completed, and will not be ready for delivery to me until the day after tomorrow. I shall doubtless be able to transmit it to Your Lordship by the steamer which sails hence on Saturday, the 1st of December . . .

I would add that Millen continues in his former relations with the Fenian organisation, and is willing to proceed to England or Ireland ostensibly in that interest if so required.

In conversation with this person I have elicited the important fact that, notwithstanding the many rumours to the contrary, Stephens is still her(and that the time for his leaving has not yet been decided upon.

Edwards enclosed with this communication a circular from the Centre Office, Fenian Brotherhood, New York, that he had presumably received through Millen. This was issued on the 23rd November by Colonel Thomas J. Kelly, who described himself as D.C.O.I.R. In it the centres were required to give immediate notice to every Volunteer, military or otherwise, who had taken the proper obligation, and who could pay his own passage to and support himself in Ireland till the 1st January, to come to New York at once and report to the Central Office. (27)

Millen never appeared in the open as an informer but there can be no doubt that he otherwise assisted the Government to the limit of his capability. This emerges from Samuel Lee Anderson's observations on Millen's inquiry in the summer of 1867 as to whether the Government had any objection to his returning to England. 'I presume', said Anderson, 'there is no objection to his doing so, so long as he does not make himself amenable to the law by engaging again in the movements of the Fenian conspiracy or otherwise. He shall never, of course, be called to account for what is past, for it may be taken for granted he has disclosed all he knows of the affairs of the conspirators. I think at the same time he should be warned that by coming to this country he incurs considerable risk of violence at the hands of his former associates, in case by any chance it should happen to be known that he gave information. The mere fact of his being here, without interference from the Government, would seem to me in itself to awaken suspicion.' (28)

Millen continued his relationship with the Fenians. He was a member of the *Clan na Gael* delegation that sought Russian aid for Ireland in 1876. Three years later he went on a secret mission to Ireland with John Devoy and conducted a military reorganising tour among I.R.B. centres. He was still an active Fenian in the 1880s. John Devoy doubted his genuineness and publicly accused him of being an adventurer, but he had defenders. In John O'Leary's view, for instance, he was 'an honorable and brave man and a good Irishman'. It was believed in 1887 that he was the head of a gang who intended to 'illuminate' Queen Victoria's Jubilee with dynamite, (29) but the plot collapsed and John Mallon, Superintendent Ryan's successor in the G Division of the Dublin Metropolitan Police, who was in a position to know the facts, simply said that 'Millen humbugged them'. (30) Lengthy though it was, however, Millen's career of deception may not have been a record for that period. Thomas Beach, under the pseudonym of Major Henri Le Caron, secured high rank in the American Fenians and kept the British supplied with information, particularly regarding their Canadian ambitions, for more than twenty years. He was, in Devoy's phrase, 'the Prince of spies', and it looks as if he would have gone to the grave undetected were it not that his employers found it necessary to produce him at the Special Commission in 1889 in an effort to sustain the serious charges brought by *The Times* newspaper against Parnell and his associates.

CHAPTER VII

Preparations for a Rising in Ireland

IT was generally believed by the Dublin people towards the end of 1866, Superintendent Ryan told the Police Commissioners, that an insurrection would take place, yet they were unable to name anything substantial or definite on which they founded their apprehensions. It might be, he thought, that because Stephens succeeded in escaping from prison and had previously expressed his defiance of the British Government, he would be equally successful in carrying out his declaration of waging war against Great Britain in Ireland by the 1st day of January 1867. 'Whatever the prevailing opinion may be,' Ryan added, 'I am induced to think that the Fenian movement in this country is quietly progressing more rapidly than at any former stage of the conspiracy.' (1)

An idea of the atmosphere in the city was given by Ryan in a report (17.11.1866) of a public lecture on the Fiscal Rights of Ireland under the Union with Great Britain. A number of 'roughs' in the gallery of the Rotunda interrupted the proceedings with shouts of 'Stephens is coming. Three cheers for Stephens! Don't forget the 1st of January!' The lecturer had finally to give up and was followed by a speaker who, according to Ryan,

> made his debut under the influence of drink. Nothing he said could be heard for shouts of 'Hang him up by his hair. Keep his hands quiet'—for he gesticulated very much, and others hoped he was not going to fly. A barrister got up to speak to a vote of thanks, wearing his gloves. He was called upon repeatedly to take them off. He is very bald and has a scanty supply of hair which he was requested to take out of his eyes, and also to leave them a lock of it . . . (2)

Cork, too was, excited by the news from America that Stephens was about to land with men and arms in Ireland. The 'most numerous' Fenian party in the city and a host of sedi-

tious sympathisers were on the *qui vive,* fully believing that
Stephens would carry out his threats. Cartridges were being
extensively made. Among working-class people there was a
noticeable change of attitude towards their employers; and wives
were pressing their husbands to withdraw their savings for safety
from the banks. Irish Americans were lately making their appearance in the district; between the 30th October and the 16th
November 800 had arrived. Some of these had only been about
nine months away, just long enough to be drilled and sent back
to lead the disloyal. They had returned in the pretence that they
could find no employment in the United States. The Resident
Magistrate who reported these developments asked for a stronger
force. (3)

It was the same in many other towns, and in rural areas throughout the country, especially in the South. Alarm spread at a
frightening rate. Dublin Castle was deluged with appeals for
protection and the banks, enlarging upon the unusually heavy
drawings of gold at branches in Tipperary and Limerick, mentioned that some respectable farmers were actually turning their
cattle and butter into gold though it involved a great sacrifice. (4)
Business was reported to be almost completely stagnated. (5)
The Attorney General supported the demand from magistrates
and local gentry for troops and police to relieve the anxieties of
the 'loyal and well-disposed' but as things stood little or nothing
could be done, save to send out every available man from the
Constabulary Depot to the most agitated districts in Cork,
Limerick, Tipperary, Clare and Kerry. (6) The Black North
would be able to look after itself, so that the troops could go to the
south and west where there might be a rising if the Yankees were
such fools as to attempt invasion. (7)

The Government took stock of the situation and re-appraised
their defences. Aid was sought from the Admiralty and the Army.
The Admiralty, accepting Naas's view that he could only allay the
panic by a display of force, (8) made no difficulty about sending
gun boats to protect the sea approaches to Ireland, and by the 1st
December, vessels were stationed at Kingstown, Waterford,
Dungarvan, Youghal, Queenstown, Crookhaven, Widdy Har-

bour (Bantry), Berehaven, Kenmare, Valentia, Foynes, Galway
and Belmullet (Blacksod Bay). All ships entering a port were
examined. The Army were helpful in supplying a thousand of the
latest breech-loading rifles for the Constabulary which were
speedily distributed to the most dangerous areas. To make one
rifle as good as half a dozen was to multiply the force six times,
Larcom said. (9) On the more important issue of the Army's own
role, Larcom was critical of Strathnairn. He would neither ask for
additional troops, he insisted, nor make use of those he had for
strengthening weak posts. 'It is always the first duty of an officer in
taking charge of a post,' Larcom said, 'to look to its defences and
provide them where they do not exist.' (10) And failing to make
progress with Strathnairn, who disliked intensely the idea of
splitting up his forces into a larger number of widely separated
weak detachments, he asked Lord Naas to bring the Prime
Minister, Lord Derby, to bear on him. 'I fear no smaller gun will
bring him down from his high war horse.'

Strathnairn was away from Ireland a good deal, presiding over
a transport committee which sat for long sessions at Army Headquarters in London. When the renewed Fenian alarm arose in
November he told Naas that if his appearance was really necessary
in Dublin he was willing to come over at once, but his committee
was important, and he disliked being brought over unnecessarily
on account of one of the numerous reports which had created the
belief, the previous year, that there would be an outbreak. He
hoped there would be one; nothing would be so advantageous to
the interests of the Government and of Ireland as that Stephens
should make the attempt which would meet with a signal defeat.
Without Stephens an outbreak was impossible, but Stephens,
having none of the things that were necessary for achieving a
military victory, was too clever and too much attached to his own
safety, to run any risks. His object, by threats of a descent, was to
collect money and to keep Ireland in that state of agitation and
alarm which paralysed all her hopes of prosperity and progress,
and multiplied the numbers of the unfortunate, the indigent and
the disaffected. And at the end of the letter in which he expressed
these views Strathnairn added: 'If you should hear of a good hun-

ter please tell me of him.' (11) He obviously did not intend his routine pleasure to be disturbed by Fenians.

Larcom told Naas on the 20th November that as the declared time for the rising approached he felt that they were not as well prepared as they ought to be, and he was going to discuss the safety of Dublin with General Cunyngham. 'We ought to have 5,000 men here at least,' he said—

> 1,500 or 2,000 in Cork, a regiment in Galway and one with artillery in Athlone. For this and the out stations we shall want I think two or three regiments more at least, and it is sad that we cannot have two or three fast steamers. The gun boats are good, and will do good work, but they cannot move. I shall be glad when you come over, because the time comes when we want the actual head of the Government on the spot, the will and the power in one hand. [This was hard on Abercorn who as Lord Lieutenant was the nominal head of the Government of Ireland]. You will hardly I suppose bring Lady Naas with you? It is only an embarrassment in troubled times. I have seen de Gernon [a resident magistrate who was being prepared for a special mission]. He will be in readiness at a moment's notice. (2)

In a letter the following day Larcom repeated that their military force was quite inadequate to their necessities: there were only 1,200 men in Dublin, after the guards were mounted, and in Cork the like disposable number of the garrison was 150 or 200. Just imagine!

> In 1848 there were 30,000 men in Ireland, and now 20,000 . . . I find every town nearly in the country had troops in it; now we have not more than a dozen occupied. I am clearly of opinion that it would not be too much to demand 10,000 men more, to be sent in successive regiments, but even half that number would be valuable. It is too late to play with the matter any longer—some three weeks being all the time we have. True it *may* never occur. But we cannot afford to stake the lives and property of the loyal people and people of property on a possibility of that kind. We must be able to say it *shall* not occur.

He suggested that Naas should raise the matter with Lord Derby and the Cabinet and insist on more troops being sent, with all despatch, and he repeated that the sooner Naas himself came over to Dublin the better. (13)

Naas wrote to Derby. They were on the verge of a general panic, which was all very unreasonable but not the less unfortunate. General Cunyngham, who was commanding the army, in the absence of Strathnairn, was looking for three more regiments, a demand he agreed with, because the best way to restore confidence was to make a show of force. One or two important arrests had been made; if they could secure a few more of the leaders he was hopeful the trouble could be stopped short. He was having great difficulty in restraining officials who were asking for the most active measures (14) but very moderate measures had to be taken and the utmost vigilance excercised. He relied upon the Home Secretary to have all the ports watched, and he supposed that Strathnairn would return to his post. A factor of concern was the disappearance of Stephens without trace in New York. He had seen it telegraphed to the papers that Stephens had left America but of course it was most desirable that it should not be known that they had authentic information of his disappearance. It was quite possible he would conceal himself in America. (15)

'If we can spare you the three regiments you ask for,' Derby replied

> (and I believe we can), you shall have them. At the same time I must say that Lord Strathnairn, when you met him at dinner at my house, intimated his opinion that the force in Ireland was amply sufficient. I shall give him a hint that his own presence there, at this moment, is very desirable. I am glad to see that your Police have got their eyes open, and that you have lately made some important captures. I do not myself believe that Stephens will show in Ireland. (16)

When Strathnairn got the hint that he ought to return to his command he said he was quite prepared to go at once, but was it not possible that his sudden and unexpected appearance with the three extra regiments would only increase the alarm it was so advisable to avoid? (17)

(2)

As important as the size of the army was the question of the diffusion of troops throughout the country. Larcom, who had been in the engineers, wrote a memorandum on this subject on the 16th November in which, having acknowledged the wisdom of the then prevailing practice of keeping the army concentrated in considerable bodies in a few places, he argued that under the conditions that had developed such large bodies were not likely to be required. Abercorn and Naas shared Larcom's views, and Naas put the whole problem as he saw it to Strathnairn in an elaborate minute. He first described the state of Ireland as one in which an effort was being made to establish an independent republic by force of arms, the effort being made in Ireland by large numbers of men of the lower class which had always been more or less disaffected, especially those living in towns. The great mass of the prosperous tradesmen in the urban areas stood aloof from the movement or were directly opposed to it; while in the rural districts the larger occupiers of land were hostile to insurrection and the smaller holders assumed a neutral attitude which a temporary success on the part of the disaffected could convert into decided hostility to the Government. So much for the masses. On the other hand every member of the upper and middle classes with scarcely an exception was ready to take an active part in the defence of the Government and the preservation of order.

In such circumstances the policy of the Government was essentially a policy of prevention, to do everything possible to avoid the necessity of a recourse to arms. The existence for even one day of a state of things approaching civil war would entail evil consequences which it would take a generation to repair. All the old animosities of creed and race, all the evils that invariably attended the success in arms of a dominant class, all the bitterness that followed the humiliation of any portion of a nation, would inevitably ensue. The Government therefore must direct all its steps—Naas argued—to preventing the possibility of a shot being fired. The first step was to restore confidence and remove the serious feeling of alarm that then prevailed. For if merchants and tradesmen deserted their business, if farmers disposed of their stock, if the gentry left their houses and sought refuge either in large towns or in England, incalculable national loss would occur and a portion of the misfortunes attendant on war would happen.

All Irish experience had shown that the presence of a military force was the only means by which a sense of security could be given to an alarmed neighbourhood. The principle had been acted upon by every successive government since 1798 with invariable success, and indeed it was clear that had the desperate circumstances of the nation permitted the plentiful distribution of troops throughout Ireland at that time, rebellion could never have occurred.

The Irish peasant in southern or western districts thought little of a military force stationed at Cork, Athlone or the Curragh, but place a small body of Red Coats in his immediate neighbourhood and he is immediately reminded of the hoplessness of any attempt at rebellion. This disposition of the Army was known to have been made under the sanction of the Duke of Wellington, and Naas enclosed an extract from Wellington's memorandum of the 15th August 1848, to show the importance he attached to the power being retained of striking simultaneously in case of necessity in various parts of the country. Was there any reason why that well-known and often tried policy should now be departed from? Troops were better armed, communications were more perfect, military posts more easily made defensible, while any opposition would be carried out with as little organisation as ever.

It was true that military leaders skilled and desperate might not be wanting on the side of the disloyal, but these desperadoes of the American Civil War were far inferior in knowledge, character and influence to the able and experienced French agents and officers who directed the insurrectionary movements in 1798 and subsequent years. Again in 1848 when the insurrectionary spirit was as strong as now, when help from France was sought for and expected, when treasonable clubs were openly established, when the leaders were men of some character, considerable ability and great courage, when a press conducted with talent and energy proclaimed treason in its most attractive form throughout the land, Lord Clarendon checked the incipient rebellion by a profuse distribution of troops in small detachments. The official return of May 1848 showed that an army of about 32,000 men were distributed in 127 different stations; in December 1866 an army of about 23,000 men was distributed in 44 posts. On the former occasion the policy was successful for no outbreak occurred.

There was nothing in the current circumstances to justify the Government from departing from the usual course. The loyal population were used to it. They were unanimous in demanding that it should be pursued. They knew that large forces were at the disposal of the Government. They asked that these forces should be utilised for the protection of their property and themselves. They professed themselves ready to remain in their homes and in their own districts to defend the authority of the Queen. They had a right to demand the assistance of the Queen's Government and the Queen's army, and this was being denied to them.

If necessity arose the Government would avail itself of the power that the law gave for the swearing in of Special Constables and for taking other measures of defence, but that was a resource only fitted for great emergencies and which the Government would not avail itself of, unless it was perfectly satisfied that the paid and disciplined forces of the State were unable to cope with whatever might be opposed to them.

But in addition to the duty which was imposed on the Government in protecting the lives and property of loyal people and the moral effect which the occupation by the troops of carefully selected posts would certainly occasion, another reason suggested itself which was in the opinion of the Government paramount to all others. In Ireland there existed a force of 12,000 men second to none in Her Majesty's services for discipline, fidelity and courage. Its inestimable services were patent to everybody. That force was essentially a part of the Imperial Army, was commanded by officers appointed by the Crown, and paid by monies annually voted by Parliament. The Irish Constabulary was as important a part of Her Majesty's forces as were Her Majesty's Guards. This splendid body of men was necessarily scattered over the country in small parties varying from five to ten men housed in small and scarcely defensible barracks, in the majority of instances far from anything approaching to armed support. To withdraw these parties from their posts for the purpose of concentration would in some districts be the signal for panic among the loyal people and possibly lead to an outbreak among the disaffected. These isolated and scattered barracks had their posts of duty and would remain there till the very last moment that was consistent with the safety of their lives. It was, therefore, the duty of the Government to make such a disposition of the military force by creating efficient supports for the police that would not only justify their officers in keeping them in their stations but would afford to them in case of an outbreak and a probable attack by an overwhelming force, an armed position within easy reach, upon which they could fall back and concentrate.

It was not, however, suggested that troops should be indiscriminately posted all over the country without regard to the necessary accommodation, easy defence and facility of support. The billeting of soldiers was most objectionable. It ought never to be necessary, as a portion of the union workhouses and other buildings could always be made available at a few days notice.

It was therefore suggested that a general scheme should be at once determined on, whereby without materially weakening their forces occupying the large towns or their reserves, such a military occupation of the most disloyal portions of the country should be immediately effected, as would encourage the loyal, remove alarm, support the police, and thus render outrage and disorder impossible. (18) The demands for protection that were arriving by every post were most pressing and numerous and it would be necessary to comply with some, and give good and sufficient reasons for refusing many.

The Lord Lieutenant, supporting Lord Naas, said that as a general principle the objections Strathnairn had raised to numerous detachments were so obvious as to require no argument; such a distribution was undoubtedly injurious to the discipline, and even the safety, of an army regarded simply as a military engine for the conquest of a country or for the *suppression* of insurrection. But the present object of the Government was to *prevent* insurrection, and to protect the lives and properties of the loyal people. With Strathnairn's assistance, this object could be achieved, for it was always to be remembered, and the history of no country more than Ireland had shown, that the recollections and the heart burnings consequent on the suppression of rebellion by warlike means, was a more enduring and greater certainty than the rebellion itself. (19)

The Irish Government's thesis was not acceptable to Strathnairn. He saw Larcom's hand in it; and Larcom he believed was not 'straight'; in any event, he should leave military matters to the experts. Nothing, he insisted, would so paralyse the means of defeating the apprehended Fenian descent on Ireland as detached or non-concentrated troops, particularly as regards operations on the coast. (20) His Commander in Chief shared his views. In fact in an earlier crisis Cambridge had warned Strathnairn not to send out detachments of insufficient strength anywhere and had laid down a high standard of strength. (21) And he pressed his strong opinions hard. So, too, did the Irish Government but they were unable to carry Walpole, the Home Secretary, with them. He consulted Disraeli and Stanley, and told the Prime Minister that all three of them were of opinion that Strathnairn's position was the correct one. Disraeli had particularly decided views on this vital matter, and declared that the Cabinet, if all of them were available, would be unanimously on Strathnairn's side. (22)

The Prime Minister, pushed into the position of having to adjudicate between the military and the Irish Government, came down largely on Strathnairn's side. 'Walpole has sent me,' he told Naas on the 8th December,

and I have read with tne deepest attention, all the papers which he has received from you within the last few days, including your correspondence with the Commander in Chief, between whom and the members of your Government I am sorry to see that there exists a serious difference of opinion as to the policy to be pursued with regard to the disposal of the troops in Ireland, or rather as to what should be the primary objects. *You* desire as wide a distribution as possible, in order to prevent an outbreak by affording extensive local protection and encouragement to the well-disposed; *he* desires to keep his forces so massed as, if it be necessary to strike a blow, to be able to strike it with irresistible force. Both objects are no doubt desirable; but in the state in which a great part of Ireland is, liable to a sudden outbreak in any quarter, and in many quarters at once, both cannot be completely attained, save with a much larger force than we could possibly send you. It is a point, therefore, which can only be settled by a compromise.

Some risk must unquestionably be run rather than have extensive districts wholly without military protection; on the other hand, you must be firm in resisting importunities for local protection to such an extent as will seriously compromise the safety of small detachments, and fritter away your military force so as to make it useless as an army. I notice in some of the requisitions statements that the nearest military station is at the distance of 25, 23, and in one case 10, miles. Now so to scatter your force as that every place should have an effective military protection within even the longest of these distances, would, I apprehend, be impossible, and, if possible, most unwise. I must own that I see very great force in the objections urged by Lord Strathnairn against multiplying small detachments, under young and inexperienced officers, in barracks or other buildings incapable of defence, commanded by neighbouring heights, at a distance from their supports, and in a country from which it might be difficult to withdraw them in case of any sudden attack. Add to this the greater risk, as suggested by Lord Strathnairn, of one or two soldiers being tampered with in small detachments, and I think you will see that there is ground for great caution as to too great a dispersion of your force. You speak of the responsibility attaching to a refusal of military protection in the event of any local outbreak; but I think your responsibility would be quite as great and the injury to the public service greater, if any disaster should occur to a weak detachment of the Queen's troops, from being insecurely posted in opposition to the opinion of the Commander of the Forces in Ireland, supported by that of the Commander in Chief in England.

I do not overlook the position of the Constabulary who, from the nature of their duties, are necessarily scattered over the country in small detachments; and it is infinitely to the credit of that splendid force that they have sustained that ordeal without the demoralisation which similar circumstances would infallibly produce in the best of the Queen's Regiments. But it is manifestly impossible to protect every outlying Constabulary Station; and much as it would be to be deplored that even one of these isolated parties should be cut off, the effect would be as nothing compared to that which would be produced by a sudden surprise and consequent destruction of a single company of the Queen's troops. Do not suppose that in what I have written I intend to find fault with the arrangements which you have made, and to which, as I understand by your last letter, the Commander of the Forces, has though reluctantly, assented; but I wish to warn you to be careful that in your natural desire to protect, as far as possible, all parts of the country, you do not make requisitions which, in a military point of view, would impair the efficiency of the Army, in case it should be called in to act ... (23)

Walpole thought that the Prime Minister's letter put the matter so clearly and so forcibly that, with a little management, a reasonable compromise in a matter that had arisen very naturally in the midst of excitement, could be effected, (24) and Naas, in letters to the Prime Minister and to Walpole, sought to explain his position and to indicate his desire to be co-operative. 'We never objected to the concentration of troops in reasonably large bodies,' he told Walpole:

on the contrary we consider it indispensable; but what we insist on is that, in addition to the large force that is now in Dublin, Cork and the Curragh and Athlone, smaller bodies should be detached, wherever it can be done with safety, for the double purpose of inspiring confidence among the loyal, and supporting the constabulary.

He recognised that they could not comply with the fiftieth part of the demands for military protection that were reaching Dublin Castle, but at the same time he considered a military occupation of the country advisable as far as was consistent with the safety of the troops. 'Garrison strongly three or four places in the country,' he said, 'and then throw out the remnant of your troops in such a manner, as they can easily, in case of need, fall back with the constabulary from post to post till they reach the main body.' Strathnairn was prepared, unwillingly and subject to his own reluctant orders, to make some concessions to this policy but he looked to fighting a regular campaign with the Fenians, an event that could never occur, for the population as a whole was absolutely devoid of discipline and unprovided with arms for 5,000 men. To prepare for such a campaign he was resorting to the cowardly policy of shutting up his troops in four or five garrisons and leaving the constabulary and the loyal people to whom they owed everything at the mercy of any gang of marauders that a few American desperadoes might bring together.

Naas assured the Prime Minister that there was no likelihood of trouble between the Irish Government and the Army. He accepted Strathnairn's offer of new detachments not to exceed four in number, leaving the remainder of the additional force that was being provided to strengthen some of the existing posts which were manifestly too weak. He did not, however, believe that Strathnairn's opinions were shared by his colleagues; many soldiers of far greater military experience saw no risk in taking the course that Naas had recommended. Strathnairn had wished to concentrate his force unduly, to withdraw the troops from many places already occupied, had actually declared the city of Galway to be unsafe and suggested the removal of the detachment from there. 'All I can say,' said Naas, 'is that if this had been done you would have witnessed a state of things such as never was seen before. The gentry would have left the country and the farmers would have had to become Fenians in their own defence. Strathnairn had asked for garrison artillery, but such a force could not possibly be wanted.'

A decided change for the better in the over-all situation had become noticeable in recent days, however, and Naas indicated that they were being more careful in making arrests. He entirely objected to Lord Kimberley's policy of filling the jails with boys and paupers.

> If you take up only the rank and file you do positive harm because you give the leaders to understand that they are not known. But if you arrest chiefs, they all begin to distrust each other and give the government credit for knowing a great deal more than we do.
>
> I can assure you that the most difficult part of our task, next to managing the Commander in Chief, is to restrain the zeal of the

officials and the magistrates. . . . The North is watching and anxious
to be up and at them. Devonshire wrote a few days since saying that
on the first alarm he would go and get sworn an Orangeman—they
suggest patrols by special constables—this in the North means
Orange walkings by armed men which always end in a fight. I have
written to implore several of my trusty friends there to set their
faces against such movements as wholly unnecessary, and calculated
to embarrass us very much. . . . However we have made no mistake
yet. I am confident that nothing very serious will happen. This I hope
is the last kick of the Fenian monster, and if we can catch Stephens
you will be able to allow the Suspension of Habeas Corpus Act to
expire in February. With such inflammable materials to deal with it
is most presumptuous to prophesy what will take place tomorrow,
but my opinion is opposed to that of Sir Thomas Larcom and
Colonel Wood of the Constabulary, and I believe that we shall get
through without a blow being struck . . . (25)

Derby was glad that a fair and reasonable compromise had been
arrived at. 'You have a difficult game to play,' he told Naas,

between excess of caution and over-confidence; and I have great
pleasure in expressing my opinion that you are playing it judiciously
and well. From all that I hear, I am every day more and more
convinced that there will be no outbreak: and if there is none it will be
mainly owing to the precautions which you have taken, and which to
some may appear exaggerated. You will of course throw no obstacle
in the way of the exodus of disappointed sympathisers. Their with-
drawal which seems to be going on rapidly, will be the the greatest
discouragement of those who have hitherto been their dupes. I
have no idea that Stephens will venture to show his face in Ireland
unless we get into hot water with the United States, and in spite of
all their bluster, I do not believe that they seriously wish to break
with us . . . (26)

(3)

Strathnairn never wavered in his belief that there would be no
descent on Ireland from outside or any internal outbreak. Never-

theless he recognised an obligation to prepare for the worst; so he called in his senior officers and unfolded to them a plan he had devised. (27) He accepted the additional regiments that were being sent over, asked for engineers and garrison artillery of which he was short, and created a second military division. He went through a list of all the police stations in Ireland with the Inspector General of the Constabulary and decided upon the military stations on which the police detachments would fall back in the event of an outbreak; he was charmed when Wood agreed with him as to the importance and inadvisability of unduly weakening military positions. 'He was a man of sound judgment and great experience,' he said. Strathnairn questioned Abercorn about a plan for the defence of Dublin he had sent to the Government the previous year. 'It was of course quite *confidential*,' he said, 'and if it has gone astray it is bad.' (28) Anyhow the defence of Dublin was again looked at carefully, in consultation with Larcom, and Strathnairn advised the Government as to the result. So far as the Castle was concerned it would be necessary to secure the houses on Cork Hill which overlooked the ground, including the City Hall and the Exchange, and to strengthen all the Castle gates and railings with half-inch boiler-iron plating, leaving loopholes. Without this plating the gates were indefensible. The Chief Secretary's Lodge in the Phoenix Park was incapable of any defensive precaution that would not disfigure it: it should be left alone. On the other hand, the Viceregal Lodge, also in the Phoenix Park, was capable of offering an effective resistance for long enough to allow of assistance being sent. The Board of Works were putting up barrier doors to isolate the centre building. The Lord Lieutenant's household could provide a garrison of fifty men who, with an officer's guard, should be quite sufficient. 2,500 sandbags had been sent.

Lord Naas raised no objection to these defensive proposals, but the Lord Lieutenant was concerned not to increase the public alarm. The least possible degree of publicity should be given to any measures undertaken. In particular, the Castle gates should not be plated; it would be better that iron shields should be constructed and kept out of sight, only to be moved to the gates in case of necessity. (29) This work on the gates had already begun, however, and when it stopped suddenly in deference to his wishes, officials of the Board of Works were blamed for acting without the sanction of the Government. (30) The water supply and drainage system were looked into at the same time, as well as the possibility of the main sewers being used for entrance into the Castle. Larcom also called for a report on the River Poddle which ran under the Castle walls. (31)

Christmas came and Naas found himself facing a happier prospect than a little earlier he had thought possible. Arrests, the seizure of arms, the proclaiming of disaffected counties, the movement into Ireland of more troops, the co-ordination of military, navy, constabulary and the coast guard, and more perhaps than anything else, the publicised dissension of the American Fenians, had had a markedly reassuring effect. (32) He poured out his optimism in a letter to the Prime Minister. Their policy had been completely successful and the conspirators, finding themselves met at every point, had begun to give up their designs. Their political opponents would say they had overdone the repression, but to this there was a complete answer. The precautionary measures that had been taken were decided and extensive, but they were not excessive, and they had had the effect in every case of allaying the alarm the Liberal Party would probably now accuse them of creating. The permanent officials assured him that the recent danger was quite as bad, if not worse, than that encountered by Lord Kimberley in February, in temporarily overcoming which he imprisoned without trial 700 men and for doing so was made an Earl. Their arrests would, he hoped, be under 100, and they would be almost all principal men in the conspiracy, A's or B's, i.e. Colonels or Captains. Naas could not call them leaders for the real leaders had never been in Ireland. Several of the prisoners had shown a disposition to 'split' which would make it easier to secure convictions at the ordinary Commission in February if they thought it advisable to try three or four of the worst of them.

There had been some difficulty in pursuing their policy with regard to these suspects. The Metropolitan Police required the arrest under warrant of three times the number of persons that it had been thought necessary to take up, while the officers of the Constabulary in *one* month sent in lists of persons whose detention they recommended, amounting to more than 1,000. 80 per cent of these were mere cases of slight suspicion which a Liberal Government would certainly have acted on, but which he, Naas, had absolutely refused to entertain. The Solicitor General had reduced the list to about 120, and Naas had further reduced it to 40, most of whom were now in Mountjoy. These arrests had been effective: in most of the localities where they had taken place the Fenians had 'dropped it' for the present.

None of the leaders had kept their promise of coming to Ireland and it looked as if the storm would soon blow over. 'The more I see of it,' he said, 'the more I am convinced that the whole thing is conducted by men of the lowest character and moderate ability. It is in the main a money swindle.' Kimberley had overstated his case in his House of Lords speech and had thereby done more to encourage Fenianism than anything Stephens ever said. They had had no cases of farmers, large or small, being engaged in the movement; it was indeed the unsympathising attitude of that class, which comprised five-sixths of the people, that had made it so easy to deal with the conspiracy. The farmers were not loyal, but they were not Fenians. They might go into a rebellion through fear but they would not turn out to put it down. They wished for peace and cared little for anything but their land.

Naas then turned to a 'pleasanter subject'. Lord Hamilton had been in America with the Prince of Wales and had spoken to him several times about the possibility of his coming to Ireland in the spring. 'He said that so far from offering any objection the Prince seemed to be quite pleased with the idea. Now I can hardly speak strongly enough on this subject,' Naas said;

> the good that the Prince's visit would do is incalculable. It would go a long way towards giving Fenianism the *coup de grace* and would afford intense gratification to the loyal and well disposed, who form such a large majority of the people. I have thought of an object for his coming which might be made the occasion of what the Irish love more than anything i.e., a Pageant. His father's blue

[St Patrick's] ribbon is still undisposed of. The Cathedral has been lately restored by the munificence of our member for the city, Mr Guinness. He might be installed a Knight of St. Patrick's with the same ceremony as was performed when George the Fourth was here. We would give him a public ball on the scale of the balls at the Hotel de Ville, while Abercorn would show an amount of magnificent hospitality as has never been witnessed in Dublin.

Every one of the gentry would on such an occasion flock into Dublin, and he would get such a reception as would show to the world what a contemptible thing Fenianism is. Now you must not laugh at this. No one knows the Irish better than you do, and I am sure you will agree with me that five or six days of festivity such as we could produce, would be more popular than all the bills, measures, projects or schemes that Parliament could pass or discuss in twenty years. I really believe that if the Queen would consent to his having the ribbon, the Prince would be quite willing to undertake all the rest. Hamilton has written to him tonight, so if you approve, I hope you will be able to recommend the plan to Her Majesty. I cannot conceive that there could be the smallest particle of risk. At this moment I consider that the effect would be electric—one that you could not possibly obtain by any other means. . .

We shall look for your reply with great anxiety.

Abercorn will write to you on the same subject. (33)

The Prime Minister, in his reply, noted with satisfaction the confirmation of his own sanguine hopes that winter would pass over without the expected outbreak in Ireland. He hoped, however, that Naas would very seriously pause before he abandoned the idea he had of not trying any of the prisoners in custody. The conviction and sentence of a few would have a great effect, and enable Naas to deal leniently with the many. As for Stephens, if he really never appeared in Ireland after all his brag, his non-appearance would serve to disabuse even a population of such unlimited credulity as the Irish lower class as well as the dupes and fools in the United States where the whole affair had been a gigantic swindle.

As regards the visit of the Prince of Wales, there were greater obstacles in the way than Naas imagined. 'I must tell you in strict confidence,' he said, that I find it would meet with very decided opposition from the Queen. It was with great difficulty that H.M. was induced to sanction the visit to Russia, which has produced so great an effect: and she expressed to me the hope that I would not encourage the Prince in going about so much as he was inclined to do, and that I would endeavour to get him to remain more quietly at home. Then you must know that the Queen is extremely jealous of the Prince taking any very prominent part, and especially so of his succeeding to any post occupied by his Father; and though, if he were to go over to Ireland, I hardly think she could object to his receiving the Ribbon of St. Patrick, the ground which would ensure a refusal would be that the Prince Consort's ribbon was still vacant. But if these difficulties could be got over, there is another of a different kind, which I think is fatal. The Princess is expecting her confinement in February; and as she has hitherto been before her time, nothing is more probable than that the event should occur just at the time you propose for the visit. At any rate he could hardly go over with that immediate prospect before him. I think therefore that it would be injudicious to propose that the Prince should go over at the time suggested; but I am as satisfied as you can be of the immense effect that his presence would produce. . . (34)

The Prince sent his regrets, but 'he says in the most pointed way,' Naas told Derby,

that he would be very glad to do *any* thing that would be useful to our Government and said that later in the spring when the Princess recovers he would not be unwilling to come. He had not heard any thing of the Ribbon. I am in hopes, therefore, that we may be able to induce him to come in the Easter week when our grand Steeple-chase meeting takes place, which would amuse him greatly. (35)

(4)

To make sure that Stephens would not escape observation if he came to Europe by a French boat, the Irish Government, in consultation with London, detached a Resident Magistrate from his district in Tipperary and sent him to France. This was de

Gernon, a man of French extraction judging by his name, and apparently a fluent speaker of French. He reached Le Havre on the 3rd December and stayed there until he satisfied himself that Stephens was not among the passengers that arrived there on *La Ville de Paris* on the 12th December. He then moved on to Cherbourg, leaving behind him, to watch the port, a young Englishman from the Consulate who had got to know Stephens when he had stopped at the Hôtel de l'Europe after his escape from Ireland. The Vice Consul at Cherbourg thought that the photograph of Stephens that de Gernon left with him bore a strong likeness to Garibaldi who was at that time very much in the news. He would show it to the *Commissaire de Police* and ask him to look out for the original. De Gernon then pushed on to Brest. On his arrival he detected a man he called D—— with whom he had apparently been told to make contact.

> He was very much astonished and (properly) placed no faith in me until I went through the process of seeing the Consul, Sir Anthony Power, a poor old gentleman, quite infirm. I found that D—— was worse than useless here. Sir Anthony could not get a man to rely upon to interpret etc., as he is very cautious, so I went to work this morning on a false alarm of a steamer from America having arrived, and in my peregrinations I met a young Norwegian who *speaks* a little English—interested him in the cause and appointed him Interpreter to D——. He will get about 2f or 3f a day, and other advantages if he does good. D—— is helpless here without some such. Major Yelverton (of the two wives) is here, and living near L'Orient. I have interested him in the matter and given him a *likeness*. I go tomorrow at 4 a.m. to St. Nazaire and Nantes . . . I find it necessary to *see* all the Consuls. They appear to awaken from a sleep . . . (36)

At Bordeaux he stayed with a cousin who introduced him to reliable persons to watch Arcachon, Poulliac, La Rochelle and Rochefort. Bordeaux was a very likely place for Stephens to spend the winter in. At a levee there he met the United States Consul, a Mr Gleeson, whose father was from Cashel and was probably related to the Fenian General of that name. De Gernon invited him, when he came to Ireland, to stay with him. He might 'perhaps learn something' from him. (37)

At Bayonne Lord Ernest Bruce and the Consul took him to see 'the ugliest man in Europe', the *Commissaire de Police* who offered to arrest Stephens, if he should appear, and hand him over to the Consul. He had to be told that that was more than was asked of him. Bruce suggested that de Gernon should go to 'the little, and little known, state, the Republic of Andorra in the heart of the Pyrenees' but to de Gernon it appeared very unlikely that Stephens, in the middle of winter, would give up the comforts of life to which he appeared so attached, to pass a dreary time in such a primitive place. So Andorra was not visited. From Biarritz de Gernon told of meeting at Gitarre 'an unfortunate scion of the nobility, calling himself Lord William de Vere and known to the villagers as M. le Vicomte'. He was willing to act because of his English blood and belongings, but, being in a state of absolute want, a little financial help was not unwelcome. At dinner with Lord William Paget at Pau, de Gernon met some French officers and country gentlemen who, he expected, would write to him if any of them should meet 'the object of our solicitude.' (38)

About the 16th January Lord Stanley said that Stephens appeared to be still in New York, which suggested that Le Havre was still the place on the European side of the Atlantic that most required to be watched. So de Gernon went back there towards the end of January, after spending some days in Paris, where the cold had been intense in the open, but the dry heat from hot air pipes in hotels and public offices much worse. The pulling down of old streets and building new ones continued to be a favourite work of the Emperors but it would take many years to complete what had been commenced. He was much interested in the news of Stephens he found in the American papers. 'I hope,' he wrote to Larcom,

> our people at home will at length open their eyes to the impositions that have been practised upon them, for by the last accounts Stephens appears to have been all through a sordid mercenary impostor and a coward also, a character not much admired *when found out*, in the green isle. It is believed by almost all the French authorities, that he is in Government employment. A great many English in France are under the same impression.

Since the frost disappeared we have had rain every day. Paris is beginning to fill. Many of the equipages here are at least equal to any to be met with in Rotten Row as regards carriages and horses but I do not think the coachmen and servants turn out as well. Coming from the Post Office today I turned into a poulterer's shop *intending* to buy a turkey to send as a present to a relative, but the price, 100f, was beyond my mark. Every thing is very dear here and will continue to get dearer. I think a family could live as well on £1000 a year in Ireland as on £2000 a year here, but then the people who live in Paris would not live in Ireland at any price. I must say I pity them. (39)

De Gernon's commission appeared to be coming to an end when he wrote home from Le Havre on the 4th February. He would wait for *La Ville de Paris* which was due in a few days and then make for London, to refit his wardrobe which had become threadbare from travelling, and on to Ireland. On the 6th he dashed off a note to Larcom in great haste. 'I have only a moment to say,' he wrote, 'that Stephens and six or seven others of his lot landed at Brest on the 4th and went on to Paris—a very ragamuffin set.' He was going back, himself, to Paris right away, but he felt isolated. He had always wanted an English detective to travel round with him in France but the Home Office had turned him down lest the French should retaliate by sending French policemen into Britain. 'I can do nothing,' he said, 'without a detective such as Mr Drascovitch . . .'

On the same day and to the same effect he wrote to Naas in London, (40) who got into touch immediately with Walpole at the Home Office. Between them it was settled that the matter from then onwards should be left to the two detectives Sir Richard Mayne had in France. Divided authority was obviously undesirable. However, de Gernon, when he got to Paris, made 'admirable' arrangements with the Honourable Mr Fane in the Embassy to ensure that Stephens would not be lost sight of; and a further stay in France being no longer necessary, he left for London, wrote a report and handed it to Naas in person. He posted a copy of this to Larcom for the information of the Lord Lieutenant with a covering note in which he remarked how he had seen with regret in the English newspapers that the Habeas Corpus Suspension Act was soon to expire. 'Look at what they [the Fenians] wanted to do at Chester,' he said, 'and you will have all these disturbers rushing over to Ireland setting the poor credulous people crazy.' His next couple of letters referred to a Fenian outbreak in Kerry, which would provide the Government with the reason they needed for a renewal of the Suspension Act. The newspapers indicated that the Kerry rising was more serious than he had at first imagined, so having seen Stanley, 'who expressed himself extremely pleased with the arrangements made in France and my mode of action all through', (41) he was cutting short his stay in London and hurrying back to Ireland. He had heard that the whereabouts of Stephens in Paris were still a mystery.

His report told how he had heard of Stephens's arrival at Brest in the smoking-room of the Hôtel de l'Europe in Le Havre from a German gentleman 'of observation and respectability' who had got into conversation with Stephens and his party on board *La Ville de Paris*. Stephens called himself Alphonse Marchand and was acquainted with German and French literature, but in his conversation with his disreputable looking companions 'he was at times imperious, coarse, familiar and very vulgar, so much so that the German was astonished that any disaffected people would adopt such a person as a revolutionary leader'. (This he obviously said after de Gernon had shown him Stephens's photo which he recognised as 'the very man and a good likeness'). The party were travelling second cabin class and appeared to be rather short of cash. One who appeared connected with the press and was called Murat Devries, evidently an Irishman, had a large heap of the *Irish People* newspaper to which he frequently referred. In Paris they were going to stop at some place in the Rue d'Amsterdam. (42)

CHAPTER VIII

Colonel Kelly in Command

DOYLE lost trace of Stephens as from the 20th November 1866 and de Gernon reported that he had arrived in Brest from New York on the 4th February 1867. Where had he been in the interval? The Government learned this later from Godfrey Massey, a member of the Fenian Executive. Massey was the illegitimate son of a William Massey of Castleconnell by a local girl, Mary Condon who brought him up as Patrick Condon. He was living in New Orleans as a commercial traveller when, as a result of reading one of Stephens's speeches, he decided to join the proposed expedition to Ireland. He threw up his employment and travelled to New York where he became a constant attendant at the Fenian Headquarters. He had served as a private and non-commissioned officer in the British army in the Crimea before emigrating to America, and in the Confederate Army he rose to the rank of Colonel before the close of the Civil War. In November 1866, about the time Doyle lost trace of Stephens, Massey went with Stephens to Washington and, through the instrumentality of Reverdy Johnson, a Southern Senator, were given an appointment with the President. They drove to the White House but Stephens refused to go in, because they were five minutes late. Massey said he denounced Stephens 'for his insincerity'—a strange accusation—and they separated. On the 15th December they met again in Stephens's lodgings in New York at a meeting Stephens had summoned, to which Kelly, Cluseret, Burke, Halpin and McCafferty also came.

Stephens's object was to announce to his colleagues that he found himself unable to fulfil his promise of taking the field in Ireland before the close of the year, and to urge that action should be postponed. (1) The meeting was opposed to delay although, according to what Stephens told O'Mahony later, it transpired from the discussion that matters, organisationally, were even worse than he had apprehended. 'We had nothing like what I promised and expected,' he said, 'and the little we had we could not forward.' During his seven months tenure of office as head of the Fenians in America the net sum he had realised for the campaign in Ireland was relatively insignificant and, at last, seeing conditions as they really were, he had decided that the rising would again have to be postponed. This was not cowardice, but a belated realism. (2) 'I then proposed,' Stephens continued, 'to go to Ireland by the next boat, even though I should be taken and hanged . . . All who spoke condemned the proposal, on the ground chiefly that if I were disposed of all would be lost. No particular plan, that I now recollect, was proposed by anybody that night, and so we parted without having determined on anything definite.' A few evenings later Stephens met another party of men—chiefly if not all officers—and on this occasion several of the officers answered affirmatively to the question put by Stephens whether they were ready immediately to start for Ireland; and some actually sailed within the next few days.

In putting such a question, at such a time, Stephens told O'Mahony, it should have been evident that he meant to bring on the fight as soon as possible, but

> words fell from Colonel Kelly and others, and hints were given me by parties then wavering in faith and undecided which side to take, from all of which it began to force itself on me, most reluctantly and sickeningly, that something was seriously wrong . . . that Colonel Kelly and his backers were . . . deep in a plot to set me down and put Colonel Kelly in my place. How had it come to this? Colonel Kelly and his backers got up the cry that I had abandoned the cause in despair, or through cowardice shrunk from the struggle, frightened by the powers I had created. . . . To come out and expose Colonel Kelly would have been certain scandal and probable ruin . . . Several times I sent for him, but he sent evasive answers and stayed away. I wanted a full explanation for even at this time I could do little more than conjecture what he was doing and had done. (3)

This explanation was given at another meeting on the 29th December when Stephens was accused by all those present of incompetence, insincerity and dishonesty. 'We quarrelled,' he said, 'and parted in anger.' This was a supreme understatement, for it was probably on this occasion that McCafferty drew a pistol to kill Stephens but was restrained by Kelly. Later Stephens heard his fate; Kelly, Halpin, Burke, McCafferty and—of all people— Massey, had deposed him. The *New York Herald* reported on the 7th January that Colonel Kelly had told the Fenians that Stephens was a coward, and that he had been foiled in an effort to appropriate all the funds and to direct his adventurous course away from Ireland to the gay capital of France, words that the Roberts wing who were, of course, overjoyed at Stephens's downfall, interpreted to mean that Stephens was making for Paris to spend the Fenian funds there on fast horses and faster women. (4) For some reason Brigadier General Gleeson was elected to the position of C.O.I.R. (Chief Organiser of the Irish Republic) in Stephens's place, but Kelly was the real boss and he was committed to action in Ireland without delay. In the police view, he was a man of a very different type to Stephens. He was as reckless and determined as Stephens was vacillating and timid. He was a most dangerous man. (5) Strathnairn saw him as the man who pulled the Fenian strings, a man who was very highly thought of by his party. (6)

Within a few weeks detectives were reporting from the South of Ireland that Stephens was being spoken of with contempt. Some people said he was a paid Government spy, others that he was just a deceiver. In Manchester a detective learned that vows of vengeance could be heard against Stephens: unless he came and fought, his life would be in danger. (7) The Government, however, did not fully realise until near the end of January 1867 the extent of the revolution within the Fenian camp, so that Stephens continued to be for them the most important person and the look-out for him at the major transatlantic ports was not relaxed. The question everybody was asking was *where is he?* 'We hear of Stephens here and there,' Larcom told Naas, 'but they are only [stories], and all is quiet. (8) 'I am quite at fault as to any scent as to his real whereabouts. I hardly think he would venture to shew here, but [he] may be leading us to believe he is here, or rather leading his followers to think so . . .' (9) A story was so persistent that Stephens and Kelly had both reached Ireland that

Wood, the Inspector General of the Constabulary, sent a note out confidentially to the County Inspectors to make sure to get them both. (10) Stephens was 'seen' in the South, at Dungarvan, Lismore and Cork, but detectives pretending they were commercial travellers could find no trace of him. (11) He was next rumoured to be travelling round in the garb of a Frenchman with a fourteen-year-old boy, but this story was likewise shown to be without foundation. Stephens, in fact, had not left Paris. When his whereabouts there were ascertained, a police watch was put on him and maintained until February 1868, by which time it was considered unlikely that he would leave the French capital. (12)

The Bantry police had other significant things to mention in their reports. In a pub they had overheard an argument between sailors from the navy ships in the Bay and soldiers from the town garrison. The sailors boasted that their guns could blow up a town four times the size of Bantry, which drew from the soldiers the retort that they were quite able to beat anything that might come their way without any help from the Navy. The reply delighted Colonel Wood when he heard of it; the soldiers were from his old regiment, the 13th. (13) This competition of loyalty to the Crown took place a few weeks after what the local police called 'a manifestation of disloyalty' on board Her Majesty's Ship *Liverpool* at Bantry. A sailor had been found in possession of photographs of Stephens, Luby and Robert Emmet, tried and given fourteen strokes of the lash. On being untied, he shouted out that he was now a better Fenian than before. There were 80 Irishmen on the *Liverpool* and the commander suspected that 35 of them were Fenians. (14) Soldiers, too, were still occasionally in trouble for voicing Fenian sentiments, and ballad singers were brought to court for singing seditious songs. Suspicious-looking strangers arriving at Dublin's North Wall were searched, usually to no effect.

It did look, however, as if the worst was over. Indeed, 'a leading notability' declared that Fenianism was extinct, and that he himself was as safe in his house in Tipperary as in any part of England. Strathnairn repeated this statement and saw no reason why he should not resume his work on that important Army

Transport Committee. The Government were also impressed by the change and announced in the Speech from the Throne that exceptional legislation for Ireland would no longer be required. At the same time a regiment was allowed to be withdrawn temporarily on the understanding that the detachments in the rural districts, such as they were, and in Dublin would not be weakened. The next three months, in Larcom's view, would be vital for all of them, for Government and Fenians alike, but particularly for the Fenians because time evaporated their funds, and the people assembling in the country would soon disappear if they were not paid. (15) And a more than optimistic Naas told the Prime Minister that public confidence had been restored and that for six months the most profound tranquillity had prevailed. (16)

(2)

Colonel Kelly, however, was determined to bring the tranquillity to an end. Money was short, so he sold the steamer that had been bought for the Campobello expedition and out of the proceeds—$14,000—he sent several officers off to Ireland, England and France, the first of them leaving in the last week of December 1866. Massey was despatched with £550 in English gold, and given a list of the officers he was to distribute it to in Ireland and London. These were men who had come over from America during the previous six or eight months in expectation that Stephens would follow them, and who had been promised support from Fenian funds. They felt 'let down', and many of them were reduced to a state of absolute destitution. Massey sailed for Liverpool on the 13th January; and Kelly, Cluseret and Vifquain who left for France a day earlier arrived in Paris on the 25th January and were joined there by Fariola on the 27th. Fariola went at once to London with Cluseret, and Kelly followed them a day or two afterwards.

The official Fenian body in Ireland, learning that Kelly had replaced Stephens, sent over representatives of the four provinces to confer with him in London. These were Edward Duffy from Connacht, William Harbison from Ulster (Belfast), Edward O'Byrne from Leinster (Dublin) and Dominick Mahony from Munster (Cork). They met him in his lodgings on the evening of the 10th February and constituted themselves a Provisional Government* to control the organisation in Ireland. They offered Kelly a seat which he accepted on condition that Cluseret and Fariola should be considered *ex officio* members by virtue of their military positions. Cluseret was confirmed as Commander in Chief of the Army of the Republic, and Fariola reappointed Adjutant General of the Army and Chief of Staff to Cluseret. Colonel Massey, otherwise Condon, was appointed Brigadier. It was also confirmed that the Commander in Chief should not proceed to Ireland until the insurrection had made fair progress and circumstances required his presence there. Likewise it was deemed proper that the preliminary arrangements should be directed by an Irishman; for that reason Fariola consented to yield his right to be the first in the place of danger to Colonel Massey until the moment of the outbreak, which was fixed to take place on the 5th March instead of the 11th February, the date fixed earlier. Massey, therefore, went to Ireland at once as Deputy of the Commander in Chief, to issue the necessary orders for the operations, to install the military officers, and generally to superintend the initial stages. For these purposes he was provided with all the funds at the disposal of the Provisional Government—these were little enough in truth—and he was given the fullest instructions. The plan of operations on which the conference agreed was deemed the only practicable one by the military men. It would enable the insurgents to hold out for at least three months, which was considered sufficient to rouse the patriotism of the Irish in America and to inspire them to energetic action. (17)

Before they separated the Provisional Government agreed to issue an address as 'From the Irish People to the World', a document whose style and character revealed to the Government that

* Richard Pigott describes this as a Directory of the civil, as distinguished from the military, management of the organisation. (*Recollections of an Irish National Journalist*, 224.)

Charles Bradlaugh of the Reform League and General Cluseret had more to do with the drafting of it than the Fenians proper. They noted particularly the references in it to the equal rights of men, to the curse of monarchical government, to the fact that the soil of Ireland was in the possession of an oligarchy, and to the necessity for the complete separation of church and state. The war the Fenians were waging was said to be directed against the aristocratic leeches who drained the people's blood, and an appeal was made to the republicans of the entire world and to the workmen of England especially to recognise that the Fenian cause was their cause; they could avenge themselves by giving liberty to their children in the coming struggle for human freedom. Kelly, Cluseret and Fariola had sought to enlist the sympathies of the leading Continental revolutionists and English republicans in the Fenian cause; and the officials in Dublin Castle considered it remarkable that they had found the English more accessible in this respect than the Continentals. Mazzini, when they approached him, would scarcely give them a hearing. He declared that the Irish must achieve something more than a prison rescue, an allusion to Stephens's escape, before he would believe they were republicans at all. Besides, while he would wish to see all Europe republican, the English Government was the last he would wish to see disturbed, for not only was it the most constitutional, but England was the only asylum in Europe for political refugees.

On the other hand, the English republicans, Bradlaugh, Cramer, and Odgers, assured them that if only they were satisfied that the Fenian principles were merely democratic and not anti-English, they would promise their support, and advocate an alliance between their respective organisations. At their first interview Cramer and Odgers said they would confer on the subject with Beales, the President of the Reform League, who had recently been holding immense public meetings in London in favour of manhood suffrage and the ballot, in defiance of official efforts to suppress them. Nothing came of these contacts but Kelly was not disappointed. He attached little importance to English support. A 'fight in Ireland' was the only measure that would advance the interests of the Brotherhood. Cluseret and Fariola were simultaneously moving in very different circles. Through Fenian influence Cluseret had been commissioned to inspect military installations abroad on behalf of the State of New York and in this capacity he, with Fariola, visited the British Army arsenals at Woolwich and Aldershot and met Sir Yorke Scarlett and other English generals at the War Office. He was introduced by the American Minister in London. (18) The inspections were cut short by McCafferty's independently planned raid on the armoury of Chester Castle.

McCafferty had come to London before his American colleagues and had met a group of Irish Fenians who, believing that the prospect of a military invasion had vanished, were intent on saving themselves from disgrace by independently making some bold attempt, no matter how hopeless it might be. This 'schismatic London directory', as it came to be called in Government circles, were glad to add McCafferty to their number and avail themselves of his experience. He had been in the Confederate army as one of Morgan's Raiders in the forays through Kentucky, Indiana and Ohio; and was recognised as an eccentric, self-willed man, with the guerrilla habit of doing what he thought proper and often disobeying orders. He had a hand in the bloody assassinations carried out by the Invincibles in 1882. He told the Irishmen of Stephens's deposition by Kelly, to whom they also gave a place on the 'board'; but they went ahead with a project McCafferty had devised and which was due to be put into operation on the 11th February, the original date fixed for the general rising. (19) This was to concentrate a body of Fenians in Chester for an attack on Chester Castle with the object of carrying away the 10,000 stand of Government arms deposited there. The train for Holyhead and the boats in the harbour there were to be seized in turn, and railway lines and telegraphic communication destroyed as the Fenians moved towards their objective, which was to secure a landing on the east coast of Ireland, in the vicinity of Dublin. The Provisional Government felt that to precipitate matters in this way would endanger the success of the general insurrection, and would be certain to lead to a renewal of the Habeas Corpus

Suspension Act then about to expire. But, in Fariola's words, they allowed a self-constituted body calling itself the Directory to carry out an attempt that was thought impracticable but which could not well be prevented for reasons of policy. (20)

The first part of McCafferty's project was far from being impracticable, for Chester Castle, with its modest guard, could easily have been overwhelmed. However, one of his adherents among the higher ranks of the Fenians in the North of England was to see that this did not occur. This was John Joseph Corydon, an old and trusted friend of Stephens, formerly a lieutenant in the Federal Army who joined the Fenian Brotherhood in 1862 at Harrison's Landing, Virginia. He met McCafferty, whom he had known since the latter part of 1865, in Liverpool in January and February 1867. McCafferty had told him that Stephens's party were played out, that he could not abide Stephens's nonsense any longer, that he had come over to fight and believed that all honest Irishmen would do the same. Corydon was a loose-living character and had been giving information for some time to the police in Liverpool, usually through Head Constable McHale of the Irish Constabulary, who was stationed in that city for the express purpose of reporting on Fenian activities. On the 10th February Corydon received details of what was planned for the morrow and promptly made them known to senior officers of the Liverpool Police whom he met in the lodgings of another Irish Constabulary man, Head Constable Meagher. They in turn communicated the information to the civil and military authorites in Chester as well as to the governments in London and Dublin.

On the morning of the 11th train-loads of Irishmen arrived in Chester from Manchester, Leeds, Preston, Liverpool and other neighbouring towns. They lounged carelessly about in small groups, all 1,200 of them, waiting to be called into action, until they observed that the guards on the Castle were being doubled, that police were taking up positions, and that military were pouring in on express trains. The secret had obviously been betrayed, but who was the betrayer? Not Corydon surely who, though purposely late for a vital train, was about to join another when he was told that the Fenians had been sold, that he was to turn back and tell the others to do the same; these were the instructions of McCafferty, and of John Flood, the head of the organisation in England. McCafferty himself had failed to reach Chester in time: his train had been put into a siding to make way for the troop specials. It was superabundantly clear that there could be no attack on Chester Castle; the Fenian body, therefore, dispersed as quickly as they could, some of them throwing away their revolvers as they did. Sixty-three of them made for Dublin but were arrested the moment they arrived.

According to the *Irish Times*, a hostile paper, these men presented a pitiable, woe-begone spectacle when marshalled by the police in the quayside sheds. It looked, the imaginative reporter said, as if the English Poor Law Guardians had practised a ruse upon the good people of Ireland, emptying out the living skeletons of their sick wards upon the Dublin quays. 'They were draggled, ragged, wan and shivering. The rough passage and a night at sea evidently had not agreed with their internal economy. They were clad in the oddest and most motley clothing, or in very little clothing of any kind. Yet, most of them had money about them, and a goodly number of revolvers were found where they had thrown them in their flight . . .' (18.2.1867)

Corydon went with these men to Dublin and made contact there with Head Constable Meagher who, by arrangement, had followed him over. To Meagher he confided the latest news. Drogheda was the first place that was to be seized when Kelly began his operations, so that a Colonel Leonard, who was already in that town preparing for 'the real thing' should be immediately arrested. (21) Corydon seems to have derived a cynical pleasure from his treachery. In a note to Head Constable McHale he said 'we have done well'; and to the Government his advice was to 'take up every man' of the Fenians who were being sent on from Chester to Ireland where fighting was expected soon. (22) The Dublin police did this, needless to say, and gave a special welcome to McCafferty and a companion from the London Directory named Flood when they arrived on the *New Draper*, a coal vessel from Whitehaven, of whose departure they had been advised by telegram. Before the *New Draper* docked, the police watching from the wharf saw the two men clambering out of the vessel into a small boat. They got another boat and went after them. McCafferty and Flood changed boats again but were finally captured, much to the delight of Superintendent Ryan of the G. Division. Up to that time few, if any, arrests had been made more detrimental to the Fenian movement than these, he told the Police Commissioners. 'Perhaps there is not a man connected with the whole movement more cold-blooded and sanguinary in his disposition than Captain John McCafferty. (23) McCafferty was later sentenced to death, commuted to a term of imprisonment, principally on the evidence of the informer Devany, for it was too early yet to expose Corydon. A warder in Mountjoy Prison testified that on searching the prisoner, he found in the lining of his coat a ring with his name and Fenian devices engraved on it.

(3)

Unrelated to the Chester Castle affair—although the contrary has often been thought—a Colonel John J. O'Connor staged a very minor outbreak in Kerry on Wednesday the 13th February. This, according to Fariola, resulted from ignorance of the change made in the government of the Brotherhood. It also presumably resulted from the change of date for the rising. At any rate, in the early hours of that day, bands of armed men collected in the neighbourhood of Killarney and Cahirciveen, attacked a coast guard station at Kells and carried away the arms and ammunition found there. About an hour later the attacking party, marching in military order, met a mounted orderly of police named Duggan on his way to Cahirciveen. He was called upon to stop, but putting spurs to his horse he tried to dash through them. He was brought to the ground, however, by a shot fired by the Fenians.

But strange to say, when his assailants discovered he was wounded, they expressed sorrow on his account and the leader O'Connor gave him some brandy out of his own flask. Having taken possession of Duggan's horse, arms and ammunition and the despatch he was carrying, the party left him with a promise to send the priest and the doctor, a promise moreover which they faithfully fulfilled. (24)

Those were the only acts of violence that marked the Kerry outbreak. At no time were more than a hundred men involved, some thirty of them returned Americans. For some days they kept together in the mountains in small groups, but then dispersed, the last of them being seen through the mist 'dropping one by one over a mountain ridge like hares seeking a covert'. (25) O'Connor got away, disguised as a priest, to America. (26)

The people of the district appear to have been apathetic, but it was recognised that had the insurgents achieved any decided success, many would have rallied to them. The police were taking no chances. One of them, Second Head Constable D. Ryan, reporting from Glencar where he was operating in disguise, wrote on the 24th February:

> I have been moving through this Glen and the surrounding mountain passes. I slept last night in the house of Darby Connor, suspected sympathiser and harbourer of the rebel refugees, and where it was supposed, and I believe correctly, that J. J. O'Connor and others of them had been staying a week since.
>
> Darby Connor believed me to be one of the gang, and he gave me shelter for the night.
>
> By a preconcerted arrangement Constable Driscoll and party visited this man's house while I was concealed there. He [Connor] assisted in secreting me during the search of the police and on their departure without having discovered me he implored of me to endeavour to effect my escape and gave me the name of a 'friend' living 12 miles away where I would be sheltered until I could manage to get off from the country.
>
> I shall sleep in that 'friend's' house (John Rahilly, P.L.G.) tonight or tomorrow night...

Elsewhere in his report Ryan criticised the local constabulary, who appear to have been scared. They shut themselves up in their barracks although a strong force of marines was in readiness to co-operate with them. If they had united their forces they could easily have disposed of the Fenians. (27)

The news of the outbreak, such as it was, caused a considerable stir in military circles. Under instructions from the Divisional Commander Cunyngham, Major General Bates lost no time in sending a detachment of soldiers from Cork to Killarney, while Sir Alfred Horsford in a few hours collected a movable or flying column of commandeered vehicles of all sorts at Limerick Junction from which he commanded the whole of the county Kerry. Strathnairn would have liked to have gone down to the outbreak area himself—he was always a man of action—but he had had rather a baddish fall in the hunting field a couple of days before, marring his beauteous visage, Larcom said, and thought it better to stay at home. (29) However, he kept his subordinates supplied with advice, arranged that the police should be supported in their search for firearms, and emphasised the importance of protecting the Valentia magnetic telegraph line. When he realised, as he speedily did, that the initial reports were grossly exaggerated, he told the 40th regiment, which had been ready to move, to stand down, and subsequently disbanded the movable column that had failed to make contact with the dwindling band of insurgents 'on the run'. Horsford would have liked to have kept a regiment of infantry in the disturbed area for some time. 'Cahirciveen I have seen', he said, 'and I have no hesitation in saying that I never saw so vile a spot. In my opinion the strongest detachment should be kept there and I should further suggest that it should be relieved as often as possible. The appearance and manner of the people of that place stamp it as a den of mischief.' (30) Strathnairn thought the suggestion well-founded, but the presence of a man of war with twenty marines on board at Valentia provided sufficient cover for Cahirciveen. (31)

He was puzzled about the origin of the outbreak and wondered whether the Americans were involved. Where had the Fenians come from? Had they landed from the sea—perhaps the Admiralty could say. He praised and blamed as he thought fit— the army had behaved uncommonly well, but the police—why

had they withdrawn from some of their barracks at the first sign
of trouble? This criticism impressed the Government, who directed
Wood, the Inspector General, to convey to the County Inspectors
concerned their hope that a Constabulary barrack would never
again be deserted by its occupants unless the officer or constable
in command was morally certain that the lives of the men would
be placed in immediate danger by remaining at their posts. The
stations referred to were to be re-occupied without delay. (32)
The Government also warned the guards on the mail trains that
they might be dismissed peremptorily from their posts if they
were found spreading lies again. They had reported that the
Fenians had risen in Dublin, attacked constabulary barracks, taken
arms and shot several men. They had also said that Stephens
had landed in Kerry and that the marines had mutinied. (33)

Killarney could well have been involved in the outbreak but
information enabling 'a disturbance' there to be anticipated and
bloodshed prevented was given by a draper's assistant to Galloway, Lord Castlerosse's agent, who passed it to the Government.
The informant had to fly the country. (34) Galloway, from his
being a Catholic, and because of his influence and exertions, was
worth all the stipendiary magistrates together, Naas was told. (35)

(4)

A few days after the Kerry affair Abercorn attended the Lord
Mayor's inaugural banquet in Dublin and replied to the toast in
his honour. He told the guests, who included Cardinal Cullen and
Lord Strathnairn, that at the close of the previous year the
Government had had reason to hope that the moral pestilence of
Fenianism had declined; and he still believed that the events in
Chester and Kerry were but as the galvanic spasm which con-
vulses the corpse in the throes of dissolution. He praised 'the
unanimous action of the intelligent and influential classes and the
admirable decision of the clergy of all denominations', and he
singled out for special commendation 'the recent most admirable

address of a distinguished prelate in the South'. The reference was cheered, for everybody recognised that Abercorn had in mind the sermon that Moriarty, the Catholic bishop of Kerry, had preached in his cathedral in Killarney the previous Sunday. This most amazing outburst was, and still is, quite unparalleled in modern Irish history. If it pleased the Establishment, it gave great offence to many people, including Cardinal Cullen who detested the Fenians and all their works, and openly supported the short-lived National Association as a constitutional alternative.

Some people in Kerry, Bishop Moriarty had said, had been betrayed into an act of madness without parallel in the annals of lunacy. Despite the spacious accommodation in the local asylum it was obvious that there were still a few lunatics at large. Some dozens of them had left the town of Cahirciveen on Wednesday evening with the avowed intention of making war on the Queen of England and of upsetting the British Empire. 'I think,' he commented, 'there is not one inmate of the asylum who would not hold his sides for laughter if he heard it.' He concentrated his fire on 'the prime movers'.

If we must condemn the foolish youths who have joined in this conspiracy, how much must we not execrate the conduct of those designing villains who have been entrapping innocent youth, and organising this work of crime. Thank God they are not our people, or, if they were, they have lost the Irish character in the cities of America; but beyond them there are criminals of a far deeper guilt—the men who, while they send their dupes into danger, are fattening on the spoil in Paris and New York—the execrable swindlers who care not to endanger the necks of the men who trust them, who care not how many are murdered by the rebels or hanged by the strong arm of the law, provided they can get a supply of dollars either for their pleasures or their wants. O God's heaviest curse, His withering, blasting, blighting curse is on them. I preached to you last Sunday on the eternity of hell's torments. Human reason was inclined to say, 'It is a hard word, and who can bear it!' But when we look down into the fathomless depth of this infamy of the heads of the Fenian conspiracy, we must acknowledge that eternity is not long enough, nor hell hot enough to punish such miscreants.

(36)

For all the pleasure that sermon gave them, the Government did not at all like Moriarty's personal political opinions. In Naas's words, he was simply 'a clever politicking Whig prelate' (37) who was not prepared to do anything to help the Conservatives to win back the prestige they had lost in Ireland. Moriarty had made this known to the Catholic Lord Denbigh when, with his eye on the next General Election, he had raised with Moriarty the possibility of Irish Catholics and the Conservative party being reconciled. Moriarty had made it absolutely clear that if all the bishops and clergy of Ireland declared for such a policy the people would not follow them. The popularity which Gladstone had recently acquired as a result of the stand he had taken on the disestablishment of the Church of Ireland had ensured for him and his party the support of the Irish people. The speeches of John Bright and Chichester Fortescue on the same issue had contributed to the same result. Already Cardinal Cullen was in overt alliance with Bright and the advanced Liberals and in recent by-elections other Irish bishops had supported the Liberal candidates on party grounds. All this indicated a settled line of action on the part of the Irish hierarchy.

During the past years the public feeling of the clergy had been very favourable to a Tory alliance, Moriarty told Lord Denbigh. The foreign policy of the Whigs, hatred of Palmerston, whom they considered the incarnation of evil, dislike and contempt of Earl Russell, promises broken and hopes deferred had made the Whig party very unpopular. But the moment the last shovel of clay was heaped upon Palmerston's corpse, the cry was 'Thou art dust and so is our enmity'. Then Gladstone was looked upon as the guiding spirit of the new ministry and Russell only a sleeping partner and the Catholic clergy found themselves in fellowship and amity with their old friends again. It was easy to find an excuse for forgiveness: *place-hunting* was the only Irish industry not destroyed by England. Under a Tory Government the Catholics of Ireland felt themselves ostracised. One or two might get a place but the Orangemen had first to be rewarded for their patience and self-denying fidelity. 'The faction must be set to rule the nation,' he went on. 'Look how the notorious champion of

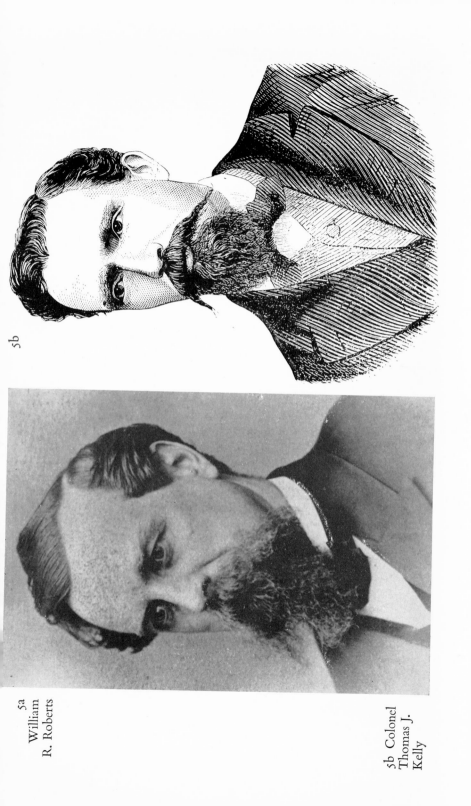

5b

5a
William
R. Roberts

5b Colonel
Thomas J.
Kelly

6 Fenian prisoners being exercised

Orangeism is now our Chief Justice of Queen's Bench and a country gentleman who it is said by the profession knows as little law as you or I placed as a judge beside him. Until the Conservatives separate themselves from the Orange faction, they cannot hope for Catholic support in this country.'

There was little difference of principle between Whig and Tory, and if it were only for the intense pleasure he felt in reading Lord Derby's translation of Homer he should like to be able to support him. Lord Naas was also a man he would trust. 'But look at the rank and file of the party. Even the English portion of it are a set of ignorant grinning sneering bigots, and the Irish worse. How could we ask our representatives to endure by their support the slanders of Newdigate or Whalley, and of all those Tory country gentlemen who cheer them.'

Whenever there existed in Ireland an inclination to support the Conservatives something occurred to stop the peace negotiations. At one time it was the Southport riots, at another the Phoenix Trials in Tralee, when Whiteside excluded the most respectable and loyal Catholic magistrates of the country from the Jury Box. Last of all there was Lord Derby's opposition to Monsell's Oaths Bill. Denbigh had apparently asked Moriarty what special measures should be adopted as steps towards reconciliation, and Moriarty outlined what should be done in the fields of education, and in land and church relations, to take the wind out of the Whig sails.

On Protestant Church Establishment, Moriarty said that he had the most certain fixed conviction that there never would be peace in Ireland, until they either levelled up or levelled down.

As long as the remnant of ascendancy remains, loyalty or cordial unity with England is an absolute impossibility. The intense love I have for the laws and constitution of England and the opportunity I have had by foreign education of comparing them with those of other lands, have made me loyal and English in heart and soul, but there is not a priest in my diocese that agrees with me. Abolish the Church Establishment 'delenda est Carthago': if not the Fenian, the rebel under some name will be in the land till doomsday...

He had written 'an unmercifully long letter' but he added a post-

FF K

script on the conduct of priests at elections which had been reported and to which Denbigh had alluded. 'I cannot answer for the truth of newspaper statements', the Bishop said,

> but if they are true, I abominate and unauthorise such horrible and unpriestly conduct. It pains and humbles me to the earth to see a display of human passion in a priest. 'Tantae ne animis caelestibus irae.'* At the last contested election since I came to Kerry I forbade every priest in the diocese to come to the election town under pain of suspension, *ipso facto*, except those who lived in the town. (38)

When he was shown this letter, Naas observed that there was a great deal of truth in it but 'when this comes from the best of the class', he said, 'what can we expect from the inferior Gods?' (39) Moriarty, in Liberal eyes, was the best of the Irish Catholic bishops. When in December 1869 Clarendon was seeking to procure a Vatican condemnation of Fenianism he cited the case of Father Ryan, the parish priest of New Inn, Cahir, who had remained uncensured by the hierarchy even though he had actually encouraged the tenants to assassinate their landlords; Clarendon instructed Odo Russell to contact Moriarty, then in Rome, as he was the only one of the bishops on whom reliance could be placed. Lord John Russell would have wished to see him in the principal See of Armagh when the vacancy occurred to which Cullen was appointed before being translated to Dublin. He was vastly to be preferred to Cullen, whom Lord Clarendon repeatedly told the Pope was 'the bitter and uncompromising enemy of the English Government in Ireland'. (40) He would have liked to prevent him from receiving the Cardinal's hat in 1866 but was prevented from doing so by Gladstone; the latter feared that the Pope might give it to the Englishman Manning who was 'infinitely worse'. Odo Russell pressed the Pope to denounce Fenianism which, he said, was the fruit of the teachings of the truculent Irish clergy for twenty years. They had been the active apostles of disaffection, having taught the people that all the misfortunes they brought upon themselves by their own idle Celtic habits were atributable to the Government. Bad harvests, emigra-

---

* Can the gods entertain such grudges? (Virgil, *Aeneid* I, 11.)

tion and the exercise of their rights by landlords were laid at the Government's door while every earthly good was promised if only the yoke of England could be shaken off. (42) Cullen was 'thoroughly disaffected' and the cleric that Clarendon distrusted most of all. These views, in appropriate terms, were conveyed to the Pope through the Papal Secretary of State, Cardinal Antonelli, whom Clarendon saw as 'a curious optimist by pessimist methods': he was praying for a European war as the bad means to the undesirable end of bringing back the Papal States under the misrule of the Papal Government. (43)

(5)

By the 18th February 1867 Larcom considered Kerry 'over for the present' but there were not wanting causes of anxiety elsewhere. They had made opportune arrests of members of the Directory in Limerick but in that town and county fire was still smouldering. In Dublin they were profiting by the revelations of their Liverpool friend (Corydon) who seemed to be 'going straight'. There was to be a meeting that night at a house they knew of, and the result of this would be given them. 'Cork, Limerick and Dublin are our main preoccupations,' he added, 'but tho' we shall be kept in hot water, it is pretty clear that nothing serious can happen to the public, and the storm so long brooding must in all probability be dispelled after a month or two.' (44)

It would be dispelled in a month or two, but its beginning was imminent. The Lord Lieutenant was convinced of this, and he based his conviction on the accordance of dates supplied by Moriarty, the Resident Magistrate in Limerick—the Bishop's brother—consistently a most reliable channel of information, and Head Constable Talbot; to this he joined the probability that the Military Directory, now free of Stephens, would favour early action beginning in Dublin with side-shows in Limerick and perhaps Cork, to draw troops off. So convinced was he that he summoned Strathnairn, who was hunting in the Queen's County, back to the city, and he strengthened the precautions already made by asking that another regiment, with a mail boat at Holyhead to take it over, be held in readiness. The boats from the Isle of Man were being watched, as the Fenians were using the island as a half-way house, and Superintendent Ryan was stirring up his informants to give him the latest news of the danger to Dublin. Sending this bag of information to Naas in London, Larcom said: 'We cannot afford to neglect warnings just now.' (45)

Government policy was obviously aimed at arresting the leaders: the ordinary rank and file did not interest them. Indeed, these very days in the aftermath of the Chester and Kerry disturbances, they proceeded to release most of the men in their hands. Colonel Lake told Naas on the 18th February that he had let 21 prisoners go from the Bridewell and was on his way to Sackville Place to discharge some more. 'It was a tedious and difficult job for they were a hard lot . . .' The next day he reported from the Richmond Bridewell as follows:

> You will see by my paper that I am spending the day up here. I paraded *all* the prisoners who have been committed by us Commissioners of Police and I gave them the option of going back to England under Police Escort at their own expense, or remaining *here*. They were *almost* unanimous in favour of the former and I selected all those who had [money] to the number of 56! The rest were to write for money today and on getting it I will let them go. Some of them certainly *cried* for joy on being allowed to go, and those who had no money looked so downcast. I drew them all up and lectured them, warning them that their appearance was known and that if ever any one of them returned he would be immediately re-arrested. Some of them said 'Catch me here again! I have had enough of it!' They were a bad lot. Tho' when I came here on Saturday and gave them the same option *not one* accepted it . . . (46)

The Government believed that the Kerry outbreak and the intended raid on Chester Castle were the work of the London-based schmismatic directory. Later they could distinguish these developments from the preparations that were being made by

Kelly, Halpin, Bourke and Massey in association with their European allies, Cluseret, Fariola and Vifquain. With McCafferty in their hands these, with a few others like Beecher, the head centre of the English Fenians, were the men they had to get hold of. Devany, the informer, knew all of them, so he was kept in Ireland till his services would be needed. Corydon, still an active Fenian, was immediately more useful. Head Constable McHale, who saw him frequently in Liverpool, learned from him on the 14th, 15th and 16th February that the final arrangements for a general rising were now completed and that Beecher had directed seventeen American officers then in Liverpool to remove themselves at once to Ireland; and they had gone over in a schooner that was partly laden with coal. He supplied a list of their names. More soldiers, he said, would be required to deal with the rising and those at Ballincollig, Athlone, Dublin and other garrisons were not to be relied on, the prisons were likely to be attacked and those in custody liberated, and he again mentioned Drogheda as a danger point. He was going over himself on the 17th and would, as before, place himself in communication with Head Constable Meagher. (47) But he was still in Liverpool on the 24th when he told the police that the American officers in Dublin had received orders to proceed to the different counties to which they had been assigned. On the same day the Head Constable of Manchester was told by *his* informant that a general rising would take place in Ireland 'before Tuesday next'. 'The plot thickens', was Larcom's comment. (48) The Dublin informants confirmed the trend of these reports.

Superintendent Ryan gathered 'from a source whose respectability and veracity cannot be questioned' that the leading Fenians were still determined to create a disturbance regardless of the results. The shedding of blood had no terror for them. Colonel Kelly, Beecher and about 150 of the men who were prominent in the Chester affair were already in Ireland and it could be inferred from their activities that their plans were cut and dried. They were disheartened by the apathy of the Kerry peasantry, and by the manner in which those who came from England for the avowed purposes of rebellion were allowed to be arrested. In fact the leaders were in near delirium respecting the turn affairs had taken, but Ryan told his chiefs that the state of desperation induced in them by the renewed suspension of Habeas Corpus could be expected to give rise to mischief. Despite police precautions some Irish Americans were succeeding in getting aboard steamers as firemen, or were concealed by the regular firemen among whom they had sympathisers. This loophole would, if possible, be closed. (49)

On the 18th February Head Constable Talbot reported that a 'friend' of his was to have attended 'a meeting of prime Fenians' at a house in Dublin that night and was to have told Talbot whatever was resolved at it. The meeting was called off, however, for fear that they had been betrayed. On the 21st February Talbot reported that

> ... on last night I met my friend of the Fenian Brotherhood. He stated that the Fenians 11,000 strong on the South side of Dublin has [sic] received orders to be ready for a rising in the force on next Saturday night (23.2.1867). All the Fenian arms at the North side of the city are to be carried to the South side on or before Saturday night. This man is positive that the arms before reported about, are in Dominick Street Chapel. There is to be a meeting of Fenians on this night (21.2.1867) at Ryan's 56 Meath St. after which it is thought final orders will be issued. I beg leave to suggest that this meeting be not interfered with as my friend will be among the leaders there and will inform me of the result. He will also before the rising give me word of the hour and place of where they are to assemble for rising on Saturday night, which I will communicate to you without a moment's delay.

Talbot's suggestion was accepted (50) and on the 23rd he reported that ' ... last night the centre for Hull, the Head Centre for Dublin, and the centre for Drogheda met at 56 Meath St. and it was there settled that the Fenian rising would not take place until the 1st of March', for lack of ammunition. 'Messages were sent to different parts of the country last night and one to Galway this morning. The night before last I went to Meath St. ... and at every corner I found Fenians on the watch.' (51)

On the 19th February one of Superintendent Ryan's informants had told him something of the plan for the 'very imminent' general rising in so far as it affected the capital.

They contemplate mustering in large numbers at some suitable place about two miles outside Dublin for an attack on the city. They expect to be several thousand strong, and to be conducted to the mustering place by guides appointed to each batch, and the locality will not be made known until the eve of battle. They hope to be able by a ruse to take some of the Barracks or perhaps the Castle by surprise and were it not that the Police in Dublin are so numerous, the mustering point would be in some place on the verge of the city, but as no house or concerns could be found sufficiently large to accommodate the number they propose to bring together they have fixed on a rural locality. Hand grenades, liquid fire in suitable quantities, various kinds of missiles as well as firearms will be supplied to the party for the attack. . . . They have unlimited hope in the disaffection of the troops in Ireland. (52)

And on the 25th February—confirming what Corydon had said—he added:

I have just now received information from a reliable source that large numbers of Irish-Americans are in the country at the present time and that several of them who are in Dublin and its vicinity have resolved to leave this evening for the North and South of Ireland and to spread themselves over the country in these quarters ready at a moment's notice to take command in an insurrectionary movement. The Irish-Americans are said to have cut off their beards and otherwise disguised themselves, and very many of them have got the new style felt hat. . . . A council of war is stated to have been held on yesterday morning but I have not yet received any information as to the nature of their proceedings but I am informed that startling news may be expected before the termination of the current week, in all probability not later than Thursday next, but certainly this week. A Frenchman whose name I have not heard but who is said to have graduated in the French Army, in which he has seen much service and attained an elevated position is said to be one of the prime movers in the contemplated insurrection here, and is in the country at the present time. It would appear that the largest proportion of the Irish American officers have gone to the South of

Ireland, and gone off in directions of lines diverging from the Mallow Junction.

During the progress of the conspiracy, especially the past eighteen months, the day for commencing an insurrection has been so often fixed, and nothing done, that it is very difficult to come to any correct conclusion on the point or to attach any credit to the various reports on the subject that are put into circulation but of one thing I feel quite certain that, if some important movement were not contemplated and that very soon Captain McCafferty and his companion would not have come here. Perhaps that at no period within the past four or five years have the Fenians residing here been less demonstrative, and there is a manifest decrease in the number of street rows, disorderly conduct and drunkenness, or in fact anything that may bring parties into collision with the Police, and this may be accounted for by the fact that meetings in public houses or at any places specially set apart for meetings are altogether abolished, but that they meet in one another's rooms in five, six or seven at a time ostensibly for some lawful purpose in connection with their trade in order to elude the police. (53)

It was bad weather for military operations. Larcom, who was feeling his years, found the climate enough to kill Hercules. After unusually mild days, it was bitterly cold, and snow fell intermittently. (54)

CHAPTER IX

On Tallaght Hill

THE Government received the exact date and hour of the rising from a variety of sources. One of these was Corydon. The date was announced by Godfrey Massey to a meeting of Fenian officers and centres held in a Dublin suburb on the 26th February. Corydon gave the information the next day to Brownrigg, the Deputy Inspector General of the Irish Constabulary: he also gave details of all that transpired at the meeting. There was to be a simultaneous rising at twelve o'clock on Shrove Tuesday night, the 5th March, all over Ireland, save the province of Ulster.* Another informant, who was in the pay of the Dublin Metropolitan Police, brought the date of the rising to Superintendent Ryan of the G. Division. He mentioned senior Fenian officers and the assignments they had been given, and one of these was Corydon. He offered to lead Ryan to Corydon's house. 'However,' said Ryan in his report to his Commissioners, 'as I was aware he [Corydon] was supplying information I did not consider it right to interfere with him lest I should do considerable mischief if the man [Corydon] is sincere. Therefore, I told my informant I would prefer watching the trains, but as a matter of course did not seem [?pretend] to have a previous knowledge of Corydon.' (1)

The Government thus had six full days' warning of the rising. They fully availed themselves of this period though Larcom told Naas that he had but little faith in what he had been told. Nevertheless he recognised that the Fenians, if they did move at all, would have to attempt 'something larger than Killarney' for their own sakes. (2) They were aware that Massey was in the country and Larcom referred to him as 'the Commander in Chief'. Later

---

* In deciding on a rising at midnight on Shrove Tuesday, the organisers apparently overlooked the fact that on the following day, Ash Wednesday, the Fenians, being Catholics, would be keeping a strict fast.

they were able to reconstruct his movements from the time he left London on the 11th February on his first visit to Ireland. His commission was to receive returns from the various circles of the fighting strength of the organisation, in arms and men, and to acquire knowledge of the country with a view to military operations. He returned to London on the 24th February, reported that the number of men available in Cork and Dublin respectively was 18,000 and 15,000 but that their arms, including pikes, numbered only 3,000 in Cork and about 1,500 in Dublin. He received additional funds from Kelly and 'final orders' from Cluseret, the Commander in Chief, whose deputy he was. It was Cluseret who had proposed to the Provisional Government at the London meeting that they should 'open the ball' on the 5th March, the day fixed for the execution of their compatriots in Canada. It was he too, no doubt, who devised the operational details for the rising which Massey communicated to the meeting in Dublin and which Corydon relayed to Brownrigg. The insurgents were to muster at the centres of railway communication, with the aim of preventing the transit or massing of troops. They were never to form in larger bodies than 500 men; nor were they to risk any encounter whatsoever unless where success seemed certain. If forced from the selected points of assembly, they were to move into the mountainous districts, driving cattle before them for sustenance, and there to carry on a system of guerrilla warfare.

Massey, as we saw, was back in Dublin on the 26th February and he was followed over within the next few days by such of the subordinate officers as were still in England. Cluseret left for Paris, Kelly remained in London and there forced Fariola, against the terms of the agreement with him, to go to Cork about the 2nd March. When he got there he found that Massey, who had arrived the previous day to tell Mahony, 'the chief of the province of Munster', of the time fixed for the rising, had disregarded his instructions in several important particulars; and having satisfied himself that the affair was utterly hopeless in any event, Fariola called upon Massey in the name of the Provisional Government to countermand the order for the rising. Massey, however, refused to acknowledge either Fariola or the Provisional

Government and as Fariola was unable to find Mahony, he let matters take their course. (3)

Leaders were now getting scarce, and the Deputy Commander in Chief, the man on whom everything depended, was himself arrested on the eve of the rising. Corydon saw to this. He sent word to Dublin Castle that 'General Massey', whose person was known only by description, was to arrive at Limerick Junction from Cork on the night of the 4th March to take command of the insurgents in and about Tipperary the following morning. The task of arresting him was given to Deputy Inspector General Brownrigg. He arranged with the Railway Traffic Superintendent that the mail train from Dublin should arrive at the Junction that night before the up train, instead of arriving, as usual, after the departure of the train for Dublin. Brownrigg and his men therefore reached the Junction in time to anticipate the arrival of the train from the South and to arrest Massey; they also found a car adjacent to the station waiting to take him to Tipperary. Brownrigg brought Massey back to Dublin, lodged him in Kilmainham jail and had him detained there under the Habeas Corpus Suspension Act. (4) On him was found a letter purporting to authorise him to act as one of the correspondents in Ireland of the New York Herald. To keep up this pretence he had also in his possession a seven page report dated the 4th March 'from our Special Correspondent'. This began:

> There is quite a lull at present after the excitement of the past few weeks, and we are all glad of it for it is much to be regretted that a country like this should be subject to periodic fits of absurd attempts at insurrection . . . (5)

The Government speedily capitalised on this capture. Hearing that Massey's indignation was deep 'at the deceit and cowardice of Stephens, Kelly and the other American leaders' they sent Robert Anderson, a member of the family that was closely involved in the secret affairs of Dublin Castle, up to Kilmainham where, having taken the Governor into his confidence, he was smuggled into and out of Massey's cell unobserved. In six hours' conversation he learned the whole story of the insurrection plot.

(6) Thereafter the prisoner's status changed dramatically. First, he was given a comfortable bedroom and his wife was allowed to stay with him. A couple of days later he was taken out of the prison and given into the custody of Colonel Lake, the Dublin Police Commissioner; later still he emerged as a Crown Witness against his former colleagues. He was well-paid, of course, for his treachery, and relatives of his had their passages paid to Australia. (7)

In Larcom's letters to Naas, whose official duties kept him mostly in London, a new informer's name appeared at this time, Curley. This was probably a slip for Corydon or a passing effort to conceal Corydon's name. 'We have nothing from Curley since he started,' Larcom wrote on the 2nd March. On the 4th, having mentioned that reports of various kinds and from separate quarters confirmed the Tipperary rising for the following evening, he said:

> Curley came back at 3 o'clock today—names the officers—he himself ordered to his post—instead of which he starts for Liverpool tonight to hide himself. Reports that Massey is to be at the Limerick Junction tonight by train going to the scene of his duties. We have sent by the train which should reach that station just before him, a party to arrest him.

Lake announced the result directly to Naas. A suspicious looking American had been arrested. His hands were by no means those of a labourer, and his whole appearance was that of 'a man of a superior class of life'. From a description and photograph he was not improbably Colonel Massey, the commander in chief of the Fenian army in Ireland. (8)

Information was coming to the Castle from other sources as well. An informant told Second Head Constable Welby in Manchester on the 14th February that the Fenians intended making a great show of numbers in two places in Ireland in order to withdraw some of the troops from Dublin, and would make similar displays in Manchester and other places throughout England. They were in great expectation that Roberts would simultaneously move towards Canada. (9) What this information covered we can only guess: it was given at the time of the Kerry outbreak.

Head Constable Thomas Talbot who, for some years had been

an officer of some importance in the Fenian Brotherhood, attending hundreds of meetings in many parts of the country, reported on the 3rd March that positive orders had been issued in Dublin the previous day for a rising on the night of the 5th March. Fenians from Dublin, Drogheda, Mullingar and Meath would concentrate outside Dublin and march on the city. (10) And de Gernon came to Larcom late on the night of the 2nd to report 'in great alarm' that a considerable number of daring spirits were to assemble, attack Thomastown Castle, take arms and valuables, and move intently on the town of Tipperary—this again to take place on the night of the 5th March. It did look to Larcom as if 'the result of the Stephens interregnum, by having thrown the military men into power for the time being, is to make some effort, as general as they can make it, probably very soon, and it may be in a few days'. But he told Naas 'there is nothing in all this to make us uneasy. We are as strong as we are ever likely to be and the sooner we come to blows the better, I believe. They will not find concentration and simultaneous movements as easy as they seem to imagine and are possibly deceived if they count upon any considerable local support anywhere.' (11)

Writing on the evening of the 5th Larcom said he had been so busy all day that he had not had time to read Naas's letters, and scarcely enough to write his own.

Our telegrams from almost all parts of the country shew apprehensions of immediate rising, with more or less appearance of grounds for the feeling. We have strengthened the principal points Tipperary, Mallow, Fermoy, Athlone etc., and have a depot at the Limerick Junction and a half-Battery of Artillery. The magistrates clamorous to draw in the out stations of Constabulary. I reply only in the last necessity—others apply for police to be stationed in the gentlemen's houses—no one thinks of the safety of the places from which the stations are to be withdrawn! or that all the police in the country distributed would not occupy half the houses.

The Dublin Fenians are to assemble at Tallaght, the Green Hills, leaving a certain chosen number in Dublin to plunder etc., as soon as the troops are withdrawn to deal with those outside, but the troops will not be withdrawn. We shall get upon their rear. I yet hope that all this bluster and threat may end in the birth of a very small mouse, but it is not the less our duty to be prepared for the worst, and laugh when it is over if it should be better than we have counted upon. (12)

The Fenian secret was not well kept in the provinces. On the 4th March word came up to Dublin Castle from Tipperary that a rising was expected the following day, and the magistrates asked for troops and permission to concentrate the constabulary. Larcom replied immediately that their wishes had been anticipated, though it might not be possible to supply them with military protection. (13) Oliver Moriarty, the Resident Magistrate in Limerick, also reported on the 4th March the likelihood of a rising that week in his district. John Daly, a Fenian prisoner awaiting trial, had said that the freedom of the country was assured and that all would be over in a few days. (14) The Government had also the benefit of a couple of anonymous letters. One of these, to Superintendent Ryan, dated the 4th March, read:

Sir,
The Dublin Fenians will assemble on Tallough [sic] Hill in large numbers on tomorrow. They will be going out in small batches all day. They will carry no arms with them. The arms will be sent out in cabs and vans and carts the best way they can in the course of the day. I hope you will act on this information in order to save bloodshed. If you do we will be troubled in Dublin no more by the Fenians.
I am, Sir,
One who would wish to save the lives of the people.

The second letter from the same person, received on the 5th, said that 'Halpin, an American officer' would command the Fenians and that 50,000 rounds of rifle bullets and powder had already gone out to Tallaght.* Ryan, on passing the letters to the Commissioners on the 5th March, said that on the previous night there were very apparent signs of a stir among the reputed Fenians

* 'They expected an American officer to take general command: however he did not come and they proposed to march to Tallaght, and in the confusion of falling in and preparing to march' John Kirwan, an ex-Dublin Fire Brigade man, who was the next senior officer, was accidentally shot. His second in command, Patrick Lennon, then took over. (15)

in the city and in Kingstown and frequent groups of five to eight men were to be met with in the streets. The men of Kingstown seemed not disposed to move to Tallaght unless arms were given to them beforehand, as they feared they would be detected before they could reach the main body and be arrested or shot without being able to resist. In a few public houses into which Fenians dropped occasionally men were overheard saying that haversacks had already been served out to them and that a rising was intended that very night. They seemed to think that if they rose and came to close quarters with the military they would be able to overpower them, and they also said that some of the disaffected soldiers would poison their comrades' food and by other means neutralise the efforts of the loyal soldiers. All the Fenians had been pledged to keep 'duly sober'. Ryan's own men were watching the movements of arms from places where they had been concealed and as he finished his statement, Ryan added 'Just now my officers report that unusual numbers of idle men may be seen at this moment in groups of five or six about the corners and particularly about the Circular Road.' (16) The Police Commissioners had already issued instructions, however, and patrols were now out along the principal roads leading from the south side of the city. Some of these were accompanied by military.

Tallaght was a constabulary district just outside the Dublin Metropolitan E Division and it was from the Superintendent of this division that the first report of a collision with Fenians was received. (17) The rising, as we have said already, was due to start at midnight and from about seven o'clock until one or two in the morning some eight or nine hundred men, if not more, were observed passing along the Crumlin Road in small groups in the direction of Tallaght Hills. Six or seven hundred of these, armed with rifles and fixed bayonets, took up a position from Doyle's forge on the Crumlin road to Mr Kavanagh's on Walkinstown road, and a police sergeant and two constables patrolling the quarter, encountered them. One of the Fenians presented a rifle but the police dashed through them, escaped into the fields and reached the barracks at Kilmainham, carrying with them a rifle and a bayonet they had wrenched from one of their assailants.

Individuals and small groups were met with on the Round-town, Milltown and Rathgar areas and detained. One man, found on the Rathgar Road, had a rifle, a sword, a bayonet, a dagger, and some ball cartridges and percussion caps. He also had a sense of humour.

He would not say anything about himself or his business except that his name was Abercorn and that he lived in the Park. (18) The police discovered 400–500 men assembled at the Palmerstown Demesne—they, too, refused to say what they were about, so the police sent for the military. It was nearly three hours, however, before a detachment of the 92nd Highlanders and the Scots Greys came on the scene, and by then the Fenian party had vanished.

One of the police patrols from the E Division—a sergeant and three constables—were met on Milltown Road near the railway arches by about 600–700 men who were armed with pikes, rifles with fixed bayonets, and revolvers. The Fenians took them pris-oner and marched them to Stepaside Police Barrack which they captured, taking away the five constables who were inside with their arms and ammunition. One of these, John McIlwain who was later 'reduced' and then resigned from the force, induced his companions to surrender at the sight of the Fenians moving to use straw and Greek fire to burn them out. (19) They were then marched to Old Connaught within half a mile of Bray where they were joined by more Fenians and a private carriage. The word halt was given by a Fenian officer who wore a white belt and sword, and who said 'here is Mr Stephens', meaning presumably the person in the carriage, with whom some of the leaders had a short consultation. From this Constable McIlwain gathered that the attack on Bray Police barrack which they had contemplated should not be proceeded with, because of its strength and position, and because British cavalry were on the way out from Dublin.

About 300 of the Fenian party then went towards the moun-tains, while the rest marched with their prisoners to Glencullen Police station into which they fired several shots, placing their police prisoners in front of the building and saying 'If you choose, shoot your men.' The police inside chose to fire, and wounded two of the Fenians, whereupon McIlwain was put in front of the

7 The Police Barracks at Kilmallock (March, 1867)

8 Prisoners in Dublin Castle on 6th March, 1867

barrack by two men who covered him with their revolvers, and he was told to say that if the barrack were not surrendered he and the other prisoners would be shot. McIlwain did as he was told, and from Constable O'Brien, who was in charge of the barrack, the reply came: 'If you give me the prisoners I'll give up my arms.' (20) To this proposition the Fenians agreed, and the prisoners were allowed into the barrack where they remained under a guard of about 100 men for two hours. After they had left the police stayed on until 8.45 a.m. when they walked over to Stepaside. There they received refreshment from a Justice of the Peace, and the Metropolitan men were driven to Donnybrook station. One of these recognised and named several of his Fenian captors; they were from the neighbouring district of Milltown and Clonskeagh. One of them had said that the Dublin police should be shot, but a Fenian officer answered that it would be dishonourable to treat prisoners in that fashion; when they reached the camp at Tallaght he would bring the matter before a general who would decide what should be done with them. (21)

By this time, however, Tallaght was not a safe place for Fenians. After dark on the night of the 5th, Sub-Inspector Burke of Rathfarnham had gone there with a small party of constabulary to strengthen the station. When within about forty yards of the building he came up with a group of Fenians who had a cart of ammunition. He seized the cart and had its contents brought into the barrack. He arrested some of the Fenian escort, but the others fled. At this point a large body of Fenians came up the road from Clondalkin and Burke called upon them to disperse, threatening to fire on them if they did not. They did not do so, but withdrew across the fields to the right, firing some shots as they went and then came up the Dublin road in close array. Burke again called on them to disperse; they replied by firing a volley of about twenty shots at a distance of about forty paces, without effect. The constabulary party, consisting of twelve men, then fired a volley at the Fenians, wounding two of them, one mortally. The rest threw down their arms and ran away. The constabulary picked up eleven long Enfield rifles with bayonets, also a great quantity of ammunition. They took upwards of fifty

FF L

prisoners and these were removed under a military escort to Dublin. (22)

(2)

On the 5th March, Strathnairn observed that the information lately received from the Government indicated 'an intention on the part of the Fenian leaders to concentrate a force in the vicinity of Dublin to assist a rising in that city, or to march upon Dublin or some country district'. (23) He had his own sources of information. On the 4th March General Bates reported from Cork the arrest of Massey (otherwise P. C. Condon), in the following terms: 'it is supposed from information received privately that he had served in the American Army and he is represented as having been the head of the Cork Fenians. It was stated that a sising would take place tomorrow night (5th inst.), that the inrurgents would march on Mallow, cutting the railway lines and destroying the telegraph wires en route' .. (24)

Strathnairn had already ordered the troops in Dublin to be held in garrison, ready to turn out instantly and occupy posts that he had specified earlier. These included the Four Courts, the Custom House, the Royal Exchange, the Broadstone and Amiens Street railway termini. (25) He doubled the guard on the Castle and had it occupied by a troop of cavalry and two companies of the 92nd Highlanders. And when it was seen that the Fenians were making Tallaght Hill the point of assembly he directed two Flying Columns, one from Dublin to take the Fenians in front and on the right flank, and the other from Newbridge, by special train, against their left flank and rear. The column from Newbridge arrived too late in consequence of defective railway arrangements. He asked the Government for a direction as to whether he, or any officer under him, could surround and attack the Fenians without being accompanied by a magistrate. It might be impossible on account of the urgency of the case to ensure that a magistrate would always be available. (25) The Law Advisers promptly advised that it was not necessary that the military should be accompanied by a magistrate to suppress an armed insurrection, which was a direct levying of war against Her Majesty and open High Treason. Strathnairn made this declaration known immediately to the army. (27) A few days later, in conversation, Naas gave Strathnairn more ample 'suggestions' from the Government as to how troops not accompanied by a magistrate were to behave when they met bodies of men engaged in rebellious or insurrectionary proceedings. If so accompanied, of course, they should act under the orders of the magistrate 'whose discretion was by no means as limited as that of parties not so accompanied.' (28)

Naas told the Prime Minister that it was quite impossible for him to get away from Dublin that night, presumably for a vital Cabinet meeting. There had been resignations from the Government on the 2nd March because of dissatisfaction with Disraeli's Reform Bill. 'The state of the country is very critical,' he said. 'Small parties are going about all over the South, demanding arms from the farmers, and there is certainly a large assembly on the Galtees in the neighbourhood of the Limerick Junction . . .' (29) Derby knew Limerick Junction well and he was sorry to find it was the very focus of the trouble, 'our rebellious district'. He had an estate there and hoped that his son Frederick who had gone to Ireland to keep his tenants straight, would be able to report to him that none of them had taken any part in the insurrection. 'My house', he told Naas,

> is little more than half a mile from the Limerick Junction, and very near the main road from Tipperary to Limerick; and if it, or any of the outbuildings attached to it, can be made of any use, I am sure that my Agent will readily place at the disposal of the Government the very limited accommodation which it can afford. (30)

He feared that this Fenian outbreak would give them much trouble and anxiety. It was quite clear that they would not stand for a moment before troops, hardly even before the Constabulary who, incidentally, had for the most part behaved admirably. Like Strathnairn he rather wished they would, but the danger was that they might carry on for some time, and in various

districts, a desultory sort of guerrilla warfare and plunder, very
harrowing to the troops, and utterly destructive of the prosperity
of the country. He recommended a Special Commission to try
the ringleaders, and especially the American Irish. It would be
quite necessary to make a prompt and severe example of them;
and much as he shrank from capital punishment, it would have,
in this instance, to be resorted to without scruple and was indeed
real mercy. (31)

The Queen echoed these sentiments in almost a paraphrase of
Derby's words, when Walpole, the Home Secretary, gave her a
full account of what had been done to suppress the insurrection.
'You would be gratified,' he told Naas, 'to hear how well satisfied
she expressed herself as being with the Lord Lieutenant and yourself . . . Let me have any accounts of interest as the Queen likes to
see them.' (32) She always liked to have intelligence that was not
already in the newspapers. (33)

Walpole had worries nearer home, with Reform League
speakers mouthing near-treason and sedition at mass meetings.
But it also fell to his lot to apprise the House of Commons. He
told them that the Government had no immediate intention, and
he trusted that there would be no necessity for them to proclaim
Martial Law in Ireland; that should the occasion for it arise, they
would be informed of the powers which would in that event be
asked for; that instead of proclaiming Martial Law they were
going to have recourse to the ordinary laws of the land, and that a
Special Commission would be directly issued to bring offenders
to a speedy trial. (34) An intense search was being made for
Colonel Kelly. The informer in his case had good knowledge but
it looked as if he was deliberately keeping it back until it was too
late to act upon it.

(3)

Strathnairn could not be contained in his headquarters in the
Royal Hospital. He was anxious to be up and about. So, as soon

as he was satisfied that Dublin city was going to remain quiet
and that Dublin Castle was safe, he joined the Dublin Flying
Column in the hope of meeting some of the rebels and bringing
them to battle. The night was pitch-black, and snow was falling.
Nevertheless 'I scoured the country,' he told the Lord Lieutenant
in the early hours of the following morning,

> to the other side of Tallaght Hill and was lucky enough to take
> 93 Fenians, amongst them some unmistakable Irish-Americans,
> arms of all sorts, some very handsome revolvers, and so much
> ammunition that we were obliged to destroy some of it, quantities
> of boxes of copper caps. We had no collision with them. They are
> trying to escape in twos and threes, throwing away their arms, which
> we found in every direction. . . .

He praised the police for their behaviour, and he prayed to be
excused for not being very bright; he had been in the saddle all
night. (35) He agreed readily with Abercorn that another regiment
would be useful; they were receiving 'unusually frequent and
proper applicants for military aid'. (36)

207 prisoners in all were marched into the Lower Castle Yard
and there brought formally before Colonel Lake, the Metropolitan Police Commissioner, in his capacity of magistrate, who
committed them for further examination on the charge of High
Treason. They were then lodged either in Kilmainham jail or the
Richmond Bridewell. (37)

In the search for other men who might have been at Tallaght,
Ryan's G-men visited the principal places of business in the city
with a view to ascertaining the number of their employees who
had been absent on the night of Tuesday and the morning of
Wednesday, the 5th and 6th March, and who might reasonably
be suspected of having been absent for an illegal purpose. Ryan
submitted a list to the Commissioners which would have been
longer, he said, had some of the employers been more co-operative. As it was, the longish list showed that most abstentions had
occurred on the G. S. & W. Railway (twenty-eight), in Martins
the timber merchants on the North Wall (fifteen) in Courtney
and Stephens, the iron founders in Blackhall Place (fifteen) and in

McSwiney's the Sackville Street drapers. (38) Most of these were soon released for lack of evidence (39) but towards the end of May the Governor of Kilmainham was complaining of the crowded state of the prison. There were then twenty cells having three prisoners in each, which was most objectionable from the angles of sanitation and discipline. (40) There was serious concern outside official circles also about prison conditions, and this came to a head when Richard J. Stowell, a Fenian prisoner, died immediately after his discharge from Naas jail. He was given a public funeral, and the police noticed that the processionists were respectable men, mainly shop assistants and clerks of the class to which Stowell himself belonged. Almost every pawnbroker's assistant in Dublin was also present out of respect for Stowell's brother, who was a pawnbroker's foreman. (41)

CHAPTER X

The Rising outside Dublin

APART from Dublin there were outbreaks in Cork, Tipperary, Limerick, Clare, Queen's County and Louth. Nothing whatever occurred in Connacht, owing it was said, to the absence of General Vifquain, who had been named to command in the West. The Connacht men, having had the promise of a French general, and hearing that Fariola was in Cork, refused to turn out without a foreign officer to lead them. A rising in Ulster does not seem to have been even contemplated.

The operations in Cork followed the Dublin pattern very closely. On the evening of the 5th March groups of young men were observed leaving the city for points of assembly in the suburbs, and from there they marched northwards in separate columns in the general direction of Limerick Junction, 'the rendez-vous for Munster', which was some sixty miles away. As they went they disrupted the telegraph service and pulled up the railway lines behind them. They were poorly equipped but among them were men like McClure, Mackey and O'Brien who tried to make sense of their predicament, and directed some attacks on police barracks. In a clash at Middleton two policemen were wounded, one of them dying subsequently. An attempt to take the barracks at Castlemartyr failed and one of the attackers was killed. At Ballyknockan the police were forced to surrender, but on giving up their arms, they were allowed to retire to Mallow. Disorganised and dejected the Fenians broke when they saw soldiers coming towards them. They were hunted, as was happening that day on the Dublin mountains, and many of them arrested. The alarm in Cork city was met by sending a cavalry patrol out on the streets, and by closing the public houses at 7 p.m. for five days. To applications for troops for Macroom, Millstreet, Queenstown and Passage Naas replied that 700 marines were in Cork harbour for garrison duty. (1)

The town of Kilmallock in the County Limerick was the scene of the most determined fight made by the insurgents. The police barrack was ill-fitted for defence; it had no fewer than twenty-one doors and windows, and was almost entirely surrounded by walls which afforded shelter to the attackers. The attack, under an Irish-American named Dunne, began before 6 o'clock on the morning of the 6th March but after a tough fight lasting three hours the barrack was relieved by a party from Kilfinane. There were no casualties apparently, but in an earlier search for arms a bank manager and a doctor had been shot, the latter fatally. At Ardagh, also in Co. Limerick, the barracks were attacked but the Fenians were easily repulsed. Trouble in Co. Clare was confined to an attack on a coast guard station at Kilbaha and the arms and ammunition carried off in circumstances which the Government felt did not reflect too well on the occupants.

There was more evidence of co-ordination in the Fenian campaign in County Tipperary. Unsuccessful attacks were made on police barracks at Emly and Gurtavoher, while two vacant stations in the Thurles district were burned down. At Kilfeakle the Fenians mobilised under Colonel Thomas F. Bourke and proceeded to Bansha, seizing arms on the way. At Bansha they broke the telegraph wires on the railways and tore up the rails. In this neighbourhood a man was shot for refusing to join the Fenians, but Samuel Lee Anderson commented that

> looking back dispassionately upon the events of the outbreak it cannot fail to be admitted that such wanton outrages were not the rule, but the rare exception, and these were almost wholly the work of American desperadoes, strangers in the country. This fact deserves to be recorded to the credit of the Irish people. (2)

(2)

To defeat the plans and actions of the Fenians, the Government on the 7th March authorised Strathnairn to set up movable or flying columns in the most disaffected districts (3) and gave him 'very good' law opinions, enabling the troops to use their arms against insurgents.(4) Lord Naas wished that this power should only be used against concentrated bands of insurgents, but Strathnairn would not listen to him. This would deprive the army of its best chance of getting at the Fenians, who had no intention of waiting to be attacked. Of course, if a surprise could be arranged, that was a very different thing: or surrounding or taking them in flank, or between two fires. (5) He egged Naas on. 'The insurrection must be stamped out, and that too with unrelenting vigour . . . and I am sure that you will agree with me that wherever it shews itself, the authority of the Government and the Queen should at once be irresistibly asserted. (6)

He had heard bad accounts of the state of things at Thurles and proposed to organise a Thurles Flying Column under a capital commander, Colonel Baker of the 10th Hussars. He could do it in twenty minutes with Government sanction and this Naas readily gave him. Strathnairn said he never remembered so rapid an organisation for service as that of the Columns already in being, and this piece of information, he suggested, might be relayed to the House of Commons, who wanted to know what was happening. The Thurles Column was very quickly off the mark. Dividing into eight smaller columns and combining with the Clonmel garrison, it scoured and searched the whole country by eight different routes between Thurles, Cashel, Fethard, Clogheen and Clonmel. Many Fenians gave themselves up in the expectation that they would be treated leniently, and this, in Strathnairn's opinion, was a favourable symptom, for it was better that Fenians should be submissive subjects in Ireland than become embittered enemies in America. (7)

As each of the Flying Columns worked under a Resident Magistrate, in the selection of whom Strathnairn had a say, de Gernon with his reputation for efficiency became an obvious choice for the Tipperary unit. In a letter to Larcom, which he wrote on the 14th March when at Thomastown with the column, he said that they were being aided by the severity of the weather and the snowfalls which prevented insurgent gatherings. 'We moved here today by Bansha,' he said, 'and through a very disaffected district and we intend pushing on by Golden, equally bad, to Dundrum where we halt for the night and continue to-morrow our movement through the mountains to Hollyford and Kilcommon which are represented as nests of Fenians.' He had heard from a person of undoubted veracity, who was well placed to get information, what the Fenians had planned to do in that area. They were to have entered the town of Tipperary from different roads on the night of the 5th March, and troops coming out to meet them were to be assailed from windows and doors in the town by the 'disaffected'. To anticipate the attack on the town, and being aware that the main contingent of the Fenians would come from the Ballyhurst direction, de Gernon took a patrol of the 31st Regiment under a Lieutenant Waldron along that road preferring it to one commanded on both sides by heights where he might have been ambushed. There they clashed with a body of Fenians who retired before them with casualties; and next day the Fenians were again defeated at Ballyhurst, a Major Lind with Lieutenant Waldron driving them from two old forts that stood about one hundred yards apart, in which they were strongly positioned. These actions 'miserable as they were on the Fenian side in a military point of view', saved Tipperary from being deluged with blood. That is what de Gernon thought. He praised the spirited conduct of Lieutenant Waldron and the steadiness of his men. As for Major Lind, a distinguished officer during the Indian Mutiny, his rout of the insurgents was worthy of the highest admiration. (8) But everywhere, Strathnairn told the Duke of Cambridge, the troops were behaving perfectly.

A sweeping movement involving a couple of the Flying Columns produced, on the 31st March, what was probably the most poignant episode of the rising. The Waterford column under Major Bell, with the local Resident Magistrate Henry Edmond Redmond (an uncle of the man who was later to lead the Irish Parliamentary Party) in support, surrounded two armed men in the wood of Kilclooney on a mountain slope. On being challenged by the soldiers the men started to withdraw down the slope, firing repeatedly as they went, and reached a river, dashed into it and made for the opposite side. At this point one of the men, Peter Crowley, received a fatal gunshot wound and fell in the water. Some of the soldiers jumped in and saved him from drowning. Redmond had meanwhile heard the firing, and rushing down the mountainside saw the armed men enter the river. He called out to the soldiers to stop firing and, as he did so, he jumped into the water and seized the second man, John McClure, an act which may have saved the Fenian's life while putting himself in the line of fire. McClure stumbled as he was caught, and fired from his revolver at Redmond. He missed him, and was about to fire a second time when a soldier wrenched the revolver from him.

The wounded Crowley, on being laid on the bank, was attended to by a staff surgeon 'with skill and Christian kindness'. While trying to staunch the wound he read from a prayer book to the dying man who 'cravingly listened and eagerly repeated the responses'. A 'respectable' farmer refused to allow Crowley to be brought into his house, so he was taken to Mitchelstown, first on a cart and then in a doctor's carriage, and died on the way. An inquest found that his death was the result of wounds inflicted by soldiers in discharge of their duty, but, afterwards, 'a very bad feeling was manifested towards Major Bell by some of the lower orders, and stones were thrown at an escort. (9)

Strathnairn was particularly impressed by the performance of his soldiers at Kilclooney Wood. It was an occasion which demonstrated the advantages of Flying Columns: they were able simultaneously to search a wide area and to concentrate on a particular spot where Fenians were known to be hiding.

> The ubiquity and rapidity of the Flying Columns, and the suddennes of their appearance in districts, some of which had never before been visited by troops, produced an excellent effect. But a still more important influence was created where the most disturbed districts which the disaffected had been brought to believe would be Fenian as soon as the insurrection had declared itself, were traversed in every direction by very small bodies of troops, proving their mastery over, and the undisputed right of the Government, to the country, whilst the insurgents, those who had asserted so continually that it would and must be theirs, were compelled to seek humiliating concealment and flight. (10)

The magistrates and the gentry generally shared this view. The Flying Columns had put confidence where there had been panic and had struck terror into the ignorant and deluded peasantry, whose little knowledge had been acquired in the columns of the, seditious Dublin press. The farmers had had a mysterious dread of the Fenians; now there was no word of approbrium they did not heap on them.

As was so frequently the case the capture at Kilclooney Wood of John McClure, and the death of his companion, was primarily the work of an informer. McClure was known to the authorities as holding the Fenian command in the Middleton area. Massey had told them this (11) and a placard offering £100 reward for McClure's capture had been put out. The reward, though earned in Kilclooney, was paid over a long way off in the city of Limerick. Neal Browne, the Resident Magistrate in Mitchelstown, explained why.

> As my motions are closely watched, I had to fix on so distant a place of meeting in order that attention might not be drawn to his meeting me. Not wishing to give him the least ground for suspicion or distrusting me I did not ask him for any receipt. . . . He had not the least expectation of getting this reward or idea that he was entitled to it. The payment has satisfied him of the good faith with which he will be treated and the care that will be taken for his security and for avoiding all reference to him. (12)

The informant told Browne that in the same quarter there were still six or seven fully armed men shifting from place to place and that, as soon as he could, he would provide the information that would enable them to be arrested. The fact of the principal persons, Godfrey Massey and company, having become approvers had done much, he said, to disgust the peasantry and to make them suspicious of the movement. On this Browne commented that it must always be borne in mind that what had taken place was against the opinion of James Stephens, and that its failure would operate to restore his prestige and give greater confidence in his judgement. It had served to free Stephens from the insubordinate, the young, hot-headed and unmanageable, and to enable him to work out his plans with more caution, confidence and certainty. (13)

On the 4th April, a day less than a month from the outbreak of the rising, the Government told Strathnairn that on account of the improved state of the public peace, the Flying Columns could be broken up and the other exceptional military measures discontinued. The police continued however to look out for the men on the run. A constabulary man, Joseph Murphy, who personated a pedlar of books and assumed an awkward gait, travelled through parts of County Tipperary looking for particular Fenians known to be in hiding, and reporting on everything he saw and heard. His was a risky duty: indeed he knew that his life would end abruptly if his real character were detected. Listening to people he formed the impression that Fenianism was not yet extinct. Very many of the conspirators condemned the recent rising as premature, but even a temporary triumph over the Queen's troops would send the vacillating and wavering people into the ranks of the insurgents and flash off a revolution. Real success for the Fenians, however, depended upon the unlikely eventuality of substantial American aid being received, or of England becoming engaged in hostilities with another country. He returned to this subject a week later (3.4.1867): in the meantime he had traversed a good portion of the country around Thurles and had made it his business, as he said, to fathom the minds of persons in various positions in life, as to the present and future prospects of Fenianism.

They all condemn the fatuity of the movement as being premature. They see the unlimited resources of the vast Empire they thought to contend against, and are unanimous in saying that without the aid of America, it is rank folly for to take the field.

It is remarkable for to note the political sagacity and shrewdness of the small farmers and the peasantry in general. I could infer from the tenor of their conversation that they expect the Eastern Question will bring England into difficulties, but Russia and the United States of America are to become firm allies, and that the difficulties which they expect and hope England will get into will materially aid the Fenian cause; that they will avail of the opportunity and expect aid, in furtherance of their plans, from the Powers named above, the idea obtaining widespread belief in and about Thurles.

At the same time, it would require great ingenuity on the part of the agents of sedition to make the people hazard their liberty in playing the game of war. The peasantry believed that even the elements, by the interposition of Providence, prevailed against them; while their leaders in some instances kept aloof in the hour of danger. Disaffection was undoubtedly rife—the people of Thurles, in particular, a deep-minded, cunning and conspiring pack, were incurable Fenians—but another rising was not imminent, except as the opportunity already named offered. Many people had fled from the district, and in dealing with those who remained the police were hampered by the absence of local informers. (14) He found that the fictitious prophecies that circulated among the peasantry were still widely believed. One of these supported the thesis that another rising would not occur until England was at war with some other country. (15)

Murphy was watching out particularly for Captain Joe Gleeson and Captain Charles Bourke but he had to be extremely careful in making inquiries about them.

I found the people very reticent on account of a report prevailing among them that 'Peelers' were going about the country in the garb of beggars as 'detectors'. However, the inference I could deduce from what I was told is, that Gleeson is still in that part of the country (the vicinity of Borrisoleigh) but his place of refuge is known only to a select few. He is not alone evading the law, but he is in dread of falling by the bullet of those who were his dupes.

It was said that on the night of the rising Gleeson got drunk at a wedding and that the Fenian party passed by the house where he was without his knowing it. After being routed by the military, men named Bourke, Kirwan and Kilmartin swore that if they met him they would shoot him. But Murphy did not 'fall in' with anybody who had seen Gleeson since Shrove Tuesday. 'I sold two books to the paternal aunt of the Gleesons (the widow Ryan who lives near Drum). She condemned the movement as prejudicial to the interests and prosperity of the country.'

As for Charles Bourke, he, too, was still lurking about the country, and allegedly with a brace of revolvers slung to a girdle depending from his waist. It would be rather difficult to arrest him, for he had friends scattered through the mountain fastnesses.

Murphy tried unsuccessfully to get the name of a priest who, contrary to the behests of his bishops and the general body of the clergy, had given the rites of the Church in anticipation of the worst to a good many of the men who figured in the rising. (16)

(3)

By the 9th March Larcom, reporting to Naas in London, was satisfied that the Fenians were finished with simultaneous risings in arms, but the scattered fragments would become marauders, a more profitable trade. This might have unpleasant consequences for loyal families scattered throughout the country, so it had occurred to him to move Naas's children into the Castle. Lady Abercorn kindly sent her carriage but they were already in bed and the nurse thought it unsafe to move them. 'I got Lake to have a special eye to your Lady and felt sure they were as safe there as here, if not more so.' Later they moved into the Shelbourne Hotel.(17)

As the month of March moved on, Larcom continued to describe the situation as 'smouldering'.

> We hold Fenianism by the throat as you would a burglar, but the moment you relax, up it springs as strong as ever. The root is in America and the manure is the discontent of a million and a half of people, mourning and brooding over a grievance—expatriation. . . . One does not now see how it is to end, or what means to use, we cannot go on throttling for ever. We can only go on trying to win away more and more from the malcontents and raise antagonism to it in contentment at home. But it is a long process, and a painful prospect. (18)

Strathnairn and his chief, the Duke of Cambridge, were agreed that it was better that Fenianism should show itself than smoulder, so that it could be dealt with. Strathnairn regretted that on account of want of heart, rather than of bad intent, the insurrectionary movement had not issued in a more decided form; the insurgents had run away instead of making a stand. He agreed with Cambridge that the guilty men who had tried to make Ireland a scene of civil war and general spoliation should be dealt with as law and policy pointed out. The ruin of Ireland was the inadequacy and uncertainty of punishment. What Ireland, more than any other country, required was the example of prompt, certain and adequate punishment of crime. When the Fenian prisoners entered Dublin the other day, he said, a respectable woman called out to her son, one of the prisoners: 'They will not hang you, thank God, and you'll all be out of prison in a few months'. This language represented the feeling of the Irish with respect to the administration of the law. Under one Lord Lieutenant, men who had committed dangerous crimes were sent to imprisonment and penal servitude, the next Lord Lieutenant, not appreciating the dangers of the past and from mistaken benevolence, remitted their punishment. Almost all the actors in the recent disturbances had appeared in the same capacity in former troubles, for which they had been punished and released before the expiration of their sentences. And mounting an old hobby-horse, he went on:

I think that people are coming round to the opinion which I wrote last year to Lord Kimberley that the suspension of Habeas Corpus is a great mistake. It is a very inefficient preventative, positively bad for the morale of the Irish, and no remedy; it is besides unjust in principle, suspending the rights of a nation for the crimes of a portion of it. The British public always views the suspension of Habeas Corpus with mistrust and unwillingness, and so much are every Irish government under the influence of this feeling that they have no sooner placed suspected men in prison under the Suspension Act than they are anxious to release them again, under engagements and promises, which are perfectly illusory, that they will go to England, Scotland or America, and not return to Ireland. The promises are no sooner made than broken. The enlarged Fenians come back again, almost by return of post, with diminished respect for the policy and power of the government which has not had the resolution to face a great state difficulty, and has applied a temporary and wholly inefficient remedy to a dangerous and lasting evil which is historical and the growth of centuries.

At this point Strathnairn produced, not for the first or last time, his idea of what should be done. There should be an Act of Parliament to put an end once and for all to the attempt to substitute a Republic for the Queen's Government, and remedies should be applied to Ireland's historical evils which were the consequence of a rude conquest and a stern Reformation. An intelligent, impassioned and vindictive race had been conquered by another race wholly different in feeling, character and customs, and forced to recognise the church adopted by the conqueror as the dominant church of a dominant race. Protestants, though few numerically in comparison with the original race who were Roman Catholics, were proprietors by right of conquest of the bulk of Irish landed properties, a circumstance which aggravated the situation still more. If ever there was a people to whom the unostentatious forms and simplicity of doctrine of Protestantism were distasteful it certainly was the impulsive and imaginative Irish, who notwithstanding all the civilisation, enlightenment and liberty of the Press which prevailed in Great Britain, were still more Roman Catholic than the French or the Italians. Ireland would not be 'justified' till the Roman Catholic clergy and their party, whose main strength were the better class farmers and shopkeepers, were reconciled and identified in interest with British rule. That this was not impossible was seen from the experience of Germany and Canada. So the starting point was the solution of the Church Question. Strathnairn believed that the way to do it was not to disestablish the Church of Ireland as Gladstone was to do within a couple of years but to lift the Roman Catholic church to an equal footing. He argued this out in great detail. (19)

He was an early ecumenist of sorts, Strathnairn. He asked an engineer he had met in the Crimea to introduce him to his brother who was the Catholic Archbishop of Cashel at the time. 'I think one cause of affairs not going on as favourably in Ireland as elsewhere,' he said,

FF M

are social separations, not differences. For instance, myself and many more whom I know are most anxious to know and be on the most friendly relations with the Roman Catholic clergy, and of course particularly with its high dignitaries. But we never have the opportunity, the means, the advantage, or the qualification of becoming acquainted with them. (20)

A point that he made to the Duke of Cambridge, recognising that it would appeal to the soldier in him, was that a settlement of the Church question would have a beneficial effect on Irish soldiers and on recruitment prospects. They drew their soldiers from the very classes that were most affected with Fenianism. Not that there ever was any apprehension for the collective loyalty of Irish soldiers. But cases of individual treason amongst them were far too numerous, and induced the conviction that there was much more of this deplorable crime which the law could not reach, or which had not come to light. The vigorous methods he had taken had brought Military Fenianism under control. Nevertheless the bad spirit fed from outside was not extinct in the army, so that it would be wise and politic to remove from the classes that supplied the army with recruits the inherited impression, however erroneous, of an injured nationality. (21)

Strathnairn himself was anything but wise at times. What could have been more foolish than to thank a Gunner Lyons, at the head of his battery in Kilkenny, for having given evidence which led to the conviction of a leading Fenian agent who had tried to tamper with him? The result was to produce such a state of intimidation in Kilkenny that two gunners of the battery were nearly murdered in the streets by a mob led by a soldier on furlough, and Lyons had to flee the country and join the growing company of men who could never return to their native land. (22)

(4)

With the Flying Columns broken up and the reinforcements gone back to England it was time to pay tribute to the troops and Abercorn sent Strathnairn a formal message of congratulation. This was not, however, in the form Strathnairn expected and he did not hesitate to send it back with a covering note in which he made it clear that he was sincerely concerned with the omission of any reference to himself. 'Of course, we all know that our little outbreak was of the mildest nature', he told the Lord Lieutenant, 'so much so that an absurdity never so approached the sublime.' It was a *tempête dans un verre d'eau*. At the same time, to eulogise the troops for their conduct against the agitation, such as it was, and not to notice their commander, who earlier had been praised by the Duke of Cambridge and the previous Lord Lieutenant for his military arrangements, was quite unusual, and an injustice with which he was sure Abercorn would not wish to associate himself. Abercorn saw the point and amended the message. A reference in it, however, to 'the prompt arrangements made by Major General Cunyngham and his staff' was never communicated by Strathnairn to those officers despite the Lord Lieutenant's specific direction to him to do so. This Cunyngham only discovered in 1870 when he was 'holding the fort' for Strathnairn's successor. (23)

Strathnairn obviously took offence easily, particularly from the civil side. He compalined to Abercorn when Larcom had the nerve to send him, a man of his vast military experience and to whom the command of over twenty thousand troops in Ireland was entrusted, a nonsensical military and strategical essay composed by Neal Browne, R.M., in which the work of the Flying Column in his district was criticised, after all it had achieved. Browne, it appears—luckily, Strathnairn now thought—had not been chosen to accompany the Column, and was writhing under this implied criticism of him. In the course of his essay he had said that the glitter of Fenian bayonets and pikes had been seen and that the entire population, especially the labouring class, was eager for fight, 'Was there ever such an invention,' said Strathnairn, 'when every report states that not an insurgent is to be *seen*, and that they are either *hiding*, *flying* or wishing to give themselves up?' (24) He also alleged that Larcom was withholding official information from him which was necessary for the correct performance of his duties, the sort of information that he had always received in Lord Kimberley's time, and he looked of course to Abercorn to put this right. Larcom, for his part, felt that Strathnairn was unco-operative. He complained to Naas that Strathnairn was writing too many letters to the Lord Lieutenant, and he suggested that Naas might speak to Sir John Pakington and have Strathnairn sent somewhere else. (25)

Naas had formally reported on the 10th March 'the deplorable events caused by the action of the Fenian conspiracy' and in reply Walpole, the Home Secretary, on behalf of Her Majesty's Government, cordially approved the prompt and judicious measures which had been adopted with such complete success. It was very gratifying to have Naas's assurance that the great majority of the people remained loyal, and were determined to afford the utmost assistance in maintaining the public peace and in upholding the authority of the law. They were also sensitive of the admirable behaviour of the Constabulary in the performance of their very difficult duties. (26) That seemed rather flat and inadequate, but better things were in the offing. The Prime Minister had mentioned to Abercorn the desirability of prompt and liberal recognition by some public reward of the 'incomparable behaviour of the constabulary' (27) so that Naas had no difficulty in inducing the usually reluctant Treasury to ask Parliament to vote a sum of £2,000 to be disbursed among the men who had particularly distinguished themselves. Bravery medals were given to nine individuals—the suggestion of a Victoria Cross or two was considered and abandoned—while on the initiative of Colonel Wood, the Inspector General, the Queen was moved to direct a letter to be written conveying her thanks and commanding that the description of the Force should thereafter be 'the Royal (or Queen's) Constabulary of Ireland'. The Harp and the Crown would be substituted on their uniform for the Shamrock. This was the Force, after all, which, in Naas's words, had resisted many efforts to corrupt its fidelity, and which had been the prime object of the insurgents' offensive operation. Had a decided success attended any of the various attacks on their isolated barracks it was impossible to say how far the rebellious

Fenian movement might have spread. It might, for a start, have meant the proclamation of martial law, an extreme measure that Derby would have grieved to introduce. 'Sharp and stern justice . . . to stamp out this most insane rebellion', to be applied by the Special Commission and juries and based on the work of the police, would be sufficient. Disorder was not general in Ireland. He had had the satisfaction of learning from his younger son who had gone over to the family property in Tipperary that among the tenants there, there was nothing wrong. (28)

The Irish Attorney General, Hedges Eyre Chatterton, prepared for the Special Commission. As he did so, he regretted that not a single leader or person of note connected with the treasonable outrages in the County of Dublin had been arrested. The leaders of some of them must have planned the movement in the city and yet the Government had no information on the subject. He had expected that with all the resources as to rewards and otherwise in the power of the constabulary and police some important arrests would have been made and information supplied for prosecutors. This had not been the case and up to that time they had but indifferent material for the Special Commissions. He was not imputing any fault to either the constabulary or the police but he would be glad if they were officially asked to use every exertion in the short intervening time to bring some of the prominent offenders to justice. (29)

To this request both Colonel Lake, for the Dublin Metropolitan Commissioners, and Colonel Wood, the Inspector General of the Constabulary, replied in a matter of days. The former said that no opportunity of arresting prominent leaders was afforded to their police. The movement from the city to Tallaght on the 5th March was certainly ordered by leaders, and the parties proceeding to the rendez-vous were informed that they would find leaders there to direct them, but no person high in authority connected with the movement turned up, nor was this ever intended. The original idea of the conspirators was to have had an outbreak in the city, as the signal for general rising in the country, but fear and the well-known and judicious arrangements made by the military and police prevented their taking this step.

Hence the general order to proceed to Tallaght. That there were no leaders was proved by the fact that the members of the constabulary and police who were taken prisoners on the night of the rising saw none, and that Sergeant Sheridan of the Dublin Metropolitan Police, whose execution was called for by some of his captors, was respited by direction of one of the party who insisted that he should be brought before the leaders, but as these never appeared he was eventually discharged, together with his comrades. Under these circumstances there were no grounds for the surprise expressed by the Attorney General. The Commissioners would do their best before the opening of the Commission to obtain further evidence, but they felt obliged to say that the great success they had hitherto had in obtaining information every day increased the difficulty in procuring more, as the conspirators took greater precautions now to guard against treachery than they had hitherto thought necessary. The greater part of the work of the conspiracy was now being carried on by women, and the tenderness hitherto shown towards the so-called Ladies Committee had greatly facilitated their work. Some of them ought to be arrested. Obviously huffed, Colonel Lake ended his minute by expressing the Commissioners' regret that the Government should have thought it necessary officially to call on them to use every exertion to bring offenders to justice, as they were not conscious of ever having neglected to discharge fully their duty in that respect. (30)

Colonel Wood likewise told Larcom that he had read the Attornoy General's letter with pain. While in common with everyone else he shared in the Attorney's regret that the originators of the eutrages had not been arrested he was less surprised at that than Mr Chatterton seemed to be, not only on account of the notorious difficulty of getting at such persons in Ireland, but because he had reason to believe that those who planned the outrages were not present at them. Wood continued:

Though the Attorney General does not directly censure the Constabulary for want of zeal or energy, and even disclaims the intentions of doing so, yet such appears to be the drift of his letter, and I can only say that it is the first intimation of the kind which I have received during the long periods in which the country has been afflicted with this movement, and it runs directly counter to the sentiments expressed by the country generally regarding the conduct of the Constabulary. I gather from the Attorney General's concluding words, that he is under the impression that the Constabulary have not already been 'officially requested to use every exertion to bring some of these prominent offenders to justice'. It may be necessary to observe that I have done so again and again, and I have reason to think that if the materials of the Special Commission are scanty, the cause is not to be found in lack of exertion on the part of the Constabulary. (31)

These minutes were sent by Larcom to the Attorney General who, on reading them, just 'ticked' them. There was no further comment. (32)

CHAPTER XI

Trials and Tribulations

FOR some months after the 5th March the main matter of interest was the trials of the Fenians at the Special Commissions in Dublin, Cork and Limerick. 169 men in all were placed in the dock. Of these 7 were acquitted, 52 convicted and 110 pleaded guilty. Of these 25 were sentenced to penal servitude for various terms and upwards of 50 to imprisonment for various periods. Eight men were found guilty of high treason; the first of them and the first men to be tried in Dublin were Thomas F. Bourke, the leader in the Ballyhurst affair and Patrick Doran who had been prominent at Stepaside and Glencullen. Both of them were sentenced to be hanged, drawn and quartered but a jury recommendation of mercy obtained a speedy reprieve for Doran while Bourke's execution was fixed for the 29th May. McCafferty was the next to be tried in Dublin and was also sentenced to die— on the 12th June. Among the important Fenians who were given long terms of imprisonment by the Dublin Commission were Edward Duffy, who had formerly been Stephens's deputy in Ireland and was a member of the Directory or Provisional Government on the 5th March, and Flood, who was McCafferty's principal abettor in the Chester affair and who had been captured with him after the tussel with the police at the North Wall. Both of these got fifteen years. Michael Cody was given another five. He had been in custody in 1866 and released. On the 4th May 1867 he was re-arrested in Grafton Street and on him was found a list of the judges and crown counsel of the Special Commission and also of the jury who had convicted Bourke. He had a revolver, too, and tried to shoot the policeman who arrested him. The authorities were in no doubt that he was one of an assassination circle that Superintendent Ryan had warned them about but in which Larcom did not at first believe though 'I dare say they are desperate enough for anything', he said. (1)

At the Cork Special Commission four men were sentenced to death including John McClure of Kilclooney fame and James F. X. O'Brien, a leader in the Ballynockan affair. The most important prisoner before the Limerick Commission was sentenced to fifteen years penal servitude: he was Patrick Walsh who had taken a leading part in the attack on Kilmallock Police Barracks. In all these presecutions the State leaned heavily on the evidence of the Crown Witnesses, especially Massey and Corydon. For that reason, and as many reports of apprehended violence had been received, their protection as they went to and from the Cork courthouse was a matter of grave concern. Colonel Kelly was said to be in Ireland: if so, he would hardly have come at such a time were not something desperate contemplated. So extreme caution was demanded.

Travelling down from Dublin, Massey and Corydon were taken in the dark late at night, by cab rather than in the conspicuous police van, to a suburban railway station and put on an express train with a pilot engine. All telegraphic communication was suspended for seven hours to cover the journey south. The train was stopped at the old terminus in Cork before entering the tunnel, which was within a few hundred yards of a police barrack (2) in which they were to be lodged for safety's sake. An alternative suggested would have involved eight or nine armed policemen in a house with sentries at the front door and at all entrances into the rooms occupied by the witnesses. Civilians were not permitted to enter the carriage assigned to the witnesses and their escort, and a caution was issued to the manner in which food was supplied. (3) The Judges had similarly to be watched over; and their train to Cork likewise preceded all the way by a pilot engine, in case of an attempt being made upon them during the journey or the rails taken up. (4)

On the 27th May Colonel Lake, the Police Commissioner, submitted to Larcom the arrangements made at Kilmainham jail for the execution of the prisoner Bourke on the 29th. The ground in front of the jail and immediately adjoining it would be kept by the police, who would assemble there at 4 a.m. There would be 190 constables, 10 sergeants and 6 inspectors, the whole under the command of a divisional superintendent. The mounted police would assemble on the ground at the same hour, and would be employed in patrolling where necessary. Each constable, both horse and foot, would be armed with sword and loaded revolver. The Commissioners were desirous that there should be as little display as possible of a military force; at the same time they did not think it altogether safe for the Civil Power to depend solely upon its own resources, and they therefore suggested that about half an hour before the time of the execution, one troop of dragoons should take up a position on the right flank of the jail, near the entrance to the Royal Hospital, and another troop on the left flank, at a corresponding distance from the jail. The Commissioners further suggested that a company of infantry should be stationed inside the jail, in addition to the military guard which was always on duty there, and that the companies of infantry should occupy the Kilmainham Court House, not appearing outside unless called upon by the Civil Power. It would be advisable to keep a portion of the troops in Richmond Barracks and those in Island Bridge Barracks ready to turn out at a moment's notice if required. (5)

The military were prepared to do whatever was reasonable but they considered that any display of troops, as had been suggested by the Governor of the prison, in front of the drop and in close proximity to the 'mob' certain to assemble upon such an occasion would be highly imprudent and be likely to lead to a collision between the soldiers and the people. (6) While these discussions were going on, and the Governor was seeking a ruling as to whether an offer of a coffin for the remains of the prisoner should be accepted and the men who offered it permitted to be present at the interment within the precincts of the jail (7) a tremendous agitation had built up in favour of reprieving Bourke. Abercorn's secretary said that the Viceregal Lodge had been inundated all day on the 27th with advocates of mercy, as opposed to justice. The appeals came from all sides, including parliamentarians of different parties. Most influential representations from inside the United Kingdom came from Cardinal Cullen, the Archbishop of Dublin who had vehemently opposed

the Fenians and who, for the first time in his career, went to see
the Lord Lieutenant to appeal for Bourke's life. Inside the official
camp there were men who believed that it would be a blunder to
execute 'the criminal Bourke'. 'Let us not re-animate the feeling
of Fenianism by making martyrs and exciting sympathy in their
favour,' a Resident Magistrate wrote to Larcom. 'It is subsiding,
let it subside.' (8)

(2)

The diplomatic pressure from the United States was very great
in respect of the Fenian prisoners generally. Bruce, the British
Ambassador in Washington, was indisposed and confined to the
house when Seward, the American Foreign Secretary, called on
him on the 20th May to inquire if Bruce knew anything as to the
fate of the Fenians who were being tried in Ireland, and particularly whether McCafferty had been sentenced to death. 'I told
him,' said Bruce in a despatch to Stanley, the Foreign Secretary
in London,

> that I had seen that Bourke and Doran had been sentenced to death
> and that the sentences had been commuted, [this was wrong so far
> as Bourke was concerned] that I had seen no account of McCafferty's
> trial or conviction, but that I should infer from what had passed that
> he would not be put to death even if convicted.
>
> Mr Seward said he wished to let me know unofficially that he had
> instructed Mr Adams [the American Minister in London] by cable
> to use his best efforts to prevent the infliction of any capital punish-
> ment but not to moot the subject unless he had reason to know that
> the sentence was to be carried out in some particular case. He said
> that Bourke's speech had produced considerable excitement in the
> country and that the President was so pressed that it was impossible
> for him to refuse taking some action in the matter. I remarked to
> Mr Seward that if the object proposed was to conciliate the Fenians
> here I could understand it, but that any interference on the part of
> this Government could only be prejudicial to the cause of the
> prisoners. That a strong feeling existed in England already with

reference to the support and countenance given to these unprincipled agitators, and that although the effect of executing these prisoners on public opinion in the United States might be legitimately alluded to by Mr Adams in friendly conversation with Your Lordship it was a very different if the subject was to be brought forward officially.

Mr Seward did not question the correctness of my remarks nor the embarrassment the Fenian element is likely to cause in the relations between the two countries. He does not deny the existence or the magnitude of the evil, on the contrary he recognises it as a fact to which the Government has no option but to submit.

The truth is that to the President and the Administration the command of the Irish vote is essential with a view to the approaching elections and they certainly will not hesitate to do anything agreeable to the Irish section of the population so long at least as it does not go beyond correspondence and diplomatic intervention however indefensible their proceedings may be on grounds of principle or usage. American orators and newspaper writers invariably talk of the Irish as an oppressed people struggling for liberty and politicians of all parties find it to their interest to adopt this view in all questions affecting Ireland. I see no remedy for this inconvenience as long as an insurrectionary spirit prevails in Ireland, unless the restoration of the Southern States to the Union and the increasing immigration from Germany diminishes the importance attached to the Irish vote. (9)

Bruce wrote again to Stanley on the 28th May, the eve of the day fixed for the execution of Bourke. He began: 'Yesterday I despatched per cable to Your Lordship the following telegram in cypher: "Seward in the name of the President earnestly recommends no executions of Fenian prisoners." '

A despatch had appeared in the newspapers that Lord Derby, the British Prime Minister, had officially declared that Bourke would be surely hanged, and this had produced great excitement among the American Fenians. 'Great pressure was brought to bear upon the President', Bruce continued,

to interfere on his behalf immediately as it was believed that the sentence would be carried out on the 29th May.

From Mr Seward's language, who came to me direct from the President, I inferred that the latter was inclined to attach more

importance to the telegraphic report than Mr Seward himself and
that Mr Seward in order that the proposed interference might be in a
form as little offensive as possible had suggested that the expression
of their opinion on the general question should be forwarded by me
confidentially to Your Lordship and not through Mr Adams.

In the course of the evening after the despatch of the message
(28th May) I received Your Lordship's telegram informing me that
the sentences on Bourke and McCafferty had been commuted to
imprisonment for life... (10)

In deciding not to go ahead with the executions, which of the
appeals for mercy impressed the Government most—was it the
American President's or Cardinal Cullen's? Or was it these two in
combination that induced the Government to change its mind?
(11) Both interventions were undoubtedly important, but the
Government were also materially influenced by a communication
of a completely different order from Judge Fitzgerald who had
tried many of the Fenian prisoners. Writing voluntarily to Naas
on the 25th May he drew attention to a fact that he thought had
not been given sufficient consideration, namely, that Bourke
(and McCafferty) had been sentenced to death, while Flood, Duffy
and Cody, who were tried for substantially the same crime and
whose guilt, in his opinion, was not less than that of Bourke and
McCafferty, were sentenced to penal servitude. The reason was,
and it was a reason the public would not understand, that in one
case the charge was High Treason for which death was the penalty,
and in the other the charge was for treason felony which carried
a lesser sentence. Gathorne-Hardy, the Home Secretary, thought
Fitzgerald's letter was 'very important and almost conclusive'.
Derby, the Prime Minister, likewise thought the letter was very
important and told Naas on the 28th May that he would be happy
to talk the matter over with him if he could call at any hour not
sooner than 4.30. It was then apparently that the decision to
reprieve was taken, and the telegrams issued. (12)

Nobody was more relieved than Bruce at the decision. 'I
think that the execution of the prisoners', he wrote,

would have had the effect of stimulating Fenianism in this country
and of acquiring for it more sympathy from the American population

than it at present enjoys. . . . Any act is if possible to be avoided
which tends to excite the popular sympathy as it serves to keep
up the influence of these hellish demagogues over their dupes. It is
not to be denied unfortunately that the men who have risked their
lives in Ireland are looked upon not as criminals but as mistaken
enthusiasts and if they are executed, they will be considered as
martyrs.

It is also very desirable that at this moment nothing should be
done to stimulate a fresh raid on Canada. . . .

Considering the irritation produced by the Civil War and the
feelings of the Irish section of the people, it was to be expected
that the attempts on Canada and Ireland would be made. It may be
anticipated that the successive failures will prove a great blow and
discouragement to such enterprises in future and will lead gradually
to a healthier tone in public opinion which will declare itself against
these proceedings, not on grounds of principle but on grounds of
expediency. As long as dissatisfaction exists on a large scale in
Ireland, and there are hopes of a successful insurrection, there will be
found desperate characters and men moved by love of adventure
and variety to incur the risk of heading them. Already however the
opinion is gaining ground that there is no chance of success unless
England be engaged in war, and that there is a growing disposition
on the part of the Legislature to deal seriously with the Irish
difficulty. (13)

Disraeli, when acting for the Prime Minister a few months later,
sent Derby a similar assurance. 'The Americans,' he told him,

are reckless partisans, and will do much for the Irish vote though,
except the Irish, nobody in America wants to go to war with us.
Nevertheless I doubt whether the Irish vote is yet strong enough to
ensure such a catastrophe. At present all the Fenians have done is to
strengthen your government. (14)

(3)

From the day that he took over from Stephens, the British
Government were particularly anxious to lay their hands on

Colonel Kelly. He had made his headquarters in London where, because the writ of Habeas Corpus still ran there, he could not be touched in the absence of information sufficient to convict him. It was some time before a photograph of him could be obtained for circulation among the police, and information about his London whereabouts usually arrived too late to enable him to be apprehended; it was suspected that the informants sometimes delayed information with that purpose in view. (15)

On the 14th March Superintendent Ryan reported that he had been informed that Colonel Kelly, General Halpin and Colonel Burke were in Dublin and were still determined on a general rising. The only obstacle was the continuing bad weather. They were declaring 'in the most confident manner imaginable' that men and money would come from America, sufficient to enable them to carry on a rebellion effectually, and that the landing of supplies on certain parts of the coast was a very feasible thing more especially if they were able to distract the attention of the Authorities by diversions in the interior of the country. St Patrick's Day was only a few days off but whether the rising would take place on that day, as had been mooted, depended entirely on the state of the weather. (16) On the next day, the 15th March, Ryan repeated that the Fenians were very sanguine about receiving substantial aid from America, and depended very much on privateering. (17)

The closeness of Ryan's informant to the inner core of Fenian affairs can be judged from a message that Kelly sent from Dublin on the 15th March to his supporters in America, though the emphasis was very different. What rebellion had taken place so far had been deliberately misreported, he said. Things were in such shape that independence could become 'a fixed fact if aid came within a fortnight'. His message also indicates Kelly's preoccupation with the effort that was being made to secure American recognition for Ireland's belligerent status. 'Don't believe a tenth of the vile newspaper reports about complete suppression—utter routs—overwhelming defeats,' he wrote.

What do our countrymen in America want? Will they wait until the last man shall be slaughtered before sending aid? I hope the Ameri-

can people believe now that our people meant to fight. If they do,
let them work like beavers. Fit out your privateers. . . .We took the
field on a little more than a thousand pounds. If those scurvy Irish
millionaires had done half their duty we would now be recognised
as belligerents. . . .When the word of the present executive business
reaches you, there should certainly be immense work done. A
landing in Sligo at the present time would be of infinite service.
That section has been reserved for just such an event, and if Fortune
should only guide your ships in that direction it would just suit our
purposes. (8)

Kelly was again in Dublin in June and attended a large meeting
of centres who were 'determined on immediate fighting'. Larcom
thought an attempt to rescue Bourke was their most likely object,
though he did not give much for their chances. Nevertheless, he
thought it better to move Bourke and some of the other Fenian
prisoners over to England. 'Talbot', he told Naas, 'is not without
hope of getting Kelly. That would cause the immediate collapse
of all open efforts.' (19)
Kelly had asked that something should be done by the Americans within a fortnight but this was out of the question since the
Fenians of New York, to whom he had appealed, had not a
privateer ready to sail nor money with which to buy or hire one.
However, they did not lack determination or influence, and some
time before the 12th April—already much too late—they obtained possession from the Collector of Customs, in circumstances that are far from clear, of a schooner or brigantine of 138
tons called the *Jackmel* and on the same day about fifty Fenians
went down the bay from New York by steamer, boarded the ship
and sailed immediately for Sligo. To avoid any vessels that might
be in pursuit of her the *Jackmel* did not follow 'the European tack'
but stood off to the West Indian course for a day. She had no
colours flying when she sailed, but English colours were hoisted
when any vessel came in sight. She had no sailing papers either,
and this was nearly the cause of a mutiny just after she sailed as
some of the crew threatened to refuse to go without them. She
must have been very crowded for, in addition to the fifty Fenians
and the crew, there was a quantity of arms on board, packed in

cases as pianos and sewing machines. These were consigned to a firm in Cuba but during the voyage the cases were opened and the carbines and rifles were packed in smaller boxes. There were also three small cannons capable of firing three-pound shot, and these were employed to fire a salute when, on Easter Sunday (21st April), a green flag with a sunburst emblazoned on it was hoisted and the brigantine newly christened with the name *Erin's Hope*.

Shortly after leaving New York, commissions were distributed by James E. Kerrigan who was in command of the Fenian party. One of the recipients was Daniel J. Buckley, later to become an informer, who had served through the American Civil War and who had joined the expedition to Campobello. After the renaming of the ship, the captain, whose name was Cavanagh, read aloud the written instruction he had received to land the men and arms on the coast of Sligo, if practicable, or if not, elsewhere in Ireland. (20)

On the 24th May the *Jackmel*, otherwise *Erin's Hope*, was off Inismurray on the Donegal coast and was boarded by a pilot, Michael Gallagher of Towny, who asked if his services were required. He was told he would be asked to take the vessel to either Sligo or Donegal, but that he must await the return of a man who had left the ship the evening before to buy provisions. Gallagher waited aboard the *Jackmel* and, in the early hours next morning he, and two men who had been wounded by the accidental discharge of a revolver Buckley had been handling, went ashore at Milk harbour on the Connacht shore of Donegal bay. Gallagher later met some coast guards who had been watching the *Jackmel* and told them what he knew; he remained an object of suspicion for a long time. The wounded men were arrested. (21)

More suspicious in the eyes of the coast guards was 'a man of gentlemanly aspect' who came up to the *Jackmel* in a small hooker and was taken to the cabin where he had about an hour's conversation with the Fenian officers, leaving the ship afterwards with three of them. This man, known as Walters, who had been spending money very freely ashore, turned out to be Colonel Ricard

O'Sullivan Burke. He had very disillusioning news for the men of the *Jackmel*: the rising they were coming to take part in had been suppressed a couple of months earlier! The projected attack on the town of Sligo was out of the question; and arms could not be landed because the local Fenians were not ready for a fresh attempt. The ship was in serious danger where it was, and would have to put to sea immediately despite the problem of provisioning and the scarcity of water. So, after cruising along the western and southern coasts for several days, about half the party were put ashore in a fog on the 10th June at Cunigar near Dungarvan in the County Waterford. Within a few hours all of them, including a Colonel John Warren and a Colonel William Nagle, were rounded up and arrested. 'They are nearly all veterans,' Lord Fermoy told Naas (6.6.1867), 'officers of the American armies, North or South. They started fifteen weeks ago ... and ... on landing expected to find the Irish Republic at least in long clothes, if not a full-grown child.' (22) While this party pined in custody, the leaders of the expedition, General Kerrigan and Colonel Tresilian, faced back to America in the *Jackmel* with the balance of the force and the consignment of arms. They had one barrel of sound bread, one barrel of mouldy bread, one barrel of rice, six pounds of pork, one box of fish, one barrel of beef, one bushel of beans, two quarters of molasses, one half-pound of sugar, a sufficiency of tea and coffee and one-third rations of water. Before reaching the Banks of Newfoundland they had run out of practically everything, but a fishing smack came to their assistance there, and off Boston they were helped by a vessel bound for San Francisco. (23) They had managed to escape, as they had managed to reach Ireland, because of the reduction of the British naval watch on Irish waters to which the Irish Government had agreed. Larcom had told Naas on the 19th May that they had nothing to fear at that moment from without, nor much prospect of it, as far as he could see. (24) Within a fortnight, as a result of the *Jackmel* affair, he had changed his view. He told Rear Admiral Frederick that they had heard in Dublin Castle that there might be another privateer or two in the offing, and that the northwestern coast was the likeliest area for landings. Would it be possible to move the *Helicon* to that coast at least for a time? Frederick did not think so. The *Helicon* was the only fast vessel under his orders and it was important that she should be at Valentia; from there she could be despatched by telegraph to any point where she might be required. But he made other adjustments to deal with the situation. (25) The *Jackmel* episode also left the gentry in the Waterford area with a sense of insecurity. As Lord Fermoy said to Naas: 'Next winter they would certainly join themselves into some sort of voluntary association. It remains with you and the Cabinet to decide whether the Government shall lead the movement or be dragged at its tail. One or the other you will have to do.' (26)

Among those landed from the *Jackmel* at Dungarvan there was a second informer, William F. Million, not to be confused with F. F. Millen. He made a statement to the police on the basis of which the Irish Government were able to give the Admiralty some help in their pursuit of the brigantine. They learned enough from him to want to know more about Gallagher, the pilot. Had he or had he not been 'sworn by Nagle in the cabin' into the Fenian Brotherhood against his will? Was he a Fenian agent from the beginning? They gave him the benefit of the doubt, later, on these questions. The Earl of Mayo—Naas had assumed the title on his father's death in August 1867—urged Larcom to make a special effort to get at the private signals known to Warren and Nagle. If discovered, they were to be taken at once to Admiral Frederick at Queenstown, who would advise how best to use them for the purpose of decoying to her capture the *Jackmel* or any other Fenian vessel. (27) The move does not appear to have yielded any success; and Million, when he returned to New York, was shot dead by a son of Michael Doheny, the 1848 man.

The killer knew Nagle, who, with seven others of the *Jackmel* prisoners, was sent down to Sligo for trial at the Spring Assizes in February 1868. A newspaper reporter could find no excitement in the town, but the authorities had taken every precaution to prevent disturbance, the local force being strengthened by the addition of 150 constabulary, two companies of the 22nd Highlanders from Dublin, and a troop of the 1st Dragoon Guards from

Waterford. The Grand Jury, under its foreman Sir Robert Gore-Booth, was duly sworn and addressed by Judge Fitzgerald, who explained that the prisoners were charged under the Treason Felony Act of 1848 with designing to depose the Queen from the Crown of Ireland and to set up instead an Irish Republic. They had taken part in what was called the *Jackmel* expedition, in what elsewhere might be termed a page of romance but which he preferred to call a wild goose chase, an exhibition of folly so remarkable that one could not conceive how reasoning and intelligent men could have engaged in it if they had not been the unthinking victims of that deception which had been so largely practised on those called Fenians in Ireland and America. The trial proceedings became farcical. First, Nagle succeeded in frustrating the Crown, as a sufficient number of aliens could not be found to constitute the jury *de medietate*, to which, as an alien himself and therefore one who owed no natural allegiance to the Queen, he was declared to be entitled. Then Patrick Nugent, one of the men who had landed on the Sligo coast, was put on trial, but by the skilful management of the Sub-Sheriff, whose sympathies were with the accused, one of the jurors was made ill, and it became necessary to discharge them all without a verdict being reached. The uselessness of proceeding further was manifest; so all the prisoners were brought back to Dublin.

Corydon, inevitably, appeared among the Crown witnesses and was brazenly described by the Solicitor General as 'entirely above suspicion'. In cross-examination he admitted that he had lived at Liverpool with a woman who was not his wife, but he denied that he had carried away a dead child in a valise from the house. He also denied that he was fatigued from swearing against his Fenian colleagues; and when he was asked how much he expected to get per head for his work, he replied 'I don't count by heads; I expect to get as much as will keep me for life . . . I expect £2,000. I'll take all I get. I assure you I am tired of this business.' He would be more contented if he had never undertaken this business. He would not retire, however, he said, until 'the entire thing' was broken up.

The United States Consul in Dublin pressed for the release of

Nagle and Warren, and Bruce, the British Minister in Washington in a 'very meagre telegram' supported him. Mayo referred the matter to the Prime Minister. He would prefer, he said, to keep the two men in custody, but they were not worth getting into a row with the Americans about and if Derby thought it desirable he would make the order for their release. (28) Derby took counsel with his son, Lord Stanley, the Foreign Secretary, and they both agreed that before coming to a decision it would be better to wait for a despatch from Bruce, who was always inclined, Derby said, to err on the side of over-caution, and to attach more importance to American 'bounce' than it was entitled to. Nagle and Warren had apparently been the leaders of a piratical attempt at invasion. It had utterly failed and, landing to avoid starvation, they had been arrested. There was nothing in the case, therefore, which would warrant any special favour being shown. (29)

Later Adams, the American Minister in London, went to the Foreign Office to plead for the two men, on the ground that, while they had intended mischief, they had not had the opportunity of doing any. (30) He left with Stanley 'unofficially and confidentially' a copy of a despatch in which Seward said he had hoped that the improved condition of society in Ireland would have made it possible for Her Majesty's Government to rescind the suspension of Habeas Corpus, which was attended by so many cases of irritation and annoyance. Stanley liked Adams: he had always found him temperate and well able to resist pressures from his countrymen, so that if Nagle and Warren could be liberated it would be much the better diplomatically, but he recognised that Irish opinion had to be considered. (31) Derby's opinion prevailed. The men were not released until May 1868 (by which time they had been a year in Mountjoy Prison), on their expressing regret for what they had done and giving assurances for the future. On reaching New York, Nagle was given a public reception and made a speech which S. L. Anderson said was a sample of the manner in which all those men might be expected to treat any clemency extended to them. (32) He had consistently taken a tough line with his captors, but his father in

America wrote privately to the Government offering to give every assistance in his power in the discovery of the Fenian plans, if his son were set free and permitted to return home. 'The father,' said Anderson, 'was no other than the famous "Captain Rock" who, during the years 1821–1823, caused so much alarm and excitement in county Cork, and who, after having been tried and convicted, was discharged on account of information he afforded to the Government. He is now in a public situation in New York where he is much respected. A communication was made to him through the Consul acknowledging his letter and informing him of his son's release.' (33)

Massey and Corydon both moved in the summer of 1867 to throw off the irksome yoke of being the Crown's principal witnesses in Fenian trials. They were feeling the effects of their exposure to public obloquy and of the continuous confinement that was necessary to ensure that they were not assassinated. Corydon asked for a change from the depot in Dublin's Chancery Lane, where Crown witnesses were usually kept, and the Government thought he might be allowed to go to Glasgow where there were a couple of R.I.C. men who could look after him. (34) Corydon wanted to go to London, however, and made what looked like an excuse that his object in wishing to go there was 'to get Kelly'.

Massey had written to Anderson. 'Believing that my obligations as Crown Witness are at an end,' he said, 'and feeling keenly the ill effects of confinement on my whole system, I respectfully request that those who have the power so to do will, at their earliest convenience, decide how I am to be disposed of.' (35) Anderson had a talk with him and explained that he could not for the present be dispensed with—there was an important case or two still pending—but some arrangement might be come to by which he would be allowed to go away for a few months. As regards a permanent settlement Anderson mentioned an annuity to be paid in monthly instalments, but Massey rejected this. 'I find such a step would most certainly endanger my personal safety. I, therefore, desire to be enabled to move at once to some other land and I have determined that no person shall know of my whereabouts.' And he added 'I have good reasons for deciding as above.' He obviously preferred to go away with a lump sum; periodical payments involved the risk of exposure. The matter was submitted to the Chief Secretary, who accepted Anderson's recommendation that, as Massey's health was apparently breaking down from want of exercise, he should be permitted to take a holiday, on condition that he reported his whereabouts. He insisted, however, that 'great circumspection must be used in allowing this man to withdraw'. (36) While a decision was awaited Massey's impatience grew apace. He wrote direct to Larcom: 'My health is much impaired and what annoys me more, the health of Mrs Massey is seriously hurt by an imprisonment which I may say, she has shared with me. I, therefore, respectfully but firmly state that, if I be not permitted to leave at once for the sea-side I shall not appear again on the witness table, and shall consequently look to the Government for an immediate settlement of my case.' (37) Larcom met this demand by asking the police whether, if Massey were permitted to go to England for a few weeks, he would undertake to report regularly his place of abode and return immediately on receiving notice. Massey gave this undertaking in writing, whereupon Larcom said he might go with a weekly allowance of £6 and with the private address of one of the Dublin Police Commisioners, Colonel Lake, to whom he was directed to write once a week. Larcom had no fear of Massey's threats. On the file he wrote 'As Massey is quite in the power of the Government as to his future prospects I do not see any risk in complying with this request.' (38)

But before Massey could get away, Colonel Lake hurried in a minute to Larcom suggesting the inexpediency of letting him leave Dublin until he had identified a prisoner just arrested. This was Fariola. Massey identified him and was then permitted to leave Dublin with the injunction that he was not to leave Ireland and was to be in Belfast when the Assizes opened there. So he went off to the north of Ireland with an allowance of £20, and with a plain clothes constabulary man to escort him. This officer, Head Constable Jacques, was brought down from Belfast and was instructed by Anderson in the nature of his duties. He was to

attend at the Police Office in Dublin next morning, proceed with
Massey to the railway station, travel in the same train with him,
though not necessarily in the same carriage, go with him to whatever hotel he stopped at, and closely watch all his movements and
any persons who might happen to speak to him or his wife, also
to be ready to afford assistance in case of necessity. Massey was
not to go outside the counties Antrim or Down and was to be in
Belfast on the appointed date.

After a few days at Portrush, Massey discharged his duties in
Belfast and was then allowed to go to England, but again on
condition that he would be back when Fariola was ready for trial.
Fariola's defection to the Government made this unnecessary, but
he had to testify in other cases. He got lodgings in London and
settled down there with his wife, crossing over to Ireland under
escort as occasion demanded. Great care was taken with him on
these journeys backwards and forwards. Scotland Yard took him
to Dublin where Superintendent Ryan's G-men looked after him
until they could hand him back on the Holyhead packet to the
English police.

It was also becoming difficult to manage Corydon, who was
now living in London. At the end of October he was very
reluctant to come forward as a witness in the prosecution of
Ricard O'Sullivan Burke, the man who met the *Jackmel* off Sligo.
'He apprehends,' said Anderson,

> that there are persons in London at present looking for an oppor-
> tunity to assassinate him; in this I may say that I have reason to
> believe his fears are well founded and that there are four men in
> London determined to take his life. He complains that the London
> police take him about from place to place in search of suspected
> parties without affording him sufficient protection, and without
> giving him any additional remuneration for his trouble. I may
> observe that the latter seemed to me to be the real grievance. He
> has been receiving £3 a week from Sir Richard Mayne [of the
> Home Office]. He says this is not enough for his support especially
> as he will have to leave London as soon as he comes forward publicly
> as a witness. Although I believed his claim to be unreasonable yet
> as he refused otherwise to give evidence, I promised that while

this prosecution is pending he should receive £5 a week, on the ground that he is obliged, for his personal safety, to drive in cabs through town instead of walking, and also frequently to change his abode. . . . (39)

CHAPTER XII

'The Manchester Martyrs'

THE belief that Fenianism had been crushed grew throughout the summer of 1867 and the Government, through the Queen's Speech at the end of July, voiced their satisfaction.

The cessation of the long-continued efforts to promote rebellion in Ireland has for some time rendered unnecessary the exercise by the Executive of exceptional powers. I rejoice to learn that no person is now detained under the provisions of the Act for the Suspension of the Habeas Corpus and that no prisoner awaits trial in Ireland for an offence connected with the Fenian confederacy.

Yet more life remained in the organisation than was imagined; and the experience of the previous year taught how erroneous was a deduction drawn from appearances. Towards the end of October Mayo told the Prime Minister that politically speaking, the country had never been in a worse state, though materially, it had never been in a better. 'The spirit of discontent and disaffection is creeping up into a better class,' he said, 'and the hatred of England is getting every day more intense among a large portion of the people.' Some of the magistrates were now affected, and the Unionist *Evening Mail* had assailed him with a malignity and bitterness that was unknown except in Ireland. As far as he could judge, however, the country would be free from active violence during the winter, but the spirit of the country was worse than it had been in the previous year. 'I own I can see no end of it,' he said, 'and it is the merest delusion to think that any thing that Parliament can do or is likely to do will have the least effect on it.' (1)

William R. Roberts, the man who split the American Fenians, seeing the failure of Colonel Kelly's projects, now urged his claims to the leadership of the conspiracy in the United Kingdom. In the month of June 1867, he established a European head-

quarters in Paris and from there sent emissaries to England and
Ireland with the intention of uniting the two branches of the
Fenian Brotherhood. He also made it known that he was hopeful
of receiving the co-operation of the French Government in an
attack on Canada. (2) The efforts of his emissaries met with some
success in England but their operations in Ireland proved con-
siderably more difficult. A vigilant police force functioning under
the cover of the Habeas Corpus Suspension Act deterred many of
them from coming into the country at all, and those who succeeded found it impossible to convene a meeting of any size.
Respect and affection for Stephens, the hero of the Richmond
Bridewell escape, had survived the stories from the Roberts camp
in America, derogatory of his character. However, the failure of
insurrection in Ireland and the continued suspension there of
Habeas Corpus appeared to make England, its north-western
area in particular, a more promising venue for Fenian activity;
and it was there in Manchester, that there occurred the first of
two highly sensational events which marked the end of 1867.
This revealed Kelly to be still very much to the fore.

At a convention in Manchester which he called in late July or
early August he was confirmed as Chief Executive of the Irish
Republican Brotherhood, the position he had taken over from
Stephens, and a plan was adopted for maintaining the American
officers who were on active service and for the establishment in
America of a new organisation to be known as Clan-na-Gael
into which it was hoped to draw 'the honest and deceived members of the Fenian wings' who shared a common hatred of England. After the convention Kelly continued to have his headquarters in Manchester, but not for long. In the early hours of the
11th September he and another American officer, Captain
Timothy Deasy who had commanded the Fenians at Millstreet,
Co. Cork, in the March rising, were found loitering about the
streets under assumed names, and were arrested on a vagrancy
charge. Corydon and Devany were brought up from London to
identify them and returned immediately, as it was considered
dangerous for them to remain in Manchester, where Corydon
at any rate was well known. Kelly facilitated identification by

having on his person a gold ornament, apparently a badge of office, with his name engraved on it. There was great rejoicing in Dublin Castle when the news arrived of Kelly's capture. (3) 'We have caught the leading Fenian of them all,' Mayo triumphantly announced to Disraeli. (4) Bitter disappointment was speedily to follow.

Colonel O'Sullivan Burke, who had met the *Jackmel* when it entered Sligo Bay, was by this time in Britain, had acted as secretary to the Manchester convention and had been appointed to take general charge of Fenian affairs in England and Wales. He conceived it his duty to organise the rescue of the prisoners, and this was brought off on the 18th September as Kelly and Deasy were being conveyed in a police van from the Court House in Manchester to the county jail. The two Fenians were handcuffed and locked in separate compartments inside the van; and there was a posse of twelve policemen to look after them. Under a railway arch, as the van passed, a man darted into the middle of the road, raised a pistol and called on the drivers to stop. At the same moment a party of about thirty men, armed with revolvers, sprang over the wall beside the road, surrounded the van and seized the horses, one of which they shot . The police, being unarmed, made little resistance before taking to flight. The rescuers, after a vain effort to burst open the van with hatchets hammers and crowbars, called on a Sergeant Brett, who was inside with the prisoners, to hand up the keys. This he refused to do, whereupon a revolver was put to the keyhole through which, unfortunately, he was looking at the time, and he was killed. The keys of the inner compartments were taken from him and Kelly and Deasy released. A tremendous chase followed but, though Kelly and Deasy got safely away, twenty-nine arrests were made. The Police Superintendent at Manchester telegraphed Mayo: 'The prisoners rescued, van horses shot. One sergeant shot through the head, dead; another officer shot through the thigh and a civilian in the foot. Three prisoners who fired revolvers in custody, including the one who shot the sergeant.'

The Irish Administration were understandably dismayed and angered. In a note to Disraeli, Mayo said that the Manchester affair showed what he had always told him, that there was no such thing as Police in England. Kelly had been allowed to escape, and he was a far more important man than Stephens. He had been very little in Ireland, and the Irish Police had missed him in March by about twelve hours. 'We have long known that he was not far off but the English Police always ridicule every thing we tell them. So I have lately left them alone.' The only use they had made of a telegram of his alerting them was to publish a lying account of it in the newspapers. (5) As usual, Dublin Castle had had advance information that an attempt would be made and had duly warned their English counterparts against it.

Mayo also wrote to the Home Secretary:

This affair at Manchester is very unpleasant but is the result of the manner in which during the whole time I have been in office all the warnings the Irish Government have given to the English Police have been disregarded. For a long time we have been almost certain that if any Fenianism existed in the United Kingdom it had its centre at Liverpool and Manchester.

On the 13th September Kelly's photo was sent to the Manchester Police. On 14th September a telegram was received from Manchester that there was very little doubt about his identity. On the same day the following telegram was sent to Commissioners of London Metropolitan Police—'Information has been received from Mancheser that our suspicions are correct—case important—great care must be taken.' On 18th September the following telegram was sent tby us to Superintendent Maybury at Manchester: 'Are the prisoners lodged in gaol? Have every precaution taken for their safe custody. Let extra guards be provided, if necessary. Consult Williamson. Telegraph reply.' This message was sent at 1.30 English Time and delivered at 2.5. On same day we telegraphed to the Home Office as follows: 'On receipt please telegraph to Manchester directing extra precautions for safe custody of Fenian prisoners on remand.'

I only mention all this to show how over confident the Manchester Police were and how the few precautions we suggested would have prevented all this mischief. . . .

. . . . There is now much more Fenian activity on your side of the Channel than here, and you should I think at once place Williamson

at the head of a Fenian Police department and insist on the police
at Liverpool, Manchester and the large towns in the North of
England giving much more attention to Fenianism than they have
hitherto done. (6)

Gathorne Hardy replied from Balmoral where he was attending
on the Queen. He was glad to find, he said, that Mayo had telegraphed direct to Manchester, as he was a good deal put out by
the delay at the Home Office, his own department. Already Sir
James Ferguson, his Under Secretary, had told Mayo by wire that
his warning message had been repeated to Manchester but arrived
too late, and he admitted later that there had been delay in
repeating the message from the Home Office. He had reorganised
procedures so as to prevent its happening again. Three hundred
pounds had been offered for the recapture of Kelly and Deasy
and notice sent to all chief constables and seaports. 'I have never
been more annoyed,' Hardy said in his message from Balmoral.

> The news that Kelly was captured arrived here by post at
> 6 o'clock and I was going to tell the Queen at dinner as she is greatly
> interested in all such matters when, while I was waiting for her to
> come down, a telegram came with the intelligence of the rescue.
> What has happened will awaken Englishmen to some notion of the
> incendiaries around them and make them take more interest in
> what so deeply affects Ireland. I agree with you that the Police have
> been supine and if the information which has reached me tonight
> that Deasy has got to France be correct negligence as well as apathy
> must be imputed to them. The railway authorities suspected him, the
> Superintendent at London Bridge spoke to him and was rendered
> more suspicious by his Irish-American accent, and yet he was
> allowed to go to Newhaven and Dieppe without interference. . . . (7)

Mayo had simultaneously taken up with the Mayor of Manchester the report given to a newspaper that his warning telegram
had reached its destination after the rescue had been effected. The
facts were that the telegram was sent from Dublin at 1.30 English
time, arrived in Manchester at 1.55 and was delivered at 2.5
whereas the van left the City court for the jail at 3.30. There was
therefore ample time to take the recommended precautions.

Mayo, having made his point, added that future telegrams received from the Government should be treated as confidential;
in the case they were discussing, the contents of official messages
had appeared in the public press.

The Mayor apologised and promised to try to prevent it happening again. The warning telegram had been received by him
at 7 p.m., and he had said so publicly, but he now knew that a
clerk in the Police Department had received it about the time
stated by Mayo. He was having a searching inquiry made. (8)
This disclosed that the telegram was addressed to Superintendent Maybury, and, in his absence, was opened at 2.5 by a
junior clerk who handed it to an inspector when he came on duty
at 2.15. The inspector went in search of another superintendent,
to whom he gave the contents of the telegram and reported that
he had seen suspicious people loitering about the courthouse. This
superintendent directed that seven or eight constables were to
accompany the police van, and that four others were to follow
close behind. As Ferguson put it: 'The local idea of precaution does
not extend to armed or mounted escort.' (9) At this point Mayo
felt the matter could not be pursued any further; he just ticked the
papers and put them away. (10) Extra precautions had been taken,
but a dozen or so unarmed police were no match for forty armed
and very determined Fenians. The only consolation from the
whole business was that they had a whole gang in custody
instead of Kelly, and a better example would be made through
their conviction. (11)

Wood, the Inspector General of the Royal Irish Constabulary
had also something to complain of. On the day of the attack on the
van he had wired Head Constable Welby, one of his men in
Manchester, inquiring 'Where is Williams [the assumed name of
Colonel Kelly] to be found', adding that he ought to be safe in
custody. The object of this query, according to Wood, was to
suggest, as best as could be done by telegram, the necessity of a
strong escort and great watchfulness in the case of a person of so
much importance and whose rescue, it was easy to anticipate,
would in all probability be attempted. Welby replied that he and
his colleague were absent from duty when Wood's telegram

arrived. He did not see it till his return at 7 p.m. by which time the rescue had taken place. He understood its meaning but he was honest enough to add that if he had received it in time he would have hesitated to show it or suggest its contents for fear of giving insult. That was that. (12)

The rank and file of the Irish Police shared the Administration's contempt for the English force. O'Farrell, a Dublin Police Commissioner, sent Mayo on the 26th September a report written by Edward Entwissell, one of the G-men who had been sent to help in Manchester. (13) This was a document intended only for the eyes of Superintendent Ryan; if Entwissell had thought it would go higher, O'Farrell said, he would probably have written with more reserve. The report went higher even than Mayo, for he let the Home Secretary see it. Entwissell and his colleague's first task in Manchester had been to inspect a number of prisoners apprehended on suspicion.

> They were just the ordinary class of Fenians, the rag, tag and bobtail of society. However, amongst the lot was one man bearing the name of John Francis Nugent, and whom we at once drew under notice, giving it as our opinion that he was the person described in the Hue and Cry as having made his escape from the R.I.C. at Drogheda, in which opinion we were borne out by the fact that subsequently we were informed that a letter from a R.C. clergyman was found upon him congratulating him upon his escape from Blue-coats and Saxons; the letter was from Drogheda.

Later, by day and by night Entwissell and his companion had been out searching houses. 'We are as hardworked almost as if the Fenian Business were at its glory in Dublin,' Entwissell said,

> and you know, Sir, our companions, English policemen are not cheap at any price. I never met such thirsty fellows in my life. . . . They know as little how to discharge duty in connection with Fenianism as I do about translating Hebrew, or marshalling troops to fight a battle; but of course a Dublin officer is only an officer from Dublin, and London leads the day—of that more anon.

Hardy, when he read this, commented to Mayo that 'Your Royal Irish' clearly did not think much of the London and

Manchester police, or of their knowledge of how to handle the Fenian problem. It was obviously a problem that he himself was not very well equipped to deal with. 'The Mayor of Manchester,' he said, 'keeps making application for money. Now we have £290 of secret service money which would not go far, and I shall certainly not put funds into the hands of local authorities to spend, though, of course, if they can prove wise expenditure within moderate limits, I would recommend repayment by the Treasury. It would be a great coup to recapture Kelly and Deasy and one would not care paying for it.' (14) The day before, there had been 'a very nasty business' in London involving the use of firearms, which showed among what desperadoes they were living. A very strong feeling of animosity was, he believed, rapidly developing in the English mind which would have for the future more sympathy with the troubles of the Irish Government. In the case to which he was referring a man had been fatally wounded in mistake for Corydon who had added to his infamous reputation by identifying Kelly for the Manchester police.

'We are kept busy at the Home Office by these horrible Fenians,' he told the Prime Minister.

Today the Mayor of Manchester telegraphed that a party was to start to-day to seize the Queen on some of her excursions. Of course we telegraphed to General Grey [the Queen's Secretary] as we found the Mayor had done, and I am afraid that the steps taken, however carefully we inculcate secrecy, must come out. The recall of troops to Ballater is alone enough to excite attention. . . . We have sent down twelve detectives for different posts in the neighbourhood of Balmoral. . . . The Queen is not without apprehension about the journey south. If she could be persuaded to travel by day the watch could much more easily be kept than at night. . . . Ruthless men in the dark may act in spite of all watching. . . . There is great uneasiness in all parts of England where Irish are, and, though exaggerated, it is not without foundation. . . . (15)

To Mayo, communicating the gist of this story, he added that there was quite a panic among local authorities. The subdivision of police into so many independent bodies made it difficult to

FF O

find trustworthy and prudent people to communicate with, while secrecy, which was so important, had been almost impossible. The press by some means or other got hold of plans the whole benefit of which rested on their not being known. (16)

(2)

Samuel Lee Anderson, the Crown Solicitor, went over from Dublin to see the Home Secretary and Sir Richard Mayne and gave them all the information he had about the escaped prisoners 'and the two Frenchmen'. Two Frenchmen had been seen at Dawlish by a man Anderson simply called 'M' and, as Fariola was already in custody, these may have been Cluseret and Vifquain. 'M' was quite possibly Millen who, as we saw, had indicated his intention of being in England about this time: it was certainly not Massey, for his treachery was now universally known and there would, therefore, be no point in concealing his name. Anderson brought 'M' to see Sir Richard Mayne and it was arranged that he should come up to lodge in London and work with the Police there. (17) The combination was unsuccessful, however, and the authorities turned to Fariola. He had been arrested in London in July as a result of information given to Mayo for which £200 was paid. (18) but the evidence against him being insufficient to send him for trial, he was kept in Kilmainham jail where, in December, Anderson interviewed him for three hours and found him very communicative. He was an uncommonly deep fellow, Anderson thought, who would disclose everything if it was made worth his while. In this preliminary conversation Fariola excluded Mazzini and some other leaders he named from any connection with Fenianism; and said that Ricard O'Sullivan Burke, then a prisoner in London, was the man who had boarded the *Jackmel* in Sligo. This was something the authorities did not know before. (19) Later, Fariola wrote to Anderson to explain that he was anxious to take his wife and child with him to Australia and for the sum he needed for that purpose he would give a written statement. This, Anderson felt, would be well worth the money, but he did not like going to Kilmainham again; two of the warders were not trustworthy. (20) So Fariola was discharged and Anderson, in his own house, wrote down the statement from him. Because of the length of time Fariola had been in custody this, Anderson explained, did not contain anything of immediate importance, but it was 'exceedingly interesting'. (21)

Fariola then went over to London and met Anderson's younger brother Robert at the Irish Office. Within three weeks he had agreed to assist in procuring the arrest of Colonel Kelly, subject to the Government promising distinctly and definitely that he would not be called as a witness in the case or brought forward in any way in connection with it. A letter containing this offer was sent to Lord Mayo with Samuel Lee Anderson's recommendation that it might be accepted: he did not think that Fariola's evidence would be at all necessary to the conviction of Kelly. Anderson was desperately anxious that the correspondence should be kept secret, and he asked Mayo not to put the papers through the registry. There were busybodies there who read everything, particularly anything marked secret. Mayo gave a verbal direction in the case, and on the papers he minuted briefly, and somewhat obscurely, that if Fariola procured the arrest of Kelly he should be released from his promise, not otherwise. (22)

Kelly, despite an intensive search, was never re-arrested, and Superintendent Ryan explained why. 'England,' he wrote on the 15th October 1867,

> may now be looked upon as the centre of the conspiracy, and it is becoming daily more formidable there, and carried out on a scale that almost renders it impossible for human ingenuity to observe its progress. No written communications whatever are sent, and special messengers whose fidelity in the cause is beyond suspicion are employed to carry orders from one place to another, and it is one of the most serious breaches of discipline for a man receiving orders from those messengers to ask . . . a question about Kelly's whereabouts, or anything else not directly bearing on the orders being delivered. . . . No person has any notion of what his [Kelly's] future movements may be. . . . (23)

(3)

By November, five of the men arrested for complicity in the Manchester rescue—William O'Meara Allen, Michael Larkin, William Goold alias O'Brien, Thomas Maguire and Edward Stone—were found guilty and sentenced to death. As there was reason to believe that the conviction in Maguire's case was erroneous he was pardoned and discharged. There was no doubt of Stone having been engaged in the affair, yet his part was less prominent and his sentence was commuted on the eve of the day fixed for his execution. In the other cases the law was allowed to take its course. (24)

The public hanging of Allen, Larkin and O'Brien—'the Manchester Martyrs'—on the 23rd November 1867, gave rise to an enormous outburst of feeling among Irish communities throughout the world. In Ireland, perhaps the greatest unforeseen effect was that almost overnight the wide rift between clergy and Fenians was appreciably narrowed, though in Kerry Bishop Moriarty prohibited public masses for the executed men. In Dublin Cardinal Cullen instructed his priests to pray for the deceased men and to say masses privately for them, and *The Nation* was able to announce with satisfaction that masses and requiem offices had been celebrated in eighteen Dublin churches. In Tuam, Archbishop MacHale attended a Solemn Requiem Mass for the decesaed men. (25) The priests, Mayo told the Prime Minister, had 'come out' very strong since the Manchester men were hanged, and were doing a lot of mischief. (26)

In a situation like this the gentry always became alarmed, and Strathnairn, making a tour in the country, admitted that the presence of troops had a calming effect. 'It is something to have brought him to that state of mind,' Larcom said. In Larcom's opinion Lord Strathnairn thought more of the safety of his troops than the safety of the country. He locked them up in places like the Curragh, thus neutralising 5,000 men. In other words, 20,000 without Strathnairn were as good as 25,000 with him, and Larcom advised Lord Mayo to make things hot for the army commander if he did not mend his ways. 'He is not a man to give way to. He must be strongly resisted and then, and not till then, will he cease to encroach, if I know his character at all.' (27)

Processions, that were sometimes described as mock-funerals, began to be organised out of sympathy for the executed Fenians. The first of these, held in the city of Cork on the 1st December, caused a hurried conference to be convened in Dublin Castle the day before at which the Lord Lieutenant, Abercorn, was present but not the Chief Secretary, Mayo, who was detained by a Cabinet meeting in London. It was there settled that the procession should be allowed to proceed as no breach of the law was anticipated; it was to be watched well, however, and an example made if the speeches were more than usually seditious. Larcom telegraphed the decision to Mayo but the message somehow did not reach him until after the Cabinet meeting.

The procession went off quietly: it was, in Strathnairn's words 'a perfectly Irish *Bull*: hearse, mourners, long funeral procession, all complete but nobody to bury'. (28) The official mind however, was disturbed by the robbery of upwards of 100 revolvers from a shop in the city, though there was some reason to believe that the robbery was a pretext put forward by a bankrupt gunsmith to obtain better terms for himself. Strathnairn was critical of the decision to permit a procession to take place which he regarded as an expression of approval of criminals who had added murder to treason, and he was very glad to learn from Abercorn that if a similar procession were proposed in Dublin, he would be against it. The wearing of green favours or rosettes, the badge of the United Irishmen and Fenian Republicans, constituted the procession a party one, in his view, and brought it under the law against party processions and demonstrations.

Abercorn made his mind known to Mayo when a procession in Dublin became likely. Whatever they felt about allowing one in Cork, and that was bad enough, how could they permit one in the vicinity of the Protestant University, in the seat of Government, and among a mixed population where there was a powerful Protestant feeling? Any procession of that nature in Dublin would only be regarded as an insult to the Protestant and loyal people, and as provoking a breach of the peace. Should it be proposed they should have plenty of informations sworn against it as likely to produce riot and breach of the peace, and on the basis of these, stop it? (29)

Mayo became very uneasy. He had received telegrams, which showed him that the Lord Chancellor and the Attorney General differed from Abercorn, and thought that the procession in Dublin could not be stopped. Then at 7.30 on a Friday night he got another telegram which was not deciphered till 8, asking for a decision as to whether the meeting was to be stopped or not and begging him to come over to Dublin at once. This placed him in a very painful position. 'I have been called on to exercise a serious responsibility at a moment's notice and without any opportunity being given of consulting my colleagues.' To go to Dublin at that hour was impossible. Had he received a message early in the day he would certainly have gone, but as it was all he could do was to consult Lord Derby by note and to send his reply to Larcom. Mayo continued his description of the sequence of events in a letter to Abercorn written on the day, a Sunday, when the procession was held.

> The lateness at which I received the telegram, the absence of any detailed information from any of my colleagues, the state of ignorance I was in as to whether the Law Officers had declared that in their opinion the meeting was an illegal one, the sudden change which appeared to have taken place in the Chancellor's mind in the afternoon of Friday placed me in almost a cruel position. It was too late to write by post. I therefore sent the telegram which appears to have induced you to decide against action.
>
> The Attorney General has written me three or four lines which, in conjunction with yours, appear to show that you did not approve of the course taken. Now there was nothing in the instructions which prevented the procession being stopped, though conditions were suggested. If there is so strong a feeling in Dublin as to its danger, as to induce numbers of persons to bring revolvers; if it was certain that its object was treasonable; surely three or four persons might have been found in ten minutes who could have deposed to that effect. The difficulty that presented itself to me was that similar demonstrations had taken place in London, Manchester and Cork without danger or disturbance but if you stopped them in

Dublin you would have been obliged to stop them all over Ireland, which, with the weak force you have in some places would probably have provoked collision and loss of life. On the other hand, I am fully sensible of the enormous evils which will attend this display, of the difficulties in store for us, principally owing to the childish folly of the Orangemen who agree that, as the Fenians do wrong, they ought to do wrong likewise. I cannot but believe however that something must happen today which will give us an opportunity of vindicating the law in the proper manner.

I shall bring the whole question before the Cabinet tomorrow, will go down by the night mail and will see you on Tuesday at 11 o'clock. You may imagine how very anxious all this makes me. However, if it precipitates the crisis it may end in good. I believe the policy of forbearance should be carried to the utmost limit and that if we are forced to act with severity we shall derive all the greater strength by being able to show that we have only acted when the law authorised us to do so and when the public peace was threatened. But the difficulty of adapting the British Constitution to the ordinary administration of Irish affairs is almost insurmountable. (30)

The procession, as it took place, was in Strathnairn's opinion 'a disgraceful exhibition' and an insult to every principle of good government and public morality. What an example to soldiers and the lower orders! He shared Abercorn's humiliation to the full at the sight of from 20,000 to 30,000 persons formally and publicly convoking together, wearing green sashes, and rebellious emblems such as the harp without the crown, and singing seditious songs, for the purpose of giving their approval to assassination and treason. He was particularly annoyed to hear that some soldiers had marched in the procession and had taken off their caps opposite the place where Emmet was executed in 1803. He had ordered a prompt and strict inquiry and the offenders immediately arrested. A very good and experienced judge of Irish matters had told him that the procession had doubled the number of Fenians and done away with the wholesome effect of the Manchester examples. He was astonished to hear that Mayo had argued that the procession could only have been put down by barricades across the streets, manned by soldiers and police. He could not conceive a more unmilitary plan, or one more calculated to ensure a collision. He would have done what the Duke of Wellington did for the suppression of the anticipated riots in London in 1848. He would not have shown the soldiers at all but kept them in positions from which they could intervene promptly if required. He did not believe they would have been required. Judging from centuries' experience of the Irish there would not have been the slightest resistance, more especially as the promoters of the procession had adopted O'Connell's watchword —'avoid collision with the law and the military'. (31)

The matter was raised in the House of Commons and Mayo, supported by the Prime Minister, explained that the Government could not legally stop the procession unless they received sworn depositions from independent persons that it was likely to produce riot, disturbance and intimidation. The opinion that was almost immediately considered to be the right one, however, was that the Common Law justified the stoppage on the ground that the object of the procession and the meeting connected with it, which was addressed by John Martin, 'a released convict guilty of treason felony in 1848', was seditious from beginning to end. The change was noted in Dublin, and Strathnairn was glad to tell the Duke of Cambridge on the 13th December that on the previous day he had attended a Privy Council meeting at which a Proclamation was issued forbidding a procession that had been announced to take place the following Sunday in Killarney. Mayo had made a mess of it, he said, but had now come around to Abercorn's and his way of thinking. (32)

Mayo, however, had been taking instructions from the Prime Minister, whose line—the one followed—was that the Dublin meeting should be allowed to proceed except upon the clearest evidence that, independently of the Party Processions Act, independent witnesses had sworn that the procession would be of such a character as to excite reasonable apprehension of disturbance. He had advised that a careful watch should be kept on the spectators, and that this question should be very carefully considered by the Law Officers: whether a meeting convened for the purpose of expressing sympathy with men condemned to death for murder in aid of treason might not be looked upon as a seditious meeting, exposing the leading actors to be prosecuted. Derby's ministerial son, Stanley, agreed with this line, putting in however, a word of extra caution. (33)

Mayo on the 11th December had in fact told Lord Derby that there was, and he was sorry to say it, a very strong feeling among the loyal Irish that they had made a mistake in not putting down by force the Dublin procession. This was very unreasonable, for how could they have known that it would have taken so decidedly treasonable an aspect? In consultation with the Chancellor, the Lord Lieutenant and the Attorney General, it had been decided to prosecute Martin for sedition, and very possibly some of the others for breaches of the Party Processions Act. He believed the time had come when public opinion would thoroughly support them in stopping the mock-funerals which could no longer be tolerated with safety. If they had erred, it had been on the side of forbearance, but they could not go on for ever witnessing passively the sort of display that had been seen in Dublin. Derby was not sorry to hear of the state of feeling among the loyal population that Mayo had described. It was much better that they should have to charge the Government with an excess of forbearance than with the opposite imputation of precipitate interference. It was much better that public opinion should anticipate Government action, and be unmistakably pronounced in favour of the course the Government proposed. Next day he approved of a proclamation on the model of that used to stop the Clontarf Repeal meeting in 1843: this was to prohibit the Killarney meeting and another announced for Tipperary.

The state of the loyal minority was one thing; what the majority of ordinary people were thinking was quite different. Derby's second son had been over to the family estate in Tipperary and had given a very unsatisfactory report of political feeling there. Disaffection was general. And Strathnairn, writing to Derby from Castlemartyr in County Cork, was of a like mind. 'I fear a very bad state of things is not far off,' he said, (34) and the nationalist newspapers, reflecting popular emotion following the Manchester executions, were largely to blame. 'I have long been of opinion,' Derby wrote to Mayo, 'that, notwithstanding all the staple objections to "interferences with the freedom of the press", a portion of that in Ireland has assumed so seditious and dangerous a character, that it had become the duty of the Government to interpose, if only they could see a fair prospect of success; for it is not to be denied that failure would have a most prejudicial effect.' (34) So the editors of the offending papers were arrested, prosecuted and sent to prison.

The ballad singers were another worry, for they, too, in their own way, reflected the spirit of the hour. They, and the printers who produced their crude, seditious sheets, were proceeded against. In Newry, one Jeremiah Cronin, with his wife Teresa who carried a child in her arms, were charged with singing seditious songs in the public streets. A police witness said that Cronin was singing a ballad to a crowd of 400 to 500 persons who blocked the footpath. The offending verse ran—

> *When those poor men they was condemned*
> *And asked what they'd to say*
> *Allen he got up and spoke*
> *In a bold and fearless way.*
> *He said that he was innocent*
> *But made this bold reply*
> *For poor oppressed Ireland*
> *On the gallows he would die.*

When the police appeared the people shouted 'Hide the ballads', and referring to the convicts (Allen, Larkin and O'Brien) said 'God help the poor fellows; they should not have been hung.' Every time the police came up the song was changed to another one. The prisoner was given a week's imprisonment, the magistrate hoping he would not repeat the offence. (36)

Poetry, as distinct from the cruder street ballads, was also being used to incite 'respectable people'. Some of these, at a lecture given in Dublin's Mechanics Institute by John Keegan Casey, were entertained to a recital of 'Shane O'Farrell', a piece whose subject was the marching of 300,000 men with pikes at the rising of the moon. This, the police reported, greatly excited the audience. (37) Prose, rather than poetry, however, was regarded as a better subject for a seditious prosecution (38) and there was much of this in circulation, especially pamphlets giving 'Speeches from the Dock' made by the Fenian prisoners.

The game of party politics continued to be played vigorously. The Liberal Lord Kimberley set about preparing an attack on the Tory Government for the course they had taken with regard to the Processions. Derby was disgusted. 'Considering the state in which he left Ireland, and his experience of the difficulties which any Government must encounter in dealing with such questions, the attack will come with peculiarly bad grace from him, and I do not think it will be very formidable.' (39)

CHAPTER XIII

The Explosion at Clerkenwell

MAYO'S willingness to agree to more repressive measures was doubtless influenced by the dire effects of an explosion that occurred on the 13th December at a House of Detention in the London suburb of Clerkenwell. This arose out of an attempt to rescue Ricard O'Sullivan Burke, who had instigated the rescue of Colonel Kelly in Manchester, and who was now detained himself on a charge of being an arms agent for the Fenians. He planned his own rescue and made arrangements with his friends outside. In what had become an almost inevitable sequence information reached Dublin Castle of what was afoot and from there the following warning was sent to the London police: 'The rescue of Ricard Burke from prison in London is contemplated. The plan is to blow up the exercise walls by means of gun powder; the hour between 3 and 4 p.m.; and the signal for "all right" a white ball thrown up outside when he is at exercise. (1) This programme was followed exactly. On the 12th December a barrel of gunpowder was brought to the place on a barrow. The white ball was thrown over the wall of the prison yard. Burke 'fell out' on the pretence of having a stone in his shoe, retired for safety to the corner of the yard and awaited the explosion. It did not come: for some reason the fuse, when lighted, failed to explode the powder. On the following day the performance was repeated. The cask of powder was rolled into position, the white ball signal given, and this time there was an infernal explosion which not merely blew down the wall of the jail but demolished tenement houses on the opposite side of the street, killing twelve people and maiming a hundred and twenty. Yet Burke did not get away. The prison authorities, under direction from the Chairman of the Middlesex Sessions, had strengthened the guard day and night and had not allowed Burke to be exercised with any of the male prisoners or in the male airing yard. He was instead exercised in one of the female yards when all the female prisoners were in their cells, and the yard was varied daily. (2)

The explosion was violently denounced by the Roberts wing of the American Fenians, their assumption being that it had been planned by Colonel Kelly. An agent of Roberts reporting to him said that the affairs both at Manchester and Clerkenwell had greatly diminished their prospects in the United Kingdom, and he urged Roberts to have nothing whatever to do with the moves that were being made to bring about a reunion of the two Fenian parties. In his view, Kelly was a curse to the organisation and to Ireland.

Apart from Burke himself, the prime mover in producing the explosion at Clerkenwell was a Captain Murphy. He succeeded in avoiding arrest, but the police got their hands on most of the other persons involved, and four of these made full confession of the facts and offered to become witnesses. In a couple of cases the offer was refused; once because the name of a person was mentioned of whom it was desirable that nothing should be made known. He was the proprietor of a well-known Dublin hotel where the leading Fenians resorted, and since 1865 he had been giving important information to the police respecting their movements. However, as the result of the two offers that were 'favourably received' a man named Michael Barrett was convicted and sentenced to death, and the execution carried out on the 26th May 1868. Burke, when his time came, got fifteen years penal servitude.

(2)

Months after the explosion Hardy, the Home Secretary, tried to explain to Parliament what had gone wrong. The police had been misled by the wording of the warning notice, he said. They had been told that the wall was to be *blown up*, which to them involved undermining, whereas in fact it was blown *down*. The cask was placed close to the wall without anybody supposing that there was any cause to apprehend mischief from it! The mode of carrying out the design of which they had received information did not strike those who were set to watch the outside of the prison; indeed a policeman walked along by the side of the wall when the cask was there, and had nearly all his clothes blown off.

This miserable explanation only convinced everybody that the police authorities had as usual grossly mishandled the whole business. 'You will see,' Mayo told the Prime Minister, 'that we gave ample notice of the Clerkenwell outrage and that it occurred exactly at the hour indicated in Inspector [Superintendent] Ryan's report. Truly the ways of the English police are wonderful. If it had not been for the sensible precautions taken by Mr Pownell [the Chairman of the Middlesex Sessions] Burke would at this moment be enjoying himself with Kelly.' (3) Behind the scenes much of the criticism was directed against Sir Richard Mayne, the Metropolitan Commissioner. He was utterly unfit for his job, Strathnairn told the Duke of Cambridge, who was a member of the Cabinet. He was not qualified by character or antecedents to deal with Fenian daring and wickedness.

The Government's immediate concern, however, was to find somebody to strengthen their secret service arm and to discover and break up whatever elements were threatening the public safety. The man chosen was not an Irish policeman—which is interesting—but Lieutenant Colonel the Honorable W. H. A. Feilding, the senior Army Intelligence Officer in Ireland, whose services were made available by Strathnairn in obedience to the *strictly confidential* wishes of the Prime Minister. (4) His task was to organise, on a temporary basis, a secret service department in London; Captain Whelan of the 8th regiment and Robert Anderson, a barrister who had previous experience of Fenian records—he had prepared for Lord Mayo a history of the Fenian conspiracy which was circulated to Ministers—were chosen to co-operate with him. Anderson was well placed to do this, being the brother and intimate collaborator of Samuel Lee Anderson, the Crown Solicitor who handled Fenian matters in Dublin Castle. (5) Robert was installed in the Irish Office in London on the 19th December 1867 and remained there until April 1868, when he moved to the Home Office 'to take charge of Irish business'. By that time it had been established that the Clerkenwell explosion was not the work of the Fenian organisation at all, but of a small number of London Irish within its ranks; and the Feilding–Whelan–Anderson trio was disbanded.

When the Clerkenwell explosion occurred, Derby was incapacitated in his home at Knowsley by one of the recurring attacks of gout from which he suffered. Disraeli, the Chancellor of the Exchequer, was acting in his place but keeping in touch with the Prime Minister on matters in which Derby had a personal interest. This was very much one of them. On the 12th December Mayo wrote to Disraeli to say that he had had a long interview with Colonel Feilding the previous day and had told him of the Government's wishes. He had also seen Lord Strathnairn who 'seemed to approve'. But he had just received a letter from Feilding which he enclosed with his own, commenting on it that he was more convinced than ever that Feilding was the man they wanted. In the letter, written from the Royal Barracks, Dublin, a post that had been offered to Feilding was declined on three grounds. It would confer no official and openly recognised status on him, so that he would be liable to be treated as a spy. His position would not be consistent with that of an officer and a gentleman. And the insinuation in the offer that the existing police authorities were either not trustworthy or were incapable would mean that his employment would be resisted. (6) Mayo had removed these scruples. The position offered would now be officially recognised. While remaining a serving officer in the Army he would be seconded for 'special service' to the Home Office. Feilding had thereupon indicated that he was prepared to accept the offer, and on being told what the Government's views and objects were, he left for London to see the Home Secretary, Gathorne Hardy. Mayo suggested that Disraeli should also see the Colonel. 'He is quick, sagacious and plucky,' he said. 'Let him choose his own staff, and give him none but general instructions. Tell him what you want and he will find means to do it.' (7)

On the 14th December, Disraeli wrote to the Prime Minister:

> Affairs here are very serious.
>
> I have contrived to get Colonel Feilding over, tho' after in-expressible difficulties, and even now doubt whether I shall be able to get him to work: so great are the obstacles at every step: but it must be done.
>
> I have not been able to see Hardy until today, and unfortunately, he has gone out of town again, but will be here on Monday.
>
> It is my opinion that nothing effective can be done in any way in these dangers, if we don't get rid of Mayne. I have spoken to Hardy who says he 'wishes to God he would resign', but, surely, when even the safety of the State is at stake, there ought to be no false delicacy on such a point?. . . I think you ought to interfere.
>
> I took upon myself to send Government aid to the Clerkenwell sufferers. (8)

When Disraeli saw Feilding he shared Mayo's enthusiasm for the man. He was 'a man equal to the occasion; young, resolute, full of resource and master of the subject' of Fenianism. He asked that Captain Whelan, with whom he had hunted Fenianism out of the army in Ireland, should be assigned to him, along with three detectives who would report to him direct, and not to Sir Richard Mayne, with whom he declined to act in any way. From experience he knew that Mayne would thwart everything. (9) As soon as they had finished their business Disraeli wrote to tell Lord Derby what the Colonel's first task was to be. He was to ascertain, if possible, the relations between the Fenians in England and the revolutionary societies abroad. 'He had much greater plans,' Disraeli wrote,

> but his operations will be limited to this head. His greater plans which would involve a discovery of the incendiaries and the in-ceddiary plots in this kingdom, must be renounced, from the absolute impossibility of furnishing him with competent agents. This morning Mr. Secretary Hardy settled with me that he (Feilding) should certainly have three or more detectives at his disposal, but Mr Hardy is of opinion that there are really no men in the force who, either from lack of honesty or intelligence, can be trusted. Colonel Feilding says his conversation with the Secretary of

9 Attack on the Prison Van at Manchester (18 September 1867)

10a
Lord Stanley

10b
Earl of Derby

10b

State was the most despairing and unsatisfactory one, as regards the position of the country, he ever knew.

There is no doubt that there is a system of organised incendiarism afloat, and we credibly hear of men crossing from America who are to take empty houses in various parts of London and set them on fire, probably simultaneously. I think the Habeas Corpus ought to be suspended now. . . . (10)

He meant in England; hitherto, suspension had been confined to Ireland.

Disraeli followed this up with an even more alarming letter. 'Affairs appear to be so serious,' he said,

that last night the Cabinet in town (seven strong) agreed to meet to confer, mainly on the critical condition of the metropolis. . . . The chief feature was a telegram from Lord Monck informing the Duke of Buckingham that some days past a Danish Brigantine left New York with a band of thirty men sworn to assassinate Her Majesty and her Ministers. (Lord Monck is not an alarmist and particularly deprecates the expense of transatlantic telegrams, but in this instance, he requests a telegram of receipt.)

We have no power to cope with such circumstances as these and others which are taking place under our nose. . . .

What are we to do? If they land and are seized, Habeas Corpus will immediately release them. If stopped on the high seas, we may be involved in a war with America.

For my part I should not hesitate advising seizure, and trusting to a parliamentary indemnity but it seems that Habeas Corpus is too strong even for such daring; and that we should violate the law without gaining our purpose. . . .

In this state of affairs and the great alarm and indignation of the public mind, there seemed an unanimous opinion that the real Cabinet should meet without loss of time and Mr Secretary Hardy says the Queen expects it. I lament this for your sake—greatly. (11)

Derby had meantime made his mind known regarding Feilding's appointment. Thanking Disraeli for 'two long and interesting, but thoroughly unsatisfactory letters', he said on the 17th December:

If I rightly understand the situation Colonel Feilding's operations

FF P

will be confined to endeavouring to trace a connexion between the disturbers of our peace at home, and the revolutionists abroad. In this I fear he will fail; as from what Mayo told us in Downing Street, I very much doubt the existence of any concert between them. Even should he be able to establish it, it would be much less effectual towards our immediate object of preserving the public safety, than an accurate knowledge of the plots and intentions of conspirators and incendiaries at home. It is really lamentable that the peace of the metropolis, and its immunity from wilful devastation, should depend on a body of Police, who, as Detectives, are manifestly incompetent; and under a chief who, whatever may be his other merits, has not the energy, nor, apparently, the skill to find out and employ men fitted for peculiar duties. There is no doubt that the public are sufficiently alarmed; but not so much, I think, as to tolerate the suspension of the Habeas Corpus Act in England. We must trust to the operation of the ordinary law, at all events unless and until we are able to bring before a Secret Committee, impartially composed, such evidence as shall satisfy all of them as to the necessity of some exceptional measures. . . . If we can bring forward all the evidence which we have of what is going on at home, irrespective of any concert with foreign revolutionists, we *may* establish a case strong enough to induce Parliament to sanction some exceptional measures. . . . (12)

Within a couple of weeks Derby was wondering whether they would be able to resist popular pressure for ultra-constitutional measures of repression in Britain as well as in Ireland. There were some indications of a revival of trade, but the Fenian scare stood in the way of a revival of confidence and seemed to be producing a bad reaction among the population. What he really feared was an indiscriminate proscription of all Irish Roman Catholics. 'You saw the account of the attempt to blow up the gas works at Warrington,' he said to Disraeli. 'An Irish Priest is trying to make out that it was all a hoax; but all the R.C. workmen have been dismissed, and one of the managers was imprudent enough to tell the priest that they were dismissed an account of their religion! Four Irish workmen (Protestants) have been kept on . . . I do not wonder, under these circumstances at home, at Stanley's anxiety about our relations with America.' (13)

In the light of Derby's views about Feilding's role, it is not surprising to find that officer's first reports coming, not from the Continent, but from Portsmouth where he found 'agents were at work to seduce sailors with a view of putting into their hands the destructive implements which are to be used against ships . . .' What success Feilding had in bringing these men to book we do not know but attempted acts of incendiarism continued, and the Home Secretary resorted to the traditional practice of offering rewards for information leading to the arrest of the persons responsible. These attempts pointed to a situation that was serious enough; but it gradually emerged that the story of the Danish Brigantine with its cargo of assassins was a complete hoax, and the Queen, who had never seen the point of the extra attention she was receiving from the police, had a good laugh at the expense of her ministers. She had been pressing for fewer restrictions at Osborne, and Hardy, who had been to see her, had found her difficult, as he explained to Lord Derby. 'Curiously enough on coming down stairs this morning very early I found a note from the Queen almost ridiculing precautions etc. . . . . . In writing to her this morning I told her that on my responsibility to her and the country I could not consent to relax precautions.' (14)

(3)

When, following the Manchester convention, Colonel Kelly appointed a staff to direct Fenian activities in the United Kingdom, he put William Mackey Lomasney, who was better known simply as Captain Mackey, in charge of southern Ireland for arms purposes. Mackey was a small man of slender build, modest and retiring in manner, who spoke with a lisp and was much wanted by the police. In the attack on the barracks at Ballyknockan in March 1867, he had wounded a constable and thereby incurred a charge of attempted murder. He celebrated his new appointment by abstracting 120 revolvers and five Snider rifles from the premises of Mr Richardson, a gunsmith, of Patrick Street, Cork—

this occurred on the 28th November 1867—and a month later he led a party into the Martello Tower at Foaty on the north side of the Cork river, made prisoners of the gunners and bore away all the arms and ammunition they could find. This action caused a major sensation but, instead of lying low as they might have done, Mackey's men returned three days later to Patrick Street, the place of their first triumph, and there, as business began on the morning of the 30th December, they entered Allport's gunshop, held up the proprietor and his assistants and filled and carried off a canvas bag full to the brim with desirable booty. Inside a couple of days they went a stage further, raiding the commercially-owned powder magazine at Ballincollig and taking away as much powder as they could handle.

The Government were gravely disturbed. 'One almost wishes that these smouldering fires would break out that we might act more vigorously,' (15) the Home Secretary told the Chief Secretary, and the Prime Minister also wrote to express his feelings. He had just been dealing with the Catholic university question and had found Mayo's 'dear countrymen' a most unmanageable team to drive;—keeping them together would defy the stick of the most practised whip, he said. Now, once more, it was the Fenians, whose successful attack on the remote Martello Tower might have been accounted for, he thought, by a very slight remission of vigilance; but the affair at Allport's seemed much more serious. It was incredible that without attracting attention eight men, fully armed, should in broad daylight enter a gunmaker's shop (the place, of all others, to be most carefully watched), should remain there ten minutes or a quarter of an hour, keeping the inmates under guard, deliberately rifle the open shop window, carry away sixty revolvers, return a second time, carry off a heavy load of ammunition and withdraw through a public street, full of people, without molestation! 'I see some of the newspapers say that the police were at breakfast—others, at parade; and that the streets were absolutely denuded! Let me know what is the truth of these reports; which, if they are well-founded, bring your Irish Police nearer down than I had thought, to the level of our Metropolitan.' (16) The Home Secretary likewise did

not like the look of what he saw reported from Cork. Unless
foiled or the perpetrators arrested, imitations would not be wanting in Britain. It was a bad lesson for the ordinary criminal
classes, though they generally lacked the pluck for such daring
schemes. (17)

That was before the raid on the Powder Magazine. When
Derby read of that in the newspapers on the 6th January 1868 he
wrote immediately to tell Mayo that this was the most audacious
outrage that had yet been committed. With the other attacks in
Cork it led to the inevitable conclusion that there must have been
connivance somewhere, if not collusion. He hoped that the
strictest possible inquiry would be instituted into all these cases,
but especially into that of the Powder Magazine. The proprietors,
he believed, were highly respectable, but either they must have
kept a very negligent watch over their premises or they must
have been betrayed by those whom they employed. It seemed
incredible that a magazine guarded by three doors, of iron, wood
and copper respectively, should have had all three broken open,
half a ton of gunpowder abstracted, and no alarm given till 11
a.m. next day. This, the Allport business, and the successful con-
cealment of all the booty, were, to say the least of it, not creditable
to the Cork Constabulary, and he hoped that Mayo would omit
no step for ascertaining where the blame rested, and if possible
for the discovery of the offenders. (18)

Mayo admitted that the situation was dire indeed. All the lower
classes in Cork were sympathisers of the Fenians and there was
little chance of catching the men responsible for the outrages
except by accident. The police arrangements were very bad and
the Government had no power to make them permanently better
without legislation which they should try to get when Parliament re-assembled. However, as a temporary measure he had
sent 100 men as a reinforcement to the constabulary, had largely
increased the garrison, and had arranged that a battalion of marines
would strengthen the defences of the harbour forts. (19) Without
any prompting from the Prime Minister, he had also made the
Government's anxiety known in all the appropriate quarters and
had promised a generous reward for Mackey's apprehension. 'We

must pay for good service,' Larcom had told him, '*pour en-
courager les autres*, as well as to reward the deserving.' The Resident Magistrate conveyed this assurance confidentially to the men
in the Cork police most likely to capture Mackey. 'Even without
such assurance,' he said, 'I know the Police, to a man, have been
most anxious, jealous and indefatigable in their exertions, and
yet—so great is the difficulty of getting information of any
offence which does not come under their own observation—
they have been as yet unsuccessful. I have used other agencies to
discover Mackey with as little success . . .' (20) The military were
also alerted and Strathnairn was given a description of Mackey.
He was a most daring, cool, plucky, and sharp fellow who, small
in size—not more than 5 ft. 5 in.—often disguised himself as a
woman, never slept more than one night in any one place, and
always had a set of ruffians about him on the watch. On a recent
Sunday night he had very nearly been caught napping, for he had
bolted out of a house only five minutes before the police were on
the spot. Cork was getting too hot for him. (21) This proved to
be the case, for on the 7th February Mackey was discovered in a
public house in a back street and arrested, but not before he had
wounded another policeman, who died after a few days. He had
now to face a murder charge.

While he was in the Cork jail somebody there got the impression that he might become an approver, and the exciting
word was passed up to Dublin Castle. Larcom minuted to Mayo
that the matter required consideration. 'It would shake the
conspirators in their very shoes, but must be approached with
extreme caution. It—if there be anything in it—must first
be proposed by himself. It is a *raison de plus* for bringing him up
here . . .' (22) There was nothing at all in it, for Mackey was
among the staunchest, as well as the toughest, of the Fenians.
He was brought up to Dublin, and soon Larcom was regretting
that this had been done because he had to be brought back to Cork
again for trial, an enormous risk with the rumour about that
Colonel Kelly was in Ireland and might try a rescue. (23) A similar
problem arose, as always, when the Crown Witnesses were being
sent down.

However, nothing untoward occurred until Mackey was in Court. Then the jury acquitted him on the charge of murder, acknowledging the probability that he had not intended to fire his revolver, that it had been struck by the revolver of the policeman who was struggling with him. On a secondary charge of treason felony, on the evidence of Corydon among others, he was found guilty and sentenced to penal servitude for twelve years. Larcom was rather surprised by the turn of events, though some of his pundits had told him that this was what would happen. The treason felony verdict would at any rate keep Mackey harmless for some time, he said, but it would make the constabulary men savage. They would be tempted to use their own weapons, and not wait in future for the weapons of the law. (24) Mackey duly served his term, joined a dynamite squad in the eighties and was blown to pieces as he placed an explosive under London Bridge.

Wood, the Inspector General of the R.I.C., fearing that the Government might attribute the Cork outrages to a want of vigilance on the part of his men, got an 'exceedingly satisfactory' report from the County Inspector, R. Barry, on what they had been doing in the previous six months. 2,213 arrests had been made for various offences—1,486 of them for intoxication—and this had been achieved by 110 policemen working among a population of between 85,000 and 90,000. Wood commented that 'the city of Cork is doubtless the most disaffected spot in the whole of Ireland . . .' (25) He was delighted to be able to send Lord Mayo a report from Barry in which he said:

> You see I have taken your good advice and succeeded in capturing Captain Mackey. I assure you I never ceased night and day since you were here, our informant behaved well, but I entrusted his arrest to Head Constable Gale only and made him dress in plain clothes. I had all your orders fully carried out to the very letter. Mackey is a most determined fellow. . . .

In a covering note Wood hoped that this report would show those high in authority in England that the Irish Constabulary were not inferior to their sister services in other countries. 'If they would only have a little more confidence in me and my men I think they would have no reason for complaint.' (26)

(4)

In the early days of 1868 the Government had a spectacular success in the arrest of most of what Strathnairn called the United Irish American Assassination Company, or what Ryan of the Dublin Metropolitan Police more simply described as a Shooting Circle. Assassination had been an intermittent Fenian weapon for a long time. Ryan's information was that even as far back as 1865 a circle existed by special direction of Colonel Kelly for the removal of obnoxious persons. He had always declared that there would have been small account of Nagle and Corydon had the policy been fully implemented. But something had in fact been done. In 1866, while the first Special Commission was sitting, such a group was active and was held responsible by the police for the murder of Clarke on the banks of the Royal Canal near Phibsborough, (27) the shooting of the soldier Meara in Bridgefoot Street and of Alfred Aylward. The informer, Eugene Smith, disappeared on the day after he gave evidence implicating a Dublin policeman in the escape of the high-ranking Fenian, Kirwan, from a hospital where he was being treated for wounds: a body resembling his was later found floating in the Liffey. Another informer, George Reilly, was set upon by half a dozen men with revolvers and wounded, while it was known that special efforts were being made to 'get' Head Constable Talbot, than whom no one was more exquisitely hated. (28) In various disguises he had entrapped many young men into the Fenian movement, had administered the I.R.B. oath to them, and in order to ingratiate himself did not scruple 'to partake of the most sacred rites of the Catholic Church of which he was not a member'. (29) He was duly assassinated in Dublin, and his assailant, though caught almost red-handed, was acquitted as the result of Isaac Butt's able defence.

On the 3rd November 1867, an attack on policemen was made in Dublin, one was killed and another seriously wounded. The attack was carried out by eight members of a circle comprising thirty men in all, directed by Colonel Kelly himself. In the search that followed, the shooting circle was broken up, much to the satisfaction of Lord Mayo, who congratulated the detective force on their work. He had an excellent personal reason for being elated, for among the men arrested was Lennon, 'the worst desperado among the Fenian assassins', the man Strathnairn called the *assassin en chef*. Ryan described Lennon as 'a very *gentlemanly* man', who apologised in the handsomest terms for shooting the two policemen: he had regretfully been compelled to do it because they tried to stop him when he was carrying papers of extreme importance to his Government. (30) But this 'very gentlemanly man' had not been arrested a bit too soon, Mayo told Derby. 'The night before last he was waiting for several hours at the Castle Gate for me, but luckily it was the only night for more than a week that I had not been home, as I had gone out hunting.' And he added: 'Ryan's information as usual is wonderful.' (31)

The Home Secretary gave the Queen a full account of Lennon's capture. She had been crowing over 'the bursting of the Canada bubble'—Lord Monck's false alarm about the Danish brigantine. The arrest of this most desperate of men who had lain in wait to murder her Chief Secretary for Ireland was a warning to Victoria that the special precautions for her safety would have to be continued. (32) Indeed a warning had reached Hardy from an American source that the Prince of Wales, the Prime Minister, and Hardy himself were to balance the account for the Manchester Martyrs. (33)

The Prime Minister, in bed with the gout, invited Strathnairn in November 1867 to second the Address to the Queen in the House of Lords. He refused because the Queen's Speech would inevitably make favourable mention of the Government's Reform Bill to which he was constitutionally opposed. He accepted an invitation to dinner, however, and availed himself of the opportunity to put Lord Derby in possession of his humble sentiments on the subject of Fenianism and Irish affairs which he believed corresponded with the Prime Minister's own ideas. His starting point was that extreme and violent measures would never pacify Ireland; they would only perpetuate the difficulties and discontent which were the sources of its disaffection. A policy of conciliation and equality of churches, without the fall of one or the triumph of the other, would alone quench the spirit of intolerance, party bitterness and sectarian animosities which lay at the root of Irish evils. This was Strathnairn's unchanging panacea, but while waiting for it to arrive he insisted that Fenianism would have to be dealt with on its own footing, specially and energetically. It was an extensive, treasonable and dangerous conspiracy that checked as long as it lasted all hopes of a better state of things.

Strathnairn was in London when the first robbery of arms in Cork occurred and Mayo asked him to hurry back, which he did, stopping a mail train *en route* to pick him up. He made a close inspection of the Cork area and was immediately critical of the police who, he believed, through carelessness were more responsible than anybody for the raids on the gunsmiths' shops, and of the Coast Guard who were not fit for action, being too comfortably married, most of them, in good quarters with gardens and poultry, to worry about Fenians. According to the unfriendly Larcom he was in a state of positive monomania about the Ballincollig affair, and could talk of nothing else to the Lord Lieutenant and the Lord Chancellor when next he met them. (34) He could not understand why the Fenians had not blown up the Powder Mills: nothing would have been easier. As for Martello Towers, they were bad in every way, he said: they were too weak for defence and vigilance and contained only two or three men, who could not be properly superintended. However, although he discounted some of the alarmist stories that came from men like Lord Fermoy, he reinforced the military garrison in Cork and then took steps to make all the forts on the Lower Shannon and on Lough Swilly safe against surprise by marauders. He also got the Duke of Cambridge to send him over some extra garrison batteries, which he distributed widely among the Cork Harbour defences and elsewhere in the country. And when he found all the worst feelings of the Cork Fenians and disaffected excited by the trial of Mackey, he increased the cavalry contingent in the city because of its usefulness on protection work and street patrols.

He was a busy man, Strathnairn, in his office and on inspections, in entertaining and being entertained; but he managed to get in a good deal of hunting and shooting. The entertaining he had to do was expensive, and for that reason he deplored the cut of 20 per cent in his official income, which the Duke of Cambridge had not approved of and which no one sought to defend. He took pains to explain to Sir John Pakington, the Minister for War, the wide range of his duties. Among other things he was one of the Lords Justices and had to function as such whenever the Lord Lieutenant was absent. This showed how important his public connection was with the ordinary administration of the country. His private and confidential co-operation was still more frequent and important. It was indispensable that the officer holding chief command in Ireland should be in constant and unreserved communication with the government of a country which, since the conquest, had been in a state of convulsion and political agitation, all directed against the Government; sometimes breaking out into war and revolt in co-operation with some great maritime power or interest, formerly France, now Irish America, sometimes taking the form of agrarian conspiracy against unpopular interests, establishing a reign of terror, and gaining its ends by a system of outrage and secret association. At other times Irish discontent had shown itself in monster meetings of which the best authority, the Duke of Wellington, acknowledged all their seriousness, for the repeal of the Penal Laws, or of the Union, or for the Abolition of Tithes, etc. In 1848 discontent and disaffection broke out in an insurrectionary movement which, although fruitless and ill-conducted, was nevertheless an expression of the feelings of the Catholic masses.

For the last three or four years, Irish malcontents, assisted by their emigrant countrymen in America, and taking a democratic lesson from that country, had joined themselves in the Fenian Brotherhood, whose avowed objects were the destruction of landlords, the spoliation of estates, and an Irish Republic. It was superfluous to observe that, if in former years the state of Ireland necessitated an intimate connection between the chief civil and military authorities, it had become still more imperative since the attempt to establish a republic by force of arms, by Irish masses led by Irish Americans who, as soldiers and officers, had acquired military knowledge and habits of daring enterprise in the great American war. And it was an important fact, bearing on the Irish question, which should always be borne in mind, that although generally speaking Americans had no particular liking for their Irish subjects, they never failed to acknowledge that of all their foreign contingents in the late war, the Irish gave the best and bravest service. (35) About the time of writing, men of all parties and creeds, civilians as well as military, were telling him not only of the extreme disaffection and disloyalty of the very great majority of the Irish people, but also of their lawlessness and studied insolence and violence, particularly towards the troops; the cases of outrage and assault quite unprovoked were frequent and continuous. 'I am sure,' he told Abercorn, 'that you will agree with me that nothing checks popular commotion, or riot, so soon or so efficiently as firm and immediate repression, and that nothing encourages and develops it so much as any appearance of hesitating concession or apprehension.' (36)

He would have liked to have made his duty in London to the Prince of Wales at a levee he was holding for the Queen, a thing he had had no opportunity of doing since he became a peer, but Mackey's trial for his life was causing much excitement amongst the very disloyal population of Cork. Regretfully, therefore, he would have to stay in Ireland and defer the pleasure of presenting himself to the Prince until later in the season. 'We are all delighted to hear,' he told the Prince's secretary 'that His Royal Highness is coming to Ireland for the Punchestown Races. I need not say how very happy I shall be if I can be of any use whatever to His Royal Highness in the way of horses or anything else.' (37) A few days later he heard the agreeable report that the Duke of Cambridge would be coming to Dublin with the Prince and he hastened to offer him hospitality. (38) Mayo, however, had got in before him, and the Duke had accepted his invitation.

CHAPTER XIV

The Fever Passes

MAYO believed and hoped that the Prince's visit, if well managed, would do more real good as regards the feelings of the Irish people than many legislative measures. (1) It would close the Fenian chapter and open one of conciliation. It might even gain the Government some votes. Mayo had always nursed the idea of such a visit, and now that it was in the offing he set about making sure that it would be a great social and political success. He told Cambridge that what he wanted was that the Prince would be enthusiastically received by every man in Ireland whose opinion was worth having and who had a shilling in his pocket, (2) but he also had his eye on the lower classes. He wanted to show that the talk of Ireland becoming impoverished and going to the devil was a lie, and that, considering all things, she was improving steadily if not rapidly. A royal visit was just the thing; so on the 3rd March he had a long talk with the Prince of Wales and told him how important it was that he should come to Ireland at Easter. The Prince was obviously keen and spoke a great deal about the steeplechasing and the Patrick Ribbon which he was told would be presented to him in a cathedral ceremony; but he emphasised that nothing could be settled until the Queen's consent had first been obtained. She was understandably nervous of her son going to Ireland; only a few years before, when training at the Curragh, he had got himself involved with a Dublin actress and had been extricated with difficulty. The affair had caused deep pain to 'dear Albert' and herself.

The way to getting the Queen's consent was through the Prime Minister and Mayo was sure there would be no difficulty if Disraeli, who had become the head of the Government on the retirement in February of Lord Derby, pressed her strongly enough. Mayo, therefore, wired Abercorn in cipher begging him to write the sort of letter Disraeli could show the Queen, (3) and this he did. Mayo simultaneously apprised Disraeli of what he had done and said he had told the Prince very frankly that the absence of the Royal Family from Ireland was very much felt, and that just at that moment his visit would be immensely appreciated.

The negotiations with the Queen were not all as easy as the Prince had predicted. The affair had given him much trouble, Disraeli told Derby, (4) whom he continued as a matter of courtesy to keep informed, on the 9th March 1868.

They [Abercorn and Mayo] invited the Prince without the previous consent of Her Majesty and the occasion chosen for eliciting the loyal feeling of Ireland was a princely visit to some races at a place with the unfortunate title of Punchestown, or something like it. The Queen did not approve of the occasion or a statement agreed to without her authority; and the matter appeared to me at one time more serious than the Irish Church [issue], but with much correspondence and the loyal assistance of General Grey [the Queen's Private Secretary] whose conduct is really admirable, I think we have got it all right. Lords Abercorn and Mayo are pardoned, and, I hope, the Prince; and, if my humble suggestion be adopted, the inauguration of H.R.H. as a knight of St. Patrick in the renovated cathedral, will be an adequate occasion for the Royal Visit, and a more suitable and stately course than a race however national. (5)

Mayo, who had seen that the whole thing was very near coming to grief (6) through his own impetuosity, was delighted to receive a note from Disraeli on the 9th March to say that at 11 o'clock the previous night he had received the Queen's consent to the visit. Mayo told Abercorn immediately to begin his arrangements. The visit, he repeated, would do a great deal of good. The installation of the Prince would be an event most gratifying to the Irish people, but Abercorn must be careful not to mention this possibility until it was first submitted to the Queen: she was very particular about such things. He thought they would be able to give the Prince a *Royal* week of it, including a Grand Ball in which 3,500 people would participate at thirty shillings a head. A Committee should be formed including some of the bourgeoisie of Dublin and the approach to the Duke of Leinster they had jointly made to offer himself as chairman would ensure that it appeared to have a spontaneous character. The Ball should be on the scale of the Hotel de Ville Balls and include the whole of the middle classes. (7)

Mayo saw the Prince from time to time and communicated his wishes to Abercorn. There had been difficulty about whether his entry into Dublin should be public, that is with soldiers lining the streets, or not. He did not wish for this, and Mayo suggested that if the Lord Lieutenant's carriages with an escort were to meet the Prince at Westland Row railway station and *trot* him up to the Castle, it would be sufficient. What was a *sine qua non* was the first day at Punchestown and a day's hunting. At a St Patrick's night ball in London the Prince had raised this matter with him. 'He spoke to me about hunting . . . so I think it must be managed. We must go to some country where there are plenty of foxes.' And, without appearing to draw breath, Mayo touched on another detail. 'I am very glad,' he said, 'you stopped the sale of tickets for Patrick's Cathedral—that was a suggestion worthy of a Dean and Chapter.' (8)

The visit was taken up with extraordinary enthusiasm by Mayo's colleagues in Dublin. Abercorn was concerned with the splendour of the occasion, the banquets and levees and the magnificent ceremony the Ulster King of Arms would prepare. The Prince might be thinking of the Punchestown Races but he would see other things besides. (9) Larcom saw other possibilities. The spectacle of Ironclads in Dublin Bay would turn people's minds away from a harangue Bradlaugh was to give at a Reform meeting in the city. (10) He had also noted a suggestion in *The Times* of some measure of amnesty, and cynically thought that it might be a useful *coup* if they could select a score or more of unimportant prisoners, and make a grace of discharging them. (11) Mayo, always conciliatory, went much further. He proceeded to clear the prisons so that by the time the royal couple arrived only one man remained who had not received an order for discharge.

Strathnairn made a tremendous fuss about the very serious

responsibilities of the Commander of the Forces on an occasion
like this. He would not only have to take measures for the safety
of the Prince and for his protection from insult, but also give the
Government a military and strategical opinion on any plan
relating to H.R.H.'s movements in which the military would be
called upon to take a part. He had much to say about lining the
rout eof a procession from Dublin Castle to St Patrick's Cathedral
with troops. This was to go, like Molly Malone, through streets
broad and narrow, the narrow ones inhabited by the low and
disaffected class esfrom whom danger might be expected. In any
event, he disapproved of the investiture of the Prince taking place
in a Protestant Cathedral. 'In the present, deplorable state of
religious party feeling, this would give umbrage', he said, 'to the
Roman Catholic party, acting under Cardinal Cullen's influence.'
He tried to make these views known to the Lord Lieutenant at an
official function in Saint Patrick's Hall and felt slighted by
Abercorn's seeming unwillingness to give him a hearing. Subsequent letters of his on the subject were left unanswered, and
when he asked for an interview it was suggested by a private
secretary that he could see the Lord Lieutenant at a concert
they were both to attend. 'However,' Strathnairn wrote, 'the
concert of 200 performers was even less favourable to an important and very delicate conversation than St Patrick's Hall. I
profited by the only opportunity I had of speaking to you . . . But
so far from corresponding with the friendly tone in which I
introduced the conversation, you answered me with much
hesitation, and in an unpleasant manner, that you had nothing
to say to me . . .' (12) Abercorn wrote to Mayo. Strathnairn
was giving a great deal of trouble as usual, he said. He had written
reams to say that the investitute ought to be held in a Catholic
cathedral and that he had not enough soldiers to protect the Prince
in going to St Patrick's. He was sending his letter, which he
believed to be entire *tosh*, to the Lord Chancellor.

Brewster, the Chancellor, could not express how great was
his surprise at what Strathnairn had said. If the military were not
prepared to man the route for the investiture procession a couple
of thousand of the Royal Irish Constabulary could easily be drafted

11a
The Earl
of Clarendon

11b

11b Lord
Strathnairn

12a
Benjamin
Disraeli

12b

12b William
E. Gladstone

into Dublin and would glory in the opportunity of giving a proof
of their willing loyalty. If he entertained the fears expressed by
Lord Strathnairn he should feel it his imperative duty to tell the
Duke of Cambridge that it would be in the highest degree
imprudent for the Heir Apparent to the Throne to visit Ireland.
But he recalled that on the occasion of his last visit there was great
dissatisfaction in consequence of his always going about shut up in
a closed carriage, so that his future subjects could not catch a
glimpse of him, and observations of a very disagreeable character
were made in reference to that error. Brewster did not think that
the Prince should pass through the streets like a captive hemmed
in by an armed soldiery, thus implying that he feared a personal
affront from the people. There was always the risk of some lunatic
having a crack at him, but from the vast majority of the people
there would be loud effusions of loyalty.

As to the unpopularity of any installation at St Patrick's Cathedral Brewster took it that this meant that Strathnairn would be
opposed to any religious ceremony unless it could be held in the
Roman Catholic Pro-Cathedral. He had never heard an objection
before to the use of St Patrick's Cathedral for such a function, not
even from the organs of treason, and he did not agree that it
would offend Roman Catholics. The alternative of going to the
Roman Catholic Cathedral, under the auspices of Cardinal Cullen,
might be considered a pleasantry if the subject were not so grave.
It was obvious that Lord Strathnairn had not informed himself
as to this serious matter before hazarding so remarkable a suggestion. He could not have been aware that the [Protestant] Archbishop of Armagh was the Prelate of the Order, that the [Protest-
ant] Archbishop of Dublin was its Chancellor and the Dean of
St Patrick's its Registrar. If his lordship knew anything about the
matter he would not have supposed it possible that these three
dignitaries could march in procession up the aisle of Marlborough
Street Chapel to do honour to Cardinal Cullen. Such a procession
would, of course, imperil the Prince's succession to the Throne.
Brewster, apologised for a long and tedious epistle. Long-
windedness was infectious, he said, and he had caught the disease
from Strathnairn. (13)

Strathnairn was not thinking of honouring the Cardinal, whom he regarded as a mischievous person, a man who was always making trouble over the treatment of Catholics in the Royal Hibernian military school. He thought much more of Moriarty, the good bishop of Kerry as he called him. If Ireland was to be rescued from her difficulties, of which the painful cause was the unforgiving nature of bigoted Protestants and Catholics, it must be by means of the tolerant and Christian frame of mind of Moriarty and his Protestant counterpart in Derry.

The conflict was finally settled by Mayo's approaching the Duke of Cambridge and obtaining from him the decision the Irish Government wanted. 'I quite enter into the spirit of the reply you have sent me in reference to Lord Strathnairn's letter,' Cambridge said. (14) 'I shall tell him that the questions he discusses must be decided entirely by the Government and I do not consider myself justified in interfering with their arrangements.' That gave satisfaction in Dublin Castle, and Mayo directed that the ceremony in St Patrick's Cathedral should not be made a sectarian affair. Cardinal Cullen would give anything to make it so, he said, and would, if he could. To avoid this, the Catholic laity and middle class would have to be profusely supplied with tickets. (15) The Cardinal and his clergy would be absent: they had absented themselves from every ceremony connected with Her Majesty or her representatives ever since the passing of the Ecclesiastical Titles Bill, but he had no reason to believe that the Catholic *laity* would absent themselves. There would be no religious services.

Strathnairn took the rebuff well but religious difficulties kept on cropping up. After the Crimea, soldiers of the 18th Royal Irish regiment, essentially a Roman Catholic troop, made what Strathnairn considered an unfavourable display of feeling about the intention of depositing their colours in St Patrick's Cathedral. A proposed procession to the Cathedral had to be abandoned, and the colours taken quietly in a car and deposited there. He was continually forced to comment on the behaviour of the Catholic clergy. Some would not allow any funeral rites for the Manchester culprits, others openly preached treason in their chapels. For this he urged they should be punished, not as priests but as British subjects. Orangemen who are punished, he said, for making fools of themsleves, and benighted Irishmen who are transported for hatching treason, have a right to complain of partial justice, if an educated clergyman advocating and exciting to treason receives no punishment whatever.

After the collpase of Fenianism, land agitation became the new expression of Irish discontent and very many of the Catholic clergy were associated with it. Whenever a parliamentary election occurred the priests were in the forefront; and in Tipperary they helped the Fenian convict, O'Donovan Rossa, to beat a Queen's Counsel who stood in the Tory interest. These were the younger men mainly. To the older ones, the Ultramontane majority, the Fenian ideal of a Red Republic was anathema. Their hope was Gladstone, to whom they were deeply grateful for his concern with the disestablishment of the Church of Ireland. Strathnairn's attitude on that question, as we saw already, was that the Roman Catholic clergy should be brought up to the Protestant level, instead of depriving the Protestants of something they already had. Gladstone would legislate against the Protestant ascendancy; but there were other more dangerous ascendancies in Ireland. He had the Roman Catholic one particularly in mind.

But for the moment Abercorn was more worried over the anomalous position of the Prince. 'The Queen is as jealous of him as possible,' he told Mayo, 'and will come down on us if we make any mistakes.' She had been angry at not being asked for her consent before the Prince was spoken to, which was rather absurd, Abercorn thought, 'as you can't treat him quite like a baby. All that was done was to know if he would come if the Queen gave permission.' (16) She would apparently allow a public entry into Dublin, but the Lord Lieutenant, her *alter ego*, was to take precedence, and there was some doubt as to whether there was to be a levee at all, certainly not one to be held by the Prince. And as for the races at Punchestown, the Prince could go there on one day only. But what about addresses? Would the Prince's capacity be sufficiently official for him to receive any? (17)

(2)

The Prince and Princess of Wales arrived on the 15th April in the Royal Yacht accompanied by several ironclads of the Channel fleet. There had been serious preparation on their part too, for the Princess wore a dress and jacket of deep-blue poplin trimmed with Irish lace and a white bonnet of Irish lace ornamented by a single rose, while the Prince wore in the breast of his blue frock-coat a rose, surrounded by a bunch of shamrocks and his cravat was of the Irish colour, green. (18) They were received by the people with what the *Freeman's Journal* called exuberant enthusiasm, proving that long suffering and wearying turmoil had not quite chilled the warmth of the Irish heart. "Tis just one year,' the paper said, 'since rebellion darkened the hills of three provinces of this country; and a month has scarcely elapsed since the last of treason's pinioned captives left the shores which yesterday trembled with the roar of artillery to bid our future Sovereign welcome.' (16.4.1868).

The royal couple spent the night in the Viceregal apartments in Dublin Castle and went next morning to Punchestown. This was some twenty miles from the city and most people reached it by rail, through a branch line from Sallins. The railway company utterly underestimated the numbers who desired to join the Prince at his favourite sport, with the result that scenes were witnessed that were 'grand, exciting, almost terrible'. At Sallins, the platforms on both sides of the track were covered with a mass of human beings as the trains, with their whistles perpetually shrieking, came in with every carriage crammed, the roofs loaded to the last inch, men hanging on the steps, and the engines even invaded by the passengers. At the racecourse things were almost as bad, and many people saw neither the royal pair nor the horses. However, on the next day—the Queen having presumably relented—the Prince went back to Punchestown alone and gave the multitude something to look at as he put his portly figure astride a grey Arab steed and pranced about the course.

The investiture in St Patrick's Cathedral took place on the third day, following the procession through the Liberties that Strathnairn had feared. The streets were crowded with cheering people, but no untoward incident occurred, though there had been threatening letters. In the Cathedral the crush was fearful: obviously, Mayo's instructions had been carried out beyond the letter. One newspaper said that when the doors were opened at 12 o'clock 'a *mob* of ladies and gentlemen immediately began to throng the building'. By the time the installation ended, hours afterwards, they were in no fit condition to enjoy Haydn's *Creation* sung, it was said, by a splendid choir. The 'mob' stood up during the entire performance, most of them on their seats, and there were cries of 'sit down, sit down'. The Prince, in his newly assumed Patrician regalia, sat still in his stall, and seldom looked down to the people who wanted to see him to the exclusion of all else. That night at a banquet in St Patrick's Hall in the Castle, he said he was deeply gratified by the reception he and the Princess had received, not only from the higher classes, but from the sons of the soil as well. After the sad times of the past year it might perhaps have been thought by some people that their reception would not have been all that could have been wished. He himself had felt confident that it would, and his hopes had been, indeed, realised.

After a week-end respite for the royal party Strathnairn staged a military review in the Phoenix Park, and a Grand Ball was given by the Lord Lieutenant. On the following day, after the unveiling of an Edmund Burke statue at Trinity College and a call at the Royal Irish Academy, the Prince went to the Catholic University. He was met there by the Chancellor, Cardinal Cullen, and escorted via the library where he saw the likeness of John Henry Newman, the University's first rector, to the Science Hall in which a throne had been erected for him under a large portrait of the reigning Pope, Pius IX. Here, with the Cardinal on his right and the Lord Lieutenant on his left, a distinguished Catholic company was presented to him, and it was noted that he bowed in a marked manner to 'the apostle of temperance in Ireland', the Carmelite Dr Spratt. After seeing the University church the Prince shook hands warmly with the Cardinal and was cheered loudly by the waiting crowds as he drove away.

Was undue attention being paid to the Cardinal? Was he being given precedence over the Protestant Archbishop of Dublin? Was it true that he was being treated as if he ranked next to the royal family? The idea gained adherence from a *Freeman's Journal* report which said that 'the Roman Catholic Prelate of this diocese is invited, with every circumstance of honour and respect, to share the Viceregal festivities, by his proper designation. "The Cardinal Archbishop of Dublin" is invited to meet the eldest son of the Sovereign, the future King of these realms and his illustrious consort' (20.4.1868). This set tongues wagging, inspired parliamentary questions and started a flurry in official circles.

Was not this of a pattern with what had happened the previous year in the wake of the Kerry disorders when the Cardinal and the Viceroy first met at the Mansion House? *The Times* had reported the occasion (22.2.1867):

> There was Archbishop Cullen . . . in his Cardinal's robes and red hat, ascending the dais . . . next after the Lord Lieutenant, having on his arm the sister of the ex-Prime Minister (Lord Russell), and chatting pleasantly with Lady Abercorn. . . . Lord Abercorn has been a bit of an Orangeman in his day, and there was a time when the portals of the Mansion House might have borne the famous inscription over the gates of Bandon [Jew, Turk, infidel and atheist may enter here, but no Papist]. But his lordship has seen the error of his ways, and a change has come over the festivities of the Round Room, and the lion and the lamb are taking turtle soup together like aldermen . . . The Archbishop of the English Church was not there . . .

Following that report Newdigate had tabled a motion in the House of Commons, and Mayo briefed Disraeli to deal with it. If Trench, the Protestant Archbishop, had been present, the Mayor would have proposed his health as 'Archbishop of Dublin' without any reserve. His absence had prevented this from being done. The Moderator of the General Assembly and many clergymen of all denominations were at the dinner, so that there was nothing in the slightest degree exclusive in Cullen's presence, and it was his person, and not his church, that was toasted. It was true that

Cullen was very much pleased, and even astonished, at the way he was treated, though this was nothing more than ordinary civility. (19)

Abercorn explained what had happened on the second occasion. The card of invitation had been correctly made out in favour of His Eminence Cardinal Cullen, which was the form Abercorn had used when writing earlier to him about the case of Bourke, the Fenian, but, by misadventure, the envelope was addressed to the Cardinal Archbishop of Dublin. Abercorn added that the invitation in any event was of no consequence, that he was presented to the Prince simply as 'Cardinal Cullen'. (20) Derby had told Mayo when the matter first came up in February 1867 that an extempore Cabinet had no doubt that Cullen should be recognised as Cardinal. This was a title, not even necessarily ecclesiastical, which had been admitted by a Committee of the House of Commons before which 'Cardinal' Wiseman appeared and which had examined him in that capacity. (21)

(3)

Apart from that little difficulty the Royal visit was an unqualified success. On his last night in Dublin the Prince further enlarged his swelling popularity by leaving the enclosure at the Great Ball in the Exhibition Palace and 'plunging into the eddies of the waltz' in the gay company of the four thousand who thronged the outer space. (22) The talk was renewed of establishing a royal residence in Ireland. On this subject Mayo sent an unusual letter to the Lord Lieutenant on the 26th April: its tone shows the relationship between the nominally subordinate Minister who was in the Cabinet to the personal representative of the Queen, who was not. Abercorn had done wonders during the visit; this Mayo acknowledged. Those who had been to Russia with the Prince of Wales said that 'his banquets beat the Muscovite' (22) but Mayo wanted something more significant from him. He wanted his firm backing for the proposal that had come into the open of setting the Prince up in Ireland in a house of his own. He wrote:

My dear Lord Abercorn,

Now that the great event of our administration is so well over we must really take advantage of it at once and endeavour to secure to Ireland that on which she has set her heart i.e., provision for the residence of the Prince of Wales in the country for a certain portion of the year. Now it is clearly our duty to press this in the strongest manner. I am prepared to push it to the utmost, and even as far as saying that we attach so much importance to it that it is scarcely fit that we should retain our offices if it is not done. Sir Colman O'Loghlin has already given notice of a motion on the subject: if we leave it in his hands we shall be in the position of voting against a proposal that we think right, and [that it] is our duty to make ourselves. The question is certain to be discussed immediately in the House of Commons and nothing will tempt me to speak against it. I hope therefore that you will write by the very next post to Disraeli, telling him that this question has now become one of the greatest moment and that he must tell the Queen without reserve that as her principal minister he cannot resist the demand made by the Irish Government backed by the whole voice of the Irish people. Write moderately but firmly. The best proposal would be that for the present year H.R.H. should occupy our Lodge—in order that he might personally superintend the arrangements for acquiring a suitable residence. He would take much more interest in the matter if he had something to do with the selection of the place and the alterations which would be necessary in any house which would be bought. Now do not lose a moment in writing this to Disraeli: there will probably be a Cabinet on Wednesday and I shall mention the question then. . . . Ever yours truly,

Mayo (24)

While the Prince was disporting himself in Ireland, a Fenian tried to kill his brother, the Duke of Edinburgh, in Australia, as a reprisal for the November executions, putting a bullet between his ribs at a public picnic when he was about to present a cheque for charity. The act confirmed the view the Queen had accepted from Lord Abercorn that the Irish lower orders were a peculiar, and rather treacherous people, so unlike the loyal Scotch.

(24) The royal visit to Ireland had ended before the news reached the country, happily, Larcom thought. 'Had it come while the Prince was here,' he said, 'go and do likewise would have been the first feeling in every Fenian heart.' It was nevertheless a terrible thing and might not long remain a solitary case. It would also not be without effect in frightening informers, as the Colonies could not long be counted on for a refuge. (26)

The Prime Minister expressed to the Queen the abhorrence of the House of Commons at the attempted assassination of the Duke and, in the same letter, told of his meeting with the Prince of Wales on his return from Ireland. Not only had all the circumstances connected with the Prince's visit been most gratifying but the Princess, notwithstanding all the fatigue and excitement to which she had been subjected, had returned in even better health than on her departure. Whatever doubts might be entertained of the *permanency* of Irish feeling, there could be no doubt but that the reception of His Royal Highness indicated a genuine, and even enthusiastic, spirit of loyalty on the part of the great mass of the community, which deserved any encouragement that could be given to it. (27) That was as far as Derby would go at the moment as regards the question of a royal residence.

If the royal visit restored their sense of euphoria to 'the well-affected', it failed to confer on the government party the political benefit they hoped for, and it most certainly did not change the attitude of 'the lower orders'. But things were quiet on the Fenian front; from March 1868 onwards Larcom had little to report, though he was none too sanguine about the long-term prospects. From America he was receiving news of 'clouds gathering', and the venom was still alive in Ireland. The vitality of the Fenian organisation and the spring that gave it motion lay, he told the Chief Secretary, in the utter hatred of England which for generations to come would, he feared, be ineradicable. The Phoenix, the name and symbol the Fenians had adopted, was most appropriate. What was needed to deal with recurring disorders was not a Suspensory Bill but a Suspensory Bandage, the case being one of rupture. (28) This was an entirely accurate prognosis. But for the time being all was quiet; indeed after the

Fenian fever of the previous two years, constitutional conflicts appeared flat to the masses. (29)

(4)

1868 was an election year: hence the Government's hope that the visit of the Prince would enhance their political fortunes. Hence also their concern to uncover the nature of a conspiracy between the Liberals and the Catholic hierarchy that it had been suggested to them existed. They were a minority government, holding office merely on sufferance, and the future looked bleak for them. However, no election is lost until the votes cast are counted, and the Tories naturally missed no opportunity to recapture the support they had previously enjoyed in Ireland. In the circumstances of 1868 this proved to be an immense task, particularly after Gladstone carried a resolution in the House of Commons in favour of the disestablishment of the Church of Ireland and of a measure of disendowment. This, Gladstone acknowledged, was an essential first step towards the reconciliation of Ireland.

What was the Liberal Party to get in return from the Irish bishops? This was what the Tories badly wanted to know, and they employed an English Catholic named Trelawney to find out. Trelawney had earlier worked for Lieutenant Colonel Feilding on the detection of Fenian secrets; it was now presumably expected, on his own suggestion, that he would uncover something with which to horrify the electorate. Lord Mayo, who was the first to inspect Trelawney, told Disraeli, who took a close personal interest in the assignment, that the young man's appearance was magnificent: he had a round English face, very fair hair and small strong blue eyes that made one believe he was a little shop boy or an usher in school. But he was born with half a dozen languages in his mouth, spoke French, German and Italian without accent, and when turned loose into a foreign town without introduction was generally found to be on important terms with a Cabinet Minister or a Cardinal within a week. 'You will see by his note,' Mayo said, 'that he proposes to follow a good scent and take a line which might give us most important news. Feilding says that his powers of investigation are quite extraordinary and that if the negotiations to which he refers *are* going on he cannot fail to find them out . . .' (30)

Trelawney's good scent was an introduction Lord Denbigh gave him to Bishop Moriarty, in whose house he met the Dean of Limerick, Monsignor R. B. O'Brien, 'a very talkative man' whom he drew out on the subject of Gladstone as an instrument of the Church of Rome. He found the Monsignor a dangerous opponent of the Conservative Administration who declared his party's intention of following up disestablishment with the Repeat of the Union. Moriarty told Trelawney that the priests had set their minds on the abolition of the Protestant establishment and, being of the people, they wielded immense influence. He had been in communication with Gladstone, who would not commit himself to a guarantee that the Catholic Church would receive material profit from the disestablishment proposals. Catholic sympathy for the Liberals was limited to this question. Feilding desired Trelawney to get a good introduction to Mr William Monsell, the leading Irish Catholic Liberal, and to Father Patrick Lavelle, the notorious Fenian priest; a letter Monsignor O'Brien wrote for him went beyond his expectations. With it Trelawney would tackle Father Lavelle 'after sucking Mr Monsell dry'.

An introduction from Monsignor O'Brien also enabled him to see Cardinal Cullen twice in Dublin. The Cardinal conversed freely on Ireland and spoke of the blindness of successive administrations with regard to Irish affairs and their audacious favouritism towards Protestants. His sympathy lay with the Liberals, as far as the measures of justice to Ireland to which they were pledged were concerned, and which 'we will take care', he said, 'they will redeem'. He sent Trelawney to see various Catholic schools, where he was astonished at the remarkable forward state of the children and the formidable anti-English feeling that was growing up among them. He dined with the Cardinal one evening and found him suave and affable beyond measure.

I sat at his right . . . and he talked to me the whole time, about Rome, books, Irish history and the future of Ireland according to his expectations. He pressed me very much to prolong my stay in Ireland so as to acquire a better knowledge of the country and people and asked me to call on him again. . . . In the course of conversation I said—suppose the Liberals, after all the indispensable support you have given them, were to deceive you (I said 'us') and do no more than carry out the mere disestablishment. 'Oh,' said Dr Doran, one of His Excellency's secretaries and a monsignor of the Papal Court, 'we will take great care of that, and *we run no risk* I assure you', and the Cardinal added, laughing, that 'it would be rather too bad if we did . . .' (31)

Trelawney's reports, ten in all, duly sent to Disraeli, disclosed nothing that was not already widely known, and certainly uncovered no plot of any kind.

When the general election took place towards the end of 1868, it was fought on the disestablishment issue, the pro-Liberal sentiment running so strongly that Bishop Moriarty told a Conservative candidate that the Pope himself, if he went forward as a Disraeli-ite, would be rejected. And when Ireland filled 65 of the 105 seats with Liberals to swell their over-all majority, he told Gladstone, in a congratulatory letter, that since the days of O'Connell the public mind had never been so deeply stirred nor the people's fate so trustingly given as it now was to him. (32)

Gladstone had already begun to look beyond disestablishment for a fuller reconciliation with Ireland, and the crude, blundering idealism of the Fenians played a part in the development of his thinking on the subject. The Clerkenwell explosion had shocked, angered and frightened the British people, but it reminded Gladstone, and he in turn reminded the people of Britain, of Ireland's grievances and of their obligations to remedy them. When this was done, instead of hearing in every corner of Europe the most painful comments on the policy of England towards Ireland, they might be able to look their fellow-Europeans in the face. And in approaching Irish problems, it was important to consider Irish ideas. So, after disestablishing the Anglican Church in Ireland Gladstone concerned himself with

Ireland's agrarian problems, and moved on gradually to espouse a policy of Home Rule. The Irish unionist lawyer Isaac Butt developed along similar lines. Out of admiration for the Fenian prisoners he had defended, he played a leading role in the subsequent amnesty campaign and then became the leader of a Home Rule movement whose principal achievement, perhaps, was to bring Charles Stewart Parnell into political life. To put the situation in perspective. however, it must be said that, while the activities of the Fenians helped to quicken the determination of Gladstone and Butt to do something for Ireland, it was the Catholic community led by the bishops who brought agitation for disestablishment and other reforms to the point at which concessions had to be made. It must also be said that the Fenians showed no interest in disestablishment despite the side-effects of their activities. They even opposed Gladstone's Land Bill of 1870, presumably because it obscured their own radical objectives. And needless to say, neither the Liberals nor the bishops felt under any obligation to the Fenians, and showed this by their actions. Gladstone propped up his Land Bill with a Peace Preservation Act, designed to control disorders for which the Fenians were blamed, while the bishops gave wide publicity to a belated Papal Decree condemning Fenianism.

(5)

A change in the Administration of Ireland was the immediate result of the election. Abercorn was replaced in the Lord Lieutenancy by Earl Spencer and, after a brief interregnum, Chichester Fortescue returned to the Chief Secretaryship. Egged on by his wife, he had pressed for the Colonial Secretaryship but, complaining bitterly, had to be satisfied with the unwelcome Irish post. (33) Kimberley became Lord Privy Seal in the new government, a second step on the road to the Foreign Secretaryship which he held towards the close of the century. When Lord Lieutenant of Ireland he had been described as 'the best clerk in the office' a tribute, though that was not intended, to the fact that he immersed himself in all the problems of the office, big and small, and strove for greater efficiency all round. Though Ireland was no longer his especial concern he maintained a close interest in her affairs and was anxious about Gladstone's appointments to the Irish Executive. He was pleased when Lord Spencer, and not Lord Dufferin, was chosen as Viceroy with Chichester Fortescue as his Chief Secretary. 'It would have been a mistake to place the Irish government entirely in the hands of two Irishmen, neither of them possessing much backbone.' (34)

Ireland presented to him a miserable spectacle, but he recognised that England for her own safety would have to continue to hold her, no matter what happened, while of course leaving no remedial measures untried. Past misgovernment had aggravated the ills from which the country suffered but the true source of Irish unhappiness was the character of the Irish race. The election of O'Donovan Rossa to be member of the House of Commons for Tipperary was an example, but just what might be expected from the ruffians who inhabited that county. 'Their blind and ignorant hatred of England is fitly represented by the rowdy felon they have chosen. What a descent from Grattan and O'Connell, or even Wolfe Tone and Emmet.' (35) Gladstone was living in the happy delusion that his policy would produce a speedy change in the temper of the Irish towards England. He would soon find out his mistake. In Portland Kimberley saw amongst the Fenian prisoners he had helped to lock up Luby, O'Leary and McCafferty. They looked well but defiant, and the Governor found them quite unmanageable. Nevertheless Kimberley thought that as political prisoners they were entitled to a better deal than they were getting. It was quite sufficient to imprison them, without treating them on the level of thieves and murderers. (36)

Within months of assuming office the new Cabinet was extremely worried over their relations with the United States, which the Fenians over the years had helped to worsen. Kimberley described one gloomy discussion when nearly all the Ministers were of opinion that it would be impossible to defend Canada successfully against the Americans and that it was much to be desired that Canada should become independent. It would be for the interest both of England and Canada and Kimberley explained why.

> We should be relieved from a constant source of weakness and danger, and the Canadians would then have nothing to fear from the United States, whose ill-will to Canada arises from a desire to injure us, and would cease when Canada no longer formed a part of the British Empire. There is no reason why an independent Canada should not be on equally good terms with both nations. Meanwhile what is to be our present policy? The United States are bent on humiliating England. Our means of damaging them in a war are much less than theirs of damaging us. Our Empire lies scattered all over the world. Our merchant ships cover every sea. They on the contrary inhabit a continent, where for thousands of miles our contiguous territory lies open to attack, whilst their merchant navy is far inferior to ours.

Such were the arguments in the Cabinet, and Kimberley recognised how plausible they were, and how they were used to justify England's timorous attitude towards the United States. In spite of all this, he was personally convinced that their wisest policy was to show a firm front and to make no further concessions. 'Unscrupulous and arrogant as the Americans are,' he wrote in his Journal, 'I am convinced they will hesitate to incur the risk of war, unless indeed we should be involved in a European contest.' (37)

(6)

Before the 1868 General Election Mayo, who had been suffering from 'the strain of his incessant labours', was appointed Viceroy of India, and was confirmed in that post by the new Government. Disraeli had recognised his services in Ireland where, as he said, 'a state of affairs so dangerous was never encountered with greater firmness, but at the same time with magnanimity'. Mayo had sought a change.

> Ireland is an infernal country to manage ... Impartiality is im-

possible, statesmanship wholly out of place. The only way to govern is the old plan (wihch I will never attempt) of taking up violently one faction or the other, putting them like fighting cocks and then backing one. I wish you would send me to India. Ireland is the grave of every reputation.*

There was another consideration. 'Though I have no debts,' he said, 'I find I have an income wholly insufficient for my position and much smaller than I expected.' (38) The appointment was publicly assailed but Mayo assured Disraeli that once he got to India he would show his countrymen that the 'malicious scribblers' were wrong. As he left the shores of England he said his farewell. 'You have made me what I am.' he told Disraeli, 'You can do nothing more for me, except keep me in remembrance. I know I shall have a brilliant career, and will make men feel that you made no mistake in sending me to India.' (39) Among the friendly notes he received was one from Sir J. Bernard Burke, the Ulster King of Arms, enclosing Mayo's 'shield of quarterings, the collar of the Star of India and the ribbon of our own St Patrick. This last will remind you,' Burke said, ' of that grand ceremonial which originated with you, and which tended so much to the increase of the splendour of the Order, and of the popular enthusiasm for loyalty and patriotic feeling.' (40) And Major General Cunyngham, likewise looking back, mentioned that another Punchestown meeting had come and gone, 'but lacked the great éclat of the Prince's presence'. (41)

But the decision to send Mayo to India was an unlucky one, for in 1872 an assassin's knife brought his career to a sudden and bloody end whilst he was inspecting a convict settlement in the Andaman Islands. What the Fenians had left undone was thus accomplished in an unexpected setting. Somewhat dull and heavy, he was in no way a man of first-rate powers, Kimberley thought, and the manner of his death raised him to a pedestal of fame altogether beyond his merits. (42)

* To a brother who had just entered Parliament for an English constituency he wrote about this time: 'I advise you to leave Ireland alone. There is no credit to be got by interfering with her politics . . .' (*Life of Earl of Mayo*: W. W. Hunter, 1891, p. 54.)

Mayo's appointment to India enabled Larcom to leave the public scene. In his case it was a simple matter of acknowledging his years, of taking his substantial pension and accepting 'deliverance from this frightful life in office'. He had raised the question of honours for the police chiefs, Wood and Lake, and for Sir Bernard Burke, the Ulster King of Arms who had done so much to make the royal visit a success, and he prodded Mayo for some recognition for himself. Mayo acted immediately and handsomely, and gave an assurance that before he left Europe Larcom would be a baronet and a member of the Irish Privy Council. Never was release from labour better earned or honour more fairly won, he said. Ireland was losing her most faithful servant, and it would be impossible to replace him. Ever zealous and laborious [sic], calm in danger, cautious and courageous, Larcom had been in troublous and anxious times the mainstay of the Irish Government. (43)

These were words Lord Kimberley endorsed. With the Liberals on their way back into office Larcom did not want to be asked to stay on for a further spell. Fenianism was as calm as it was likely to be in that generation, he told Kimberley, but he dreaded another winter like the previous three, when, day and night, he had had to labour ceaselessly to undo the work of the Fenians. He was now being visited with that constant fainting and collapse that in 1858 had pretty nearly put an end to him. Kimberley saw the point. There was such a thing as a willing horse being worked to death. (44)

(7)

Strathnairn found Spencer, the new Viceroy, very amiable and hospitable. 'I inaugurated him in the hunting field,' he told a friend, 'by lending him one of my best horses for the Meath Stag Hounds and he was delighted with him as were the Hunt. Some of the members said: "By Gad, if he governs Ireland after that fashion, divil a Fenian will there be after the hunting season." '

FF R

But for what was left of his term Strathnairn regretted that he could not hunt or go shooting woodcocks as often as he would have wished. The country was still too disturbed. There was too much agrarianism, too much intimidation, too many death notices being served, an occasional murder and too many inflammatory speeches by priests. In 1870 reinforcements were again called for and the Flying Columns revived on the initiative of the Government. Strathnairn thought the politicians were unduly nervous, but he nevertheless geared the Columns to meet any eventuality. 'I have thought of everything from the smallest to the highest detail . . .' he wrote, 'from coffee and sugar to the relief of the men of the columns when required.' The Columns did not go into action on this occasion, and in May 1870, as Strathnairn was preparing to quit Ireland for good, they were disbanded.

Strathnairn was looking forward to an active career in the House of Lords, and hoped to enlighten public opinion about the country he was leaving. He would always be happy, he said, to be an humble friend to Ireland and to advocate any measure which was for her welfare. Nothing, he thought, would conduct so much to that welfare as the charitable union of all sects; and on Home Rule, when it became an issue, he was more open-minded than most of his Tory associates. He advised some of them who were defeated in parliamentary elections on that issue not to react so stiffly. There was all the difference in the world, he said, between separation from England and what he saw as a modification of the Lord Lieutenancy. In other words, a safe degree of Home Rule was possible which would satisfy Protestant loyalists. If managed with tact it could conduct to the pacification of a distracted country and strengthen the Conservative Party. He reminded them that the Home Rule leader, Isaac Butt, was a Conservative and a Protestant; the Protestant element in Butt's party were chiefly Conservative, some of them Orangemen, others staunch Protestants, all of them devoted to Britain. This was a great improvement, an acceptable alternative to Fenian republicanism and the Repeal of the Union alike. But he left behind him a larger distribution of troops than he had countenanced in 1867. Major General Cunyngham, writing to Mayo almost gleefully, reported

that there was now an immense number of detachments all over
Ireland, for 'during the last year our Commander of the Forces
has even sent out more than the Government requested, reversing
the plan for [sic] to which he took so much exception to my
doing, at your desire, by increasing the outer small stations. The
country is very quiet—they of course delight in having the troops,
and if a company is withdrawn, protest most vehemently.' (45)

(8)

Our story began with Stephens; it can well end with him.
The Dublin police never lost interest in the man and reported
every scrap of information about him that came their way. The
failure of the 1867 rising and talk of embezzlement in the higher
Fenian ranks had caused a revival of confidence in him. He had
never been deserted by the 'Old Guard' and there were converts
from other groups during the Franco-Prussian War when 'the
Captain', as he was often called, showed signs of re-asserting
himself. The war had awakened in Ireland an old enthusiasm for
republican France: men volunteered for service in the French
army in contravention of the Foreign Enlistment Act, an ambul-
ance brigade was fitted out and despatched, and Stephens,
through his Dublin contacts, raised hopes that French Republicans
would recognise the Irish Republicans. Indeed a day might come
when Ireland would be a partner in a Federal Republic of Europe.
To provide him with the money he needed to develop his plans,
some three thousand people paid for admission to a concert in the
Rotunda in Dublin, at which the *Marseillaise* was sung, but the
police learned that half the proceeds were to be spent on bringing
in arms that were concealed in Liverpool. (46) Nothing came of all
this, and Stephens in 1871 began a long precarious odyssey which
took him backwards and forwards between France and America
several times before he was finally permitted by the British
Government, through the intervention of Parnell, to return to
Ireland in the late eighteen-eighties. There he lived in retirement

until his death. He made an effort during his last visit to the United States to regain the lost leadership but this ended in failure. The American Fenians were badly riven: other attacks on Canada in 1870 and 1871 failed hopelessly, and some of Stephens's former lieutenants, returning from prisons and convict settlements, though recognising the need for reunions, would have nothing to do with him. At the time of his death in 1901, however, the Irish Republican Brotherhood, the Irish Fenian wing, which he had created and whose first leader he had been, was at the beginning of a revival. New men were coming forward to take up the leadership and to continue the old fight; their initial failure and final substantial success are now the subject of many books.

Notes

CHAPTER I

1. Clarendon Deposit, c. 143, 25. 11.1865. **2.** Fenian Papers, Police Reports, 19.8.1864 and 12.9.1864. **3.** Devoy, *Recollections of an Irish Rebel*, 55. **4.** Fenian Papers, 8.5.1865. **5.** Clarendon Deposit, c. 99, 26.2.1865. **6.** Ibid. **7.** Ibid., 14.5.1865. **8.** Ibid., 23.6.1865. **9.** Ibid., Wodehouse to Clarendon, 20.9.1865. **10.** Chief Secretary's Office Registered Papers, 1865/7556. **11.** Ibid. 1866/14212. **12.** Ibid. 1866/20355. **13.** Clarendon Deposit, c. 99, 11.11.65.

CHAPTER II

1. Anderson Papers, Ms. 5964. **2.** Ibid. **3.** Ibid. **4.** Ibid. **5.** Ibid. **6.** Ibid. **7.** Ibid. **8.** Ibid. **9.** Ibid. **10.** Ibid. **11.** Devoy, *Recollections of an Irish Rebel*, 75. **12.** A files 78, 6.1.1866. **13.** Fenian Papers, Police Reports, 12.11.1865. **14.** Clarendon Deposit, c. 99, Wodehouse to Clarendon, 27.11.1865. **15.** Ibid., 5.12.1865. **16.** Ibid., 28.2.1866. **17.** Ibid., 29.3.1866. **18.** Devoy, op. cit., 87. **19.** Larcom Papers, Ms. 7517. **20.** Devoy, op. cit., 94–96. **21.** Ibid. 65. **22.** Ibid. 115.

CHAPTER III

1. Strathnairn Papers, B.M. Add. Mss. 42825, Rose to Wodehouse, 30.11.1865. **2.** Ibid., 11.12.1865. **3.** Ibid. 42830, to Spencer, 20.12.1869. **4.** Ibid., 42824, Rose to Cambridge, 27.1.1866. **5.** Ibid., 3.1.1866. **6.** Ibid. **7.** Ibid., 21.6.1866. **8.** Ibid., 3.1.1866. **9.** Devoy, *Recollections of an Irish Rebel*, 149. **10.** Strathnairn Papers., B.M. Add. Mss. 42829, to Cambridge, 2.4.1868. **11.** Ibid. 42325, to Cambridge, 18.6.1865. **12.** Ibid., to Wodehouse, 6.12.1865. **13.** Ibid., B.M. Add. Mss. 42824, 10.12.1865. **14.** Ibid., 13.12.1865. **15.** Ibid., 12.12.1865. **16.** A Files 30, 29.9.1865. **17.** A files 34, 7.10.1865. **18.** A files 36, 10.10.1865. **19.** A files 37, 14.10.1865. **20.** A files 42, 24.10,1865. **21.** A files 54–57 18.11.1865 to 23.11.1865. **22.** A files 65, 9.12.1865. **23.** A files 84, 13.1.1866. **24.** A files 88, 20,1.1866. **25.** A files 90, 26.1.1866. **26.** A files 93, 24.1.1866. **27.** Clarendon Deposit, c. 99, 11.11.1865. **28.** Mac Giolla Choille, *Fenian Documents in the State Paper Office*, 273. **29.** Clarendon Deposit, c. 143, 24.4.1866. **30.** Ibid., c. 99, Wodehouse to

Clarendon, 5.4.1866. **31.** Ryan, *Fenian Chief*, 236. **32.** Ibid. 231. **33.** A files 120. **34.** A files 123. **35.** A files 124, 16.7.1866 and 17.7.1866. **36.** A files 125. **37.** Between A files 129 and 130, 2–4 April 1866.

CHAPTER IV

1. D'Arcy, *The Fenian Movement in the United States*, 84–85. **2.** A files 51, Bruce to Clarendon, 31.10.1865. **3.** Ibid., Clarendon to Bruce, 7.11.1865. **4.** Ibid. **5.** A files 53, 14.11.1865. **6.** Clarendon Deposit, c. 90, Bruce to Clarendon, 10.3.1866. **7.** A files 53, 14.11.1865. **8.** A files 87, Bruce to Clarendon, 8.1.1866; and Clarendon Deposit, c. 143, Clarendon to Gladstone, 14.2.1866. **9.** Clarendon Deposit, c. 90, 12.12.1865 and 26.12.1865. **10.** Ibid., 31.12.1865; and D'Arcy, op. cit., 110. **11.** Clarendon Deposit, c. 142, 16.12.1865. **12.** Ibid., 13.1.1866. **13.** Ibid., 3.2.1866. **14.** Clarendon Deposit, c. 90, 9.1.1866. **15.** Ibid., 9.2.1866. **16.** Clarendon Deposit, c. 142, 6.1.1866. **17.** Clarendon Deposit, c. 90, 9.2.1866. **18.** Clarendon Deposit, c. 143, 14.2.1866. **19.** Clarendon Deposit, c. 90, 10.3.1866. **20.** Clarendon Deposit, c. 142, 24.2.1866. **21.** Ibid., 3.3.1866. **22.** Ibid., 24.3.1866 and 31.3.1866. **23.** Ibid., 31.3.1866. **24.** Ibid., 7.4.1866. **25.** A files 96–98, 3.2.1866 to 9.2.1866. **26.** A files 99, 13.2.1866. **27.** A files 96 and 97, 3.4.1866 and 4.2.1866. **28.** A files 109, 2.3.1866. **29.** A files 129, 3.4.1866. **30.** A files 130, 6.4.1866. **31.** A files 129, 3.4.1866. **32.** A files 131. **33.** D'Arcy, op. cit., 140–141. **34.** A files 139, 28.4.1866. **35.** Clarendon Deposit, c. 90, Bruce to Clarendon, 23.4.1866. **36.** Clarendon Deposit, c. 142, 14.4.1866. **37.** Clarendon Deposit, c. 99, 21.2.1866 and 16.3.1866. **38.** Ibid., 8.4.1866. **39.** Ibid., 14.4.1866. **40.** Clarendon Deposit, c. 142, 19.5.1866. **41.** A files 150, 18.5.1866. **42.** A files 145. **43.** Ibid., 11.5.1866. **44.** A files 149, 16.5.1866. **45.** A files 150, 18.5.1866. **46.** A files 156, 2.6.1866. **47.** Ibid. **48.** A files 157, 158, 159, 5.6.1866 to 12.6.1866; and Clarendon Deposit, c. 90, 4.6.1866. **49.** D'Arcy, op. cit., 159. **50.** Ibid., 169. **51.** A files 165, despatch of 13.6.1866. **52.** Ibid. **53.** A files 165, Bruce to Monck, 15.6.1866. **54.** A files 165, 18.6.1866. **55.** Clarendon Deposit, c. 142. **56.** Clarendon Deposit, c. 99, 4.6.1866 and 20.6.1866. **57.** Clarendon Deposit, c. 142. 30.6.1866. **58.** Ibid., 7.7.1866. **59.** Clarendon Deposit, c. 90, 22.7.1866.

CHAPTER V

1. Clarendon Deposit, c. 99, 12.7.1866. **2.** Derby Papers, 191/1, 10.7.1866. **3.** Larcom Papers, Ms. 11191, undated (sometime in

October 1868). **4.** Derby Papers 191/2, 18.8.1866. **5.** Larcom Papers, Ms. 7590, 5.7.1866. **6.** Mayo Papers, Ms. 11144, 27.8.1866. **7.** Derby Papers 155/2, Naas to Derby, 20.8.1866, 31.8.1866 and 3.9.1866. **8.** Mayo Papers, Ms. 11144, Derby to Naas, 6.9.1866. **9.** Derby Papers 155/2, 31.8.1866. **10.** Ibid., 3.9.1866. **11.** Devoy, *Recollections of an Irish Rebel*, 156. **12.** Mayo Papers, Ms. 11188. **13.** Ibid., 17.9.1866. **14.** Chief Sec. Off. Reg. Papers, 1866/22285. **15.** Devoy, op. cit., 157, 183. **16.** Chief Sec. Off. Reg. Papers, 1866/19362 and 20355. **17.** Larcom Papers, Ms. 7517. **18.** Chief Sec. Off. Reg. Papers, 1866/21218. **19.** Derby Papers 155/2, 3.9.1866.

CHAPTER VI

1. A files 224, 27.10.1866. **2.** Ibid., Bruce to Stanley, 30,10,1866. **3.** Ibid., Bruce to Seward, 18.11.1866. **4.** Ibid., 19.11.1866. **5.** Derby Papers 161/2, 10.11.1866. **6.** A files 169, 14.7.1866. **7.** A files 166. **8.** A files 169 and 175, 14.7.1866 and 3.8.1866. **9.** A files 176, 10.8.1866. **10.** A files 175 and 179, 3.8.1866 and 24.8.1866. **11.** A files 180, 28.8.1866. **12.** A files 182. **13.** A files 184, 14.9.1866. **14.** A files 189, 28.9.1866. **15.** A files 197, 26.10.1866. **16.** A files 200, 29.10.1866. **17.** A files 185, 18.9.1866. **18.** A files 186, 21.9.1866. **19.** A files 215, 16.11.1866. **20.** Ryan, *The Fenian Chief*, 238. **21.** Ibid. **22.** Ibid. 239. **23.** Larcom Papers, Ms. 7517 (a history of Fenianism probably compiled by Samuel Lee Anderson). **24.** A files 221, 27.11.1866. **25.** A files 233, 30.11.1866. **26.** A files 238, 7.12.1866. **27.** A files 223, 27.11.1866. **28.** Chief Sec. Off. Reg. Papers, 1867/13084, 19.7.1867; and Foreign Office Papers, 5/1110, Archibald to Stanley, 1.7.1867. **29.** Ryan and O'Brien (eds.), *Devoy's Post Bag*, Vol. 2, 299. **30.** Bussy, *Irish Conspiracies*, 161.

CHAPTER VII

1. Chief Sec. Off. Reg. Papers, 1866/21554. **2.** Ibid., 1866/21105. **3.** Ibid. 1866/20839. **4.** Ibid. 1866/21090. **5.** Ibid., 1866/22417. **6.** Ibid. 1866/21127. **7.** Montgomery Papers 627/252, 7.12.1866. **8.** Derby Papers 141/11, Pakington to Derby, 5.12.1866. **9.** Mayo Papers, Ms. 11189/3. **10.** Larcom Papers, Ms. 7590. **11.** Mayo Papers, Ms. 11189/2. **12.** Ibid., Ms. 11189/9. **13.** Ibid. **14.** Derby Papers 155/2, 25 11.1866. **15.** Ibid., 27.11.1866. **16.** Mayo Papers, Ms. 11189/4, 26.11.1866. **17.** Strathnairn Papers, B.M. Add. Mss. 42826, Strathnairn to Lt.-Gen.

Peel, 26.11.1866. **18.** Mayo Papers, Ms. 111888/2. **19.** Larcom Papers, Ms. 7590, Nov. 1866. **20.** Strathnairn Papers, B.M. Add. Mss. 42826. **21.** Ibid., Rose to Wodehouse, 24.2.1866. **22.** Derby Papers 153/3, 3.7.1866. **23.** Mayo Papers, Ms. 11144. **24.** Derby Papers 155/3, to Derby, 10.6.1866. **25.** Ibid., 9.12.1866. **26.** Ibid. 192/1, 16.12.1866. **27.** Strathnairn Papers, B.M. Add. Mss. 42826, to Col. Somerset, 29.11.1866. **28.** Ibid., 15.12.1866. **29.** Chief Sec. Off. Reg. Papers, 1866/22375. **30.** *The Times*, 24.12.1866. **31.** Chief Sec. Off. Reg. Papers, 1866/21912. **32.** Ibid. 1866/23144, to Military Sec., 22.12.1866. **33.** Mayo Papers, Ms. 11188/6, 23.12.1866. **34.** Derby Papers 192/1, 24.12.1866. **35.** Ibid. 155/2, 4.1.1867. **36.** Larcom Papers, Ms. 7590, de Gernon to Larcom. **37.** Ibid., 1.1.1867. **38.** Ibid., 6.1.1867 and 16.1.1867. **39.** Ibid., 28.1.1867. **40.** Mayo Papers, Ms. 11150. **41.** Larcom Papers, Ms. 7590, 15.2.1867. **42.** Ibid., 12.2.1867.

CHAPTER VIII

1. Larcom Papers, Ms. 7517. **2.** D'Arcy, *The Fenian Movement in the United States*, 224. **3.** Ibid., 220. **4.** Ibid. 225. **5.** Larcom Papers, P. J. Murray (of Prisons Service) to Larcom, 5.1.1867. **6.** Strathnairn Papers, B.M. Add. Mss. 42828, to Col. Sir E. Wetherell, 21.9.1867. **7.** Fenian Papers, F. 2185. **8.** Larcom Papers, Ms. 11191/1, 13.1.1867. **9.** Ibid., 14.1.1867. **10.** Fenian Papers, F. 2361. **11.** Ibid., F. 2528. **12.** Mayo Papers, Ms. 11188. **13.** Fenian Papers, F. 2292. **14.** Ibid., F. 2228. **15.** Larcom Papers, Ms. 11191/1, to Naas, 20.1.1867. **16.** Ibid., Ms. 11150, 30.1.1867. **17.** Larcom Papers, Ms. 7517; and D'Arcy. op. cit., 251–252. **18.** Larcom Papers, Ms. 7517. **19.** Ibid. **20.** D'Arcy, op. cit., 251–252. **21.** Fenian Papers, F. 2473 and 2455. **22.** Ibid., F. 2379. **23.** Chief Sec. Off. Reg. Papers, 1867/6870. **24.** Larcom Papers, Ms. 7517. **25.** *Irish Times*, 19.2.1867. **26.** Devoy, *Recollections of an Irish Rebel*, 181. **27.** Fenian Papers, F. 3564. **28.** Mayo Papers, Cambridge: enclosure to letter from Cunyngham, 16.6.1870. **29.** Larcom Papers, Ms. 11191/4, Larcom to Naas, 23.2.1867; and Strathnairn Papers, B.M. Add. Mss. 42826, Strathnairn to Naas, 15.2.1867. **30.** Kilmainham Papers, quoted by Curzon to Larcom, 4.3.1867. **31.** Strathnairn Papers, B.M. Add. Mss. 42826, 4.3.1867. **32.** Fenian Papers, F. 2477. **33.** Ibid., F. 2413. **34.** Mayo Papers, Ms. 11150, Lord Denbigh to Mayo, 5.9.1867. **35.** Ibid., Longfield to Naas, 23.2.1867. **36.** *Irish Times*, 19.2.1867. **37.** Derby Papers, 155/3, Naas to Derby, 24.1.1867. **38.** Ibid., 20.1.1867. **39.** Ibid. **40.** Clarendon Deposit,

c. 143, 4.6.1866. **41.** Bodleian Ms., file 468, March 1866. **42.** Ibids, 26.3.1866. **43.** Quoted from Clarendon Papers in E. R. Norman'. *The Catholic Church and Ireland in the Age of Rebellion*, 129–130. **44.** Larcom Papers, Ms. 11191/3, to Naas. **45.** Ibid., Ms. 11191/4, 21.2.1867. **46.** Mayo Papers, Ms. 11153, to Naas, 18.2.1867 and 19.2.1867. **47.** Chief Sec. Off. Reg. Papers, 1867/3004; and Fenian Papers, F. 2391. **48.** Larcom Papers, Ms. 11191/4. **49.** Chief Sec. Off. Reg. Papers, 1867/3086, 22.2.1867. **50.** Fenian Papers, F. 3563. **51.** Ibid., F. 2542. **52.** Chief Sec. Off. Reg. Papers, 1867/6341. **53.** Ibid., 1867/6352. **54.** Larcom Papers, Ms. 11191/1, 12.1.1867 and 20.1.1867.

CHAPTER IX

1. Mayo Papers, Ms. 11153, 28.2.1867. **2.** Larcom Papers, Ms. 11191/4. **3.** Ibid., Ms. 7517. **4.** Government Letter Book, 1867. **5.** Chief Sec. Off. Reg. Papers, 1867/10079. **6.** Anderson, *Sidelights on the Home Rule Movement*, 71. **7.** Chief Sec. Off. Reg. Papers, 1867/10078 and 10256. **8.** Mayo Papers, Ms. 11153, 5.3.1867. **9.** Fenian Papers, F. 2444. **10.** Larcom Papers, Ms. 11191/5. **11.** Ibid. **12.** Ibid. **13.** Chief Sec. Off. Reg. Papers, 1867/3475 and 3536. **14.** Ibid. 1867/3476. **15.** Ibid. 1867/14141 and 21588. **16.** Ibid. 1867/3820. **17.** Ibid. 1867/3750 and 3821. **18.** Ibid. 1867/3821. **19.** Ibid. 1867/6011 and 6809. **20.** Ibid. 1867/6011 and 3819. **21.** Ibid. 1867/3819. **22.** Ibid. 1867/4783. **23.** Kilmainham Papers, Strathnairn to Larcom, 5.3.1867. **24.** Kilmainham Papers, Ms. 1305, p. 347. **25.** Chief Sec. Off. Reg. Papers, 1867/3653. **26.** Kilmainham Papers, Strathnairn to Larcom, 5.3.1867. **27.** Ibid. **28.** Ibid., 8.3.1867. **29.** Derby Papers 155/2, 8.3.1867. **30.** Ibid. 192/1, 10.3.1867. **31.** Ibid. **32.** Mayo Papers, Ms. 11189, 9.3.1867. **33.** Ibid., 4.5.1867. **34.** Ibid., 11.3.1867. **35.** Strathnairn Papers, B.M. Add. Mss. 42826, 6.3.1867. **36.** Ibid., 6.3.1867. **37.** Chief Sec. Off. Reg. Papers, 1867/4527. **38.** Ibid. 1867/4715, 16.3.1867. **39.** Ibid. 1867/5624. **40.** Ibid. 1867/1737, 20.5.1867. **41.** Ibid. 1867/8894.

CHAPTER X

1. Chief Sec. Off. Reg. Papers, 1867/3682–3683. **2.** Larcom Papers, Ms. 7517. **3.** Chief Sec. Off. Reg. Papers, 1867/3731. **4.** Strathnairn Papers, B.M. Add. Mss. 42826, Strathnairn to Bates, 8.3.1867. **5.** Ibid., Strathnairn to Naas, 9.3.1867. **6.** Ibid., 9.3.1867 at 12 p.m. **7.** Chief Sec. Off. Reg. Papers, 1867/7568. **8.** Ibid. 1867/4537. **9.** Ibid. 1867/9163,

10. Ibid. 1867/7568. **11.** Larcom Papers, Ms. 11191/6, Larcom to Naas.
1.4.1867. **12.** Chief Sec. Off. Reg. Papers, 1867/8371, to Larcom,
1.5.1867. **13.** Ibid. **14.** Ibid. 1867/8957. **15.** Fenian Papers, F. 3597. **16.**
Ibid. **17.** Larcom Papers, Ms. 11191/4. **18.** Ibid., Ms. 11191/5. **19.**
Strathnairn Papers, B.M. Add. Mss. 42826, 16.3.1867. **20.** Ibid., to
Edmund Leahy, 16.7.1867. **21.** Ibid., 16.3.1867. **22.** Ibid., to A.G.,
Horse Guards, 22.7.1867. **23.** Mayo Papers, Cambridge, Cunyngham
to Mayo, 16.6.1870. **24.** Strathnairn Papers, B.M. Add. Mss. 42826,
20.3.1867. and 22.3.1867. **25.** Larcom Papers, Ms. 11191/8, 7.5.1867,
26. Chief Sec. Off. Reg. Papers, 1867/4737. **27.** Derby Papers, 193/2,
12.3.1867. **28.** Ibid. **29.** Fenian Papers, F. 3520, 2.4.1867. **30.** Ibid., to
Larcom, 4.4.1867. **31.** Ibid., 6.4.1867. **32.** Fenian Papers, F. 3520.

CHAPTER XI

1. Larcom Papers, Ms. 11191/8, to Naas, 10.5.1867. **2.** Ibid. **3.** Fenian
Papers, F. 3755. **4.** Ibid., F. 3785. **5.** Chief Sec. Off. Reg. Papers,
1867/9300. **6.** Ibid. 1867/9420. **7.** Ibid. 1867/9394. **8.** Ibid. 1867/9315.
9. A files 629. **10.** Ibid. 270. **11.** MacSuibhne, *Paul Cullen and his
contemporaries*, Vol. 3, 419–428. **12.** Mayo Papers, Ms. 11150. **13.**
A files 270, 28.5.1867. **14.** Derby Papers 146/4, 1.1.1868. **15.** Mayo
Papers, Ms. 11189, Walpole to Naas, 9.3.1867 and 11.3.1867. **16.**
Chief Sec. Off. Reg. Papers, 1867/4536. **17.** Ibid. 1867/4717. **18.**
D'Arcy, *The Fenian Movement in the United States*, 243. **19.** Larcom
Papers, Ms. 11191/11, 17.6.1867. **20.** Chief Sec. Off. Reg. Papers,
1867/18637. **21.** Ibid. 1867/10684. **22.** Mayo Papers, Ms. 11189/7.
23. Sullivan, *Speeches from the Dock*, 300. **24.** Larcom Papers, Ms.
11191/9. **25.** Chief Sec. Off. Reg. Papers, 1867/10553. **26.** Mayo
Papers, Ms. 11189/7. **27.** A files 273, 10.11.1867. **28.** Derby Papers,
155/2, 26.8.1867. **29.** Mayo Papers, Ms. 11188/16, 24.8.1867 to
28.8.1867. **30.** Ibid. 23.9. 1867. **31.** Ibid., 21.9.1867. **32.** Ibid., Ms.
11188/15. **33.** Larcom Papers, Ms. 7517. **34.** Chief Sec. Off. Reg.
Papers, 1867/14459. **35.** Ibid. 1867/17990, 28.6.1867. **36.** Ibid., 6.7.1867.
37. Ibid., 8.7.1867. **38.** Ibid., 11.7.1867. **39.** Ibid., 1867/20992, S. L.
Anderson to Mayo.

CHAPTER XII

1. Derby Papers 155/3, 20.10.1867. **2.** A files 271, 1.6.1867. **3.** Larcom
Papers, Ms. 11191/17, 17.9.1867. **4.** Disraeli Papers, B/XX/BO/37,

17.7.1867. **5.** Ibid., B/XX/BO/38, 22.9.1867. **6.** Mayo Papers, Ms. 11189/8, 19.9.1867. **7.** Ibid., 21.9.1867. **8.** Chief Sec. Off. Reg. Papers, 1867/18150. **9.** Mayo Papers, Ms. 11188, to Mayo, 24.9.1867. **10.** Chief Sec. Off. Reg. Papers, 1867/18190. **11.** Mayo Papers, Ms. 11188, Ferguson to Mayo, 24.9.1867. **12.** Chief Sec. Off. Reg. Papers, 1867/11878. **13.** Mayo Papers, Ms. 11189/9, 26.9.1867. **14.** Ibid., Ms. 11189/8, 30.9.1867. **15.** Derby Papers, 164/6, 14.10.1867. **16.** Mayo Papers, 11189/8, 18.10.1867. **17.** Ibid., Ms. 11146. 28.9.1867. **18.** Ibid., Ms. 11188/20. **19.** Ibid., Ms. 11146. 7 or 17.12.1867. **20.** Ibid., 13.12.1867. **21.** Ibid., 18.12.1867. **22.** Ibid., Mss. 11146, 11189/8 and 11161. **23.** Chief Sec. Off. Reg. Papers, 1867/18458. **24.** Larcom Papers, Ms. 7517, f. 347. **25.** O Fiaich, *The Clergy and Fenianism.* **26.** Derby Papers 155/4, 3.1.1868. **27.** Larcom Papers, Ms. 11191/18, 9.11.1867; Ms. 11191/21, 28.1.1868; and Ms. 11191/23, 28.2.1868. **28.** Strathnairn Papers, B.M. Add. Mss. 42828, to Lt.-Gen. Sir H. Grant, 3.12.1867. **29.** Mayo Papers, Ms. 11146, 4.12.1867. **30.** Mayo Papers, Ms. 11189/10, 8.12.1867. **31.** Strathnairn Papers, B.M. Add. Mss. 42828, 9.12.1867. **32.** Ibid., to Captain Wellesley, 18.12.1867. **33.** Derby Papers 155/1, 6.12.1867. **34.** Mayo Papers, Ms. 11146, 12.2.1867 and 13.2.1867; and Derby Papers, 195/2, 12.2.1867. **35.** Derby Papers, 195/1, 4.1.1868. **36.** Fenian Papers 572R. **37.** Ibid., Ryan to Commissioners, 11.8.1868. **38.** Chief Sec. Off. Reg. Papers, 1867/17844. **39.** Derby Papers, 195/1, to Gathorne Hardy, 6.1.1868.

CHAPTER XIII

1. Chief Sec. Off. Reg. Papers, 1867/21787. **2.** Derby Papers, Box 55, Home Office to Mayo, 13.12.1867. **3.** Ibid. 155/2, 14.12.1867. **4.** Ibid. 157/7, Cambridge to Derby, 9.12.1867. **5.** Anderson, *Sidelights on the Home Rule Movement,* 74; and *The Lighter Side of My Official Life,* 23. **6.** Disraeli Papers B/XX/BO/42. **7.** Ibid., 13.12.1867. **8.** Derby Papers, 146/3. **9.** Ibid., 16.12.1867. **10.** Ibid., 16.12.1867 (a second letter). **11.** Ibid., 17.12.1867. **12.** Disraeli Papers, B/XX/5/457, 17.12.1867. **13.** Ibid., B/XX/5/470, 3.1.1868. **14.** Derby Papers 164/6, 30.12.1867. **15.** Mayo Papers, Ms. 11189/11, Gathorne Hardy to Mayo, 1.1.1868. **16.** Mayo Papers, Ms. 11164, 1.1.1868. **17.** Ibid., Ms. 11189/11, Gathorne Hardy to Mayo, 1.1.1868. **18.** Ibid., Ms. 11164. **19.** Derby Papers, 155/2, 10.1.1868. **20.** Mayo Papers, Ms. 11189/11, J. F. Hamilton to Mayo, undated. **21.** Kilmainham Papers, Ms. 1305, p. 371, 24.1.1868. **22.** Larcom Papers, Ms. 11191/21, 13.2.1868. **23.** Ibid.,

Ms. 11191/24, Larcom to Mayo, 4.3.1868. **24.** Ibid., Larcom to Mayo, 12.3.1868. **25.** Chief Sec. Off. Reg. Papers, 1868/653, to Larcom, 13.1.1868. **26.** Mayo Papers, Ms. 11188, 9.2.1868. **27.** Devoy, *Recollections of an Irish Rebel*, 38. **28.** Larcom Papers, Ms. 7517, f. 330; and Strathnairn Papers, B.M. Add. Mss. 42828, Strathnairn to Feilding, 18.1.1868. **29.** *Sidelights on British Conspiracies*, Vol. 1, 101 (a typescript of W. H. Joyce in author's possession). **30.** Strathnairn Papers, B.M. Add. Mss. 42828, Strathnairn to Feilding, 18.1.1868. **31.** Derby Papers, 155/4, 9.1.1868. **32.** Ibid., 164/7, Gathorne Hardy to Derby, 10.1.1868 and 14.1.1868. **33.** Ibid., 15.1.1868. **34.** Larcom Papers Ms. 11191/21, 16.2.1868. **35.** Strathnairn Papers, B.M. Add. Mss. 42828, 10.2.1868. **36.** Ibid., B.M. Add. Mss. 42829, 8.3.1868. **37.** Ibid., 10.3.1868. **38.** Ibid., 12.3.1868.

CHAPTER XIV

1. Mayo Papers, Ms. 11163, 7.3.1868 and 10.3.1868. **2.** Ibid., Ms, 11161, 22.3.1868. **3.** Abercorn Papers, 4.3.1868. **4.** Derby Papers, 146/4. **5.** Ibid. **6.** Abercorn Papers, 11.3.1868. **7.** Ibid., 16.3.1868. **8.** Ibid., 18.3.1868. **9.** Larcom Papers, Ms. 11191/25, 14.3.1868. **10.** Ibid., 19.3.1868. **11.** Ibid., 20.3.1868. **12.** Ibid., 10.3.1868. **13.** Mayo Papers, Ms. 11161, 20.3.1868. **14.** Ibid., 11163, 24.3.1868. **15.** Ibid., Mayo to Brewster, 23.3.1868. **16.** Ibid., 10.3.1868. **17.** Ibid., 23.3.1868. **18.** *Annual Register* 1868, 42. **19.** Disraeli Papers, B/XX/BO/260, February (?) 1867. **20.** Mayo Papers, Ms. 11161, letters of 11, 12 and 15 May 1868. **21.** Derby Papers, 192/1, 15.2.1867. **22.** *Annual Register* 1868. **23.** Disraeli Papers, B/XX/BO/63, 20.4.1868. **24.** Abercorn Papers. 26.4.1868. **25.** Elizabeth Longford, *Victoria R.I.*, 360. **26.** Larcom Papers, Ms. 11191/26, to Mayo, undated. **27.** Derby Papers, 197/1, 28.4.1868. **28.** Larcom Papers, Ms. 11191/27, 23.5.1868. **29.** Disraeli Papers, B/XX/BO/70, Mayo to Disraeli, 12.8.1868. **30.** Ibid., B/XXI/F/80, 20.9.1868. **31.** Ibid. B/XXI/F/190, 30.10.1868. **32.** Thornley, *Isaac Butt and Home Rule*, 45 and 62. **33.** Kimberley Journal, 10.12.1868. **34.** Ibid., 10.12.1868. **35.** Ibid., 14.12.1869. **36.** Ibid. **37.** Ibid., 8.5.1869. **38.** Disraeli Papers, B/XX/BO/36. **39.** Ibid., B/XX/BO/71 and 84. **40.** Mayo Papers, Cambridge, 9.4.1869. **41.** Ibid., 16.6.1870. **42.** Kimberley Journal 10.2.1872. **43.** Larcom Papers, Ms. 7572, 9.11.1868. **44.** Ibid., Oct. 1868. **45.** Mayo Papers, Cambridge, 16.6.1870. **46.** Fenian Papers, 6756R.

Bibliography

MANUSCRIPT SOURCES

National Library of Ireland: Mayo Papers, Larcom Papers, Samuel Lee Anderson Papers, Kilmainham Papers and Monsell Papers.

State Paper Office, Dublin Castle: Chief Secretary's Office Registered Papers, Government Letter Books, Police Reports on Fenianism, A files and Fenian Papers.

British Museum: Strathnairn Papers and Gladstone Papers.

Public Record Office, Belfast: Abercorn Papers and Montgomery Papers.

Public Record Office, London: Foreign Office Papers.

Bodleian Library, Oxford: Clarendon Deposit.

Knowsley Hall, Lancashire: Papers of 14th Earl of Derby.

Hughenden Manor, Buckinghamshire: Disraeli Papers.

Cambridge University Library: Mayo Papers.

BOOKS CONSULTED

Anderson, Robert (1906) *Sidelights on the Home Rule Movement.* (1910) *The Lighter Side of my Official Life.*

Annual Register, The.

Blake, Robert (1966) *Disraeli.*

Bourke, Marcus (1967) *John O'Leary.*

Brown, Thomas N. (1966) *Irish-American Nationalism.*

Bussy, Frederick Moir (1910) *Irish Conspirators.*

Corish, Patrick J. (1967) 'Political Problems, 1860–1878' (in *History of Irish Catholicism*, Vol. 3).

D'Arcy, William (1947) *The Fenian Movement in the United States.*

Denieffe, Joseph (1906) *A Personal Narrative of the Irish Revolutionary Brotherhood.*

Devoy, John (1929) *Recollections of an Irish Rebel.*

Hammond, J. L. (1938) *Gladstone and the Irish Nation.*

Hunter, W. W. (1875) *A Life of the Earl of Mayo.*

Jenkins, Brian (1969) *Fenians and Anglo-American Relations during Reconstruction.*

'Kimberley Journal' (*Cambden Miscellany* XXI).

Le Caron, Henri (1892) *Twenty-five Years in the Secret Service.*

Longford, Elizabeth (1964) *Victoria R.I.*

McCartney, Donal (1967) 'The Church and Fenianism' (in *University Review*, Vol. iv, 3).

McDowell, R. B. (1964). *The Irish Administration, 1801–1914.*

Mac Giolla Choille, Breandán 'Fenian Documents in the State Paper Office' (in *Irish Historical Studies*, XVI 63).

MacSuibhne, Peadar (1961–1965) *Paul Cullen and his Contemporaries.*

Magnus, Philip (1954) *Gladstone.*
(1964) *King Edward the Seventh.*

Moody, T. W. (1961) 'Irish-American Nationalism' (in *Irish Historical Studies*, XV.60).
(1967) 'Fenianism, Home Rule and the Land War' (*The Course of Irish History*, chapter 18).

Moody, T. W. (ed.) (1968) *The Fenian Movement.*

Norman, E. R. (1965) *The Catholic Church and Ireland in the Age of Rebellion 1859–1873.*

O Fiaich, Tomás (1968) 'The Clergy and Fenianism 1860–1870' (in *Irish Ecclesiastical Record*, Vol. 109, No. 2).

O'Leary, John (1896) *Fenians and Fenianism.*

O Lúing, Seán (1961) *John Devoy.*

Pigott, Richard (1882) *Recollections of an Irish National Journalist.*

Rutherford, John (1877) *The Secret History of the Fenian Conspiracy.*

Ryan, Desmond (1937) *The Phoenix Flame.*
(1967) *Fenian Chief.*

Ryan, Desmond and O'Brien, William (eds.) (1948–1953) *Devoy's Post Bag.*

Sheppard, Edgar (1906) *H.R.H. George Duke of Cambridge.*

Sullivan, T. D. (1905) *Troubled times in Irish politics.*

Sullivan, T. D., A. M. and D. B., *Speeches from the Dock.*

Tansell, Charles C. (1957) *America and the fight for Irish freedom.*

Thornley, David (1964) *Isaac Butt and Home Rule.*

Index